D0072856

The Black Market

Patterson Smith Reprint Series in
Criminology, Law Enforcement, and Social Problems

A listing of publications in the Series *will be found at rear of volume*

Publication No. 87: Patterson Smith Reprint Series in Criminology, Law Enforcement, and Social Problems

The Black Market

A STUDY OF WHITE COLLAR CRIME

MARSHALL B. CLINARD

Professor of Sociology · University of Wisconsin

ST. JOSEPH'S UNIVERSITY   STX
HF5415.1.C55 1969
The black market;

3 9353 00154 8195

HF
5415.1
.C 55
1969

Reprinted
With a New Preface by the Author

Montclair, New Jersey
PATTERSON SMITH
1969

155831

Copyright 1952 by Marshall B. Clinard
Reprinted 1969 by arrangement with Holt, Rinehart and Winston, Inc.
Patterson Smith Publishing Corporation
Montclair, New Jersey

New material copyright ©1969 by
Patterson Smith Publishing Corporation

SBN 87585-087-1

Library of Congress Catalog Card Number: 69-16233

TO MY MOTHER

PREFACE TO THE REPRINT EDITION

Some fifteen years have elapsed since the first appearance of this study of the World War II black market, or illegal behavior in the form of price and rationing violations. Written originally as a study of white collar crime, it has come to be regarded as a significant contribution to criminological theory, to the study of law in action, and to the general social and economic history of the war period. For those with an interest in deviant behavior and social problems, it analyzes some of the value conflicts confronting people in higher-status positions who are caught between the state regulation of commercial transactions and the business values of a free-enterprise system. The study of white collar crime thus brings into focus the relationships among criminal behavior, criminal law, penal sanctions, and the social structure.

"White collar crime" is a term which denotes lawbreaking in the middle and upper ("white collar") socio-economic classes. This type of criminal behavior differs from the conventional criminal behavior committed by lower socio-economic groups and is subject to different types of sanctions. The concept of white collar crime is a relatively new addition to criminological theory. Although the need for a term to cover such illegal behavior was suggested in 1907 by one of the founders of American sociology, E. A. Ross, and reaffirmed by Morris in the 1930's, it was not until 1940 that the distinguished criminologist E. H. Sutherland coined the term in a paper. Later (in 1949), Sutherland published the first major study in the area, called *White Collar Crime*. An effort has recently been made by Quinney and Clinard to introduce the broader notion of "occupational crime," i.e., violations of law in connection with one's occupational role regardless of social status, while retaining the term "white collar crime" as a designation limited to occupational violations committed by persons of high status.

Although white collar crime is a worldwide phenomenon, research in this field has come almost uniquely from American criminologists. The present study of black market violations, originally published in 1952, was the second major study in this area. Together with Cressey's study of embezzlement and other violations of trust, and Sutherland's work, it constitutes one of the three major books in the field to date. (Other important studies, all by American criminologists, are Hartung's study of black market violations in the wholesale meat industry, Lane's study of employers' violations of labor laws, Newman's of pure-food laws, Quinney's of illegal activities of pharmacists, and Geis's of price-fixing violations of antitrust laws by leading U. S. electrical concerns. Several theoretical articles on white collar crime have been written by American criminologists and a few by British, German, and Norwegian criminologists.)

This study of the black market has added significance for the contemporary scene. In demonstrating the extensive violation of the law by businessmen and other persons of means and education, it draws our attention to the fact that crime is not limited to the lower classes or to slum dwellers and thus serves as additional proof that crime cannot be explained by poverty. Moreover, the theoretical significance of white collar crime has still not been adequately recognized in the more individualistic explanations of psychiatry, psychology, and social work. A useful theory of crime should apply alike to the ordinary criminal and to the white collar criminal.

—MARSHALL B. CLINARD

March, 1969

PREFACE TO THE ORIGINAL EDITION

This is not a story of one of the more pleasant aspects of American life. It describes a situation on the home front during World War II which seems almost inconceivable when compared with the sacrifices of the men in the armed forces. During the war at least a million cases of black market violations were dealt with by the government. Illegal profits ran into billions of dollars. Business interests and the government vied with one another in estimating the seriousness of the black market; business estimates, curiously, often being higher than those of the government. Such extensive conniving in the black market in illegal prices and rationed commodities took place among so many business men, ordinary criminals, and even average citizens that serious questions might be raised as to the strength of the moral fiber of the American people. Black market violations of law were on such a grand scale that the American people, instead of forgetting about them after the war, should have felt the same concern that they feel about the periodic investigations of organized crime and the corruption of public officials and politicians.

Some have stated that the black market was unnecessary, since we did not need wartime price and rationing controls. Others have placed the entire blame on the government administration of the program, while still others have pointed to the lack of cooperation on the part of business and to public indifference. In this, the first book to describe the extent and nature of the black market, I have tried to present an objective appraisal of the entire situation. I have particularly emphasized the black market in meat, gasoline, and rent, and in the case of gasoline I have shown how there was ex-

tensive collusion between filling-station operators and professional criminals who sold them stolen and counterfeit ration currency. I have told how the government went about
controlling the black market and the mistakes it made. I have
also described the attitudes of the average citizen toward
this black market, and I have offered some observations on the
relative blame which might be assigned to government, business, and the public. Finally, I have discussed the implications
of these past experiences for future national emergencies.

I have pointed out that most black market behavior involved violations that were both complex, evasive, and willful
in nature, and that from a sociological point of view they
should be considered "crimes." Moreover, much of this black
market activity was also in violation of many peacetime laws,
such as those dealing with tax collections and pure foods.

Black market violations, on the whole, fall within the
area of what is termed "white collar crime," namely, illegal
activities among business and professional men. The material
presented in this book demonstrates the similarity between
some of this wartime disregard for law and ordinary criminal
activities, insofar as both constitute violation of law. While
this book discusses illegal activities among businessmen, it
does not imply that American business is for the most part
dishonest. In fact, it is a defense of American capitalism and
the honest businessman. The repetition of such illegal behavior as the black market cannot be avoided merely by pre-
tending it never occurred; positive methods of preventing its
reoccurrence must be devised. One important implication of
this book is that a wider development of business ethics will
do more than anything else to convince the American people
of the integrity of American business.

My interest in the black market was the result of work I

did with the Enforcement Department of the Office of Price Administration in Washington, D. C., from December, 1942, until September, 1945. As Chief, Analysis and Reports Branch, I had the opportunity of gathering and interpreting material, as well as observing other aspects of this problem. Trips during the war to various field offices also gave me a more intimate acquaintance with the black market and the difficulties of controlling it. While this experience has been invaluable to me in this study, I have tried to approach the issues in as unbiased a manner as possible.

Much of the data which I have used grew out of the enforcement of regulations, such as case records, field reports, and administrative orders. Other data have included newspaper and magazine accounts, interviews with businessmen, and various opinion polls dealing with public and business attitudes toward price control, rationing, and the black market. I found congressional hearings conducted at the time an extremely useful source of information. Data from other government agencies and the few materials available in secondary sources have also been useful. I should like particularly to acknowledge my indebtedness to Professor Frank E. Hartung of Wayne University, whose doctoral dissertation dealt with the black market in the Detroit wholesale meat industry.

In the preparation of this manuscript I have received generous aid from the University of Wisconsin Research Committee, from the Social Science Research Council's Committee on War Studies, and from the Institute for Research and Training in the Social Sciences of Vanderbilt University. I am also grateful for the assistance of Harvey Mansfield, Chief, Policy Analysis Branch, Office of Temporary Controls, Office of Price Administration, although the statements and conclusions in this book, which makes use of some materials gathered in the course of my work with the OPA, are my own personal views and do not necessarily reflect those of the agency.

Among those who have read all of the manuscript and offered suggestions are Professors Ernest W. Burgess of the University of Chicago, John L. Gillin of the University of Wisconsin, and the late Edwin H. Sutherland of Indiana University, who first called my attention, while I was a graduate student at the University of Chicago, to the implications for criminology of law violation among business and professional groups. Professor Harold M. Groves made several helpful suggestions. I also wish to acknowledge the assistance given by several former members of the staff of the Office of Price Administration, Robert W. Arthur, George M. Austin, and Professors Carl A. Auerbach, James S. Earley, and Erwin A. Gaumnitz, who have read parts of the manuscript for factual accuracy. None of them, however, are in any way responsible for my conclusions. Finally, appreciation should be expressed to my wife who, as editor, typist, and housewife, is one of those rare persons who make it possible for college professors to do research.

MARSHALL B. CLINARD

Madison, Wisconsin
February, 1952

Contents

Tables

CHARTS

FIGURE

The Black Market

CHAPTER ONE

The Black Market

Profiteering by some businessmen and the securing of unfair advantages by many civilians have probably characterized all wars. Even Washington is said to have wished that he could have hanged some of the men who made excessive profits from sales to his ragged soldiers. In the Civil War, the Spanish-American War, and World War I there were stories of men who enriched themselves at the expense of others. Much of this activity was not illegal, however, since there were few clearly defined wartime restrictions prohibiting the sale of commodities above a certain price. While people generally frowned on such behavior, they seldom had any laws with penalties to prevent it.

With the coming of World War II all this changed. Drastic regulations were issued making it against the law to charge more than a certain fixed price for nearly all commodities, and for the first time in American history there was compulsory rationing of certain goods by the government. As a result, this country was swept with a new type of danger, as serious a threat to our political, social, and economic welfare as major military reverses. This insidious new attack on the home front came in the form of what was called a "black market," a term previously almost unknown in this country but one which developed rapidly in significance. The actual origin of this term is not quite clear, although it appears to have been identified with "black" to indicate illegal activities occurring under conditions of great secrecy.[1]

Whatever the origin of the term might be, the black market and what it signified became a great wartime interest in this country, involving attempts to circumvent economic controls set up by the government to guarantee more adequate and equal distribution of certain essential goods and to prevent inflation. In general, these controls concerned the allocation of scarce industrial materials, the regulation of prices and rents, and the distribution by rationing of vital commodities in scarce supply. These regulations were in effect not only in this country but in all those at war, regardless of the form of government. Great Britain, for example, instituted price controls at the outbreak of war in 1939 and extended these controls in 1941, while rationing was begun in 1940. Such controls helped to make available the maximum amount of materials necessary for conducting total war.[2]

---

[1] The *Columbia Encyclopedia* does not include the term as a part of American speech, and the *Encyclopedia Americana* first listed it in the *Annual* of 1944. "The etymology of the term [black market], as of the continental *marché noir* which already flourished in World War I, is doubtless to be sought in comparable expressions denoting forbidden activities carried on in dark secrecy to escape detection and punishment, e.g., 'black bourse,' 'black mass,' 'black hand.' "—*Britannica Book of the Year 1944*, p. 112. The term "black marketeer" did not appear until 1945 in Webster's or in Funk and Wagnall's *Dictionary*, or in H. L. Mencken's *The American Language* (New York: Alfred A. Knopf, Inc., 1945), in which it was stated in *Supplement 1* (p. 360) that it carried a disparaging significance.

[2] Black marketing in Europe after World War II was chiefly on an individual basis but had much wider ramifications than ever was the situation in the United States. In Germany, for example, Germans and the occupation troops sold cigarettes, coffee, foodstuffs, and the like at prices far above those set by the authorities concerned. In addition, occupation scrip was frequently sold at any price from ten to twenty times the legal rate. Further, there was a great deal of direct barter, particularly among the peasants, who withheld foodstuffs from the market, and either sold them for reichsmarks at high rates, or, much more frequently, insisted on the direct bartering of radios, sewing machines, rugs, and other things, in exchange for foodstuffs. There was some

The issuance of economic controls on the outbreak of a national emergency in our country had been in the plans of the War Department for some time prior to World War II, and there can be no adequate understanding of the black market without realizing the close relationship between price, rationing, and other economic controls and military success in modern war. There had been little coordinated economic planning or enforced controls during World War I, and the difficulties which arose, together with the greater mechanization of recent warfare, made it obvious that tight economic controls would be essential in any subsequent war effort. The modern concept of war, viewed as much as a battle between industrial societies as a matter of the bravery and skill of the armed forces, has made adequate war procurement not only a military function but a task for the entire nation. Victory in modern warfare goes to those nations with a preponderance of materials, a superior number of adequately trained armed forces, and a sufficient will to win. Warfare today is not simply combat between soldiers, airplanes, and ships; it is a war of attrition not only in the supplies of war munitions and steel but of food, clothing, gasoline, and other materials which are also consumed by the civilian population: "A fighting army is only the cutting edge of a militarized industrial system. A nation's fighting strength depends on how well and to what extent its entire sources have been mobilized and managed toward the ends of war."[3] In this connection President Wilson once said: "It is not an army that we must shape and train

---

currency manipulation. Reichsmarks were traded for occupation francs, Swiss francs, pounds, and the like. Except for the barest necessities of life the black market was all-pervasive.

[3] *The United States at War*, No. 1 of the Historical Reports on War Administration, United States Bureau of the Budget (Washington: Government Printing Office, 1946), p. 3.

for war; it is a nation." True of World War I, this was even more applicable to World War II.

Whether John Q. Citizen likes governmental controls over his business, employment, or personal life is immaterial once a nation embarks upon preparedness for or enters a "hot" war. A wartime economy must rely on drafted men for the armed services and not volunteers; it must determine what and how much goods can be produced by various industrial plants including those which are the most powerful and influential in our economy; it must have control over the amount a man can earn in essential industries and where he can work; and it must levy heavy taxes and encourage savings not only to pay for the war but to hold down inflation of commodity values. This inflation is swelled by the decrease in available consumer goods arising from the diversion of material, labor, and manufacturing facilities from the production of consumer goods and services, and the enormous outlay of funds necessary for the production of war goods with a consequent rise in purchasing power in the form of wages, salaries, profits, and dividends. The government in wartime must institute price controls on nearly all goods, not only to prevent the bidding up of prices to civilians due to increased purchasing power, but to keep down the costs of military supplies which would eventually have to be paid for by taxes or indebtedness incurred for future generations. Finally, a wartime economy must control rents and must ration essential goods in limited supply, not only to bring about a more equitable distribution but also to help control the prices of extremely scarce and vital goods.

In such an economy a fight on inflation is almost as important as the fight against the enemy. The experience of every nation at war, whether a democracy or a totalitarian government, has indicated that economic stabilization is "as essential to effective prosecution of the war as staffing the armed forces or providing material for war production."[4] Bernard Baruch has estimated that inflation during World War I, when we had little economic control, increased war costs to the American taxpayers by about 40 per cent.[5] World War I with its relatively unchecked inflation was followed by a depression, unemployment, extensive business failures, and farm foreclosures. The inflationary situation was particularly serious in World War II because although expenditures of World War I were less than 20 billion dollars, World War II cost the United States over 360 billion dollars. While it is estimated to have cost about $25,000 to kill one of the enemy in 1917–1918, in World War II this cost had risen to from $75,000 to $100,000.[6]

Along with the need for price controls in modern industrial warfare is the necessity for the compulsory rationing of essential supplies. Voluntary rationing to regular consumers, or those with sufficient money on a first-come, first-served basis, may be used for less essential goods or during temporary shortages. This system does not work if the conditions are reversed and the goods are necessities in short supply over a longer period of time. By compulsory rationing it is possible to make a limited supply available to each consumer. This avoids the bidding up of the price with sales to a favored few and the irritation to the people caused by purchasers lining up for sales, generally with the purpose of hoarding. While our abundance of agricultural production suggests little need for rationing controls, at least as compared with an importing country like Great Britain, closer inspection of the problem reveals this conclu-

---

4 *Ibid.*, p. 239.
5 *Ibid.*, p. 240.
6 Chester W. Wright, "American Economic Preparations for War, 1914–1917 and 1939–1941," *Canadian Journal of Economics and Political Science*, VIII (February–November, 1942), 159.

sion to be wrong. The need for rationing is great in a nation such as ours where, because of our abundant production, we must carry the responsibility for feeding not only our own armed forces and civilian population but also some of our allies. We need to ration our civilians to feed others. The food requirements in World War II of the more than ten million men in our armed forces were enormous. The navy, for example, provided for monthly allotments for each 1,000 sailors of 32,000 pounds of meat, 2,400 pounds of butter, 4,500 pounds of eggs, and 800 pounds of cheese, in addition to considerable quantities of dry groceries and fresh fruits and vegetables. "These menus gave each sailor more than twice as much meat, three-fourths again as much butter, one-third again as many eggs, and two-thirds again as much cheese as the average citizen ate in 1942."[7]

Throughout the war a tremendous amount of our supplies was needed to keep our allies, such as Great Britain and Soviet Russia, in the war. "To keep British and Russian diets at the subsistence level in 1943 would take about 10 per cent of our total food supply."[8] Large amounts of fats and oils were sent by the United States to the Soviet armies. There was, in addition, the need for feeding liberated peoples in North Africa, France, Yugoslavia, the Balkans, Poland, and Italy, as well as the defeated enemy. Moreover, large amounts of food and other supplies were lost by submarine warfare, by bombing attacks on supply ships, and in the actual invasion.

The 1920 amendment to the National Defense Act charged the Assistant Secretary of War with the responsibility for providing assurances of adequate material and industrial organization essential to wartime needs. From 1920 until the outbreak

---

[7] *The United States at War*, pp. 323–324.
[8] *Ibid.*, p. 324.

of World War II the Planning Branch of the Office of the Assistant Secretary of War and the Army Industrial College, under the sponsorship of the Joint Army and Navy Munitions Board, formulated several plans for industrial mobilization[9] The War Department's first published Mobilization Plan provided for a price control section, and the 1939 revised plan stated that all economic functions which must be exercised in time of war are interrelated and interdependent. In this plan the War Department proposed a War Resources Administrator who would have under him agencies controlling war finance, war trade, war labor, and price control.[10] Accordingly, in the event of war, regulations were to be imposed on production, wages, prices, and the allocation of scarce materials. All of these measures were considered essential to the prosecution of modern warfare, which requires the expenditure of huge outlays of capital and consumer goods, and all were acknowledged as vital by the military authorities of every country concerned.

Economic controls were eventually imposed by the United States government in World War II, but not exactly as planned. In its total war program the government "faced the greatest administrative test since its founding."[11] It developed new agencies in areas like price control and rationing where there had been no precedent or previous experience. It made mistakes; occasionally even the entire control procedures looked chaotic and confused; yet as time went on the machinery in these new areas of government controls became better organized. Industrial controls were established between 1941 and

---

[9] These plans were published as the *Industrial Mobilization Plan of 1931*, with revisions of 1933, 1936, and 1939. See Harold W. Thatcher, *Planning for Industrial Mobilization, 1920–1940.* Office of the Quartermaster General, General Administrative Services Division, Historical Section, Q.M.C. Historical Studies, No. 4, August, 1943.

[10] *Industrial Mobilization Plan, Revision of 1939.*

[11] *The United States at War,* p. 3.

1945 which enabled us and our allies to defeat two of the most ruthless military systems in the history of the world, Germany and Japan, the Nazi war machine with its blitzkrieg and Stuka dive bombers having been regarded by many Americans in 1940 as almost invincible. "Yet it managed to do these dictatorial things within the framework of the democratic system, and even in the forms and changes of its administrative machinery it preserved the methods of democracy so that the resolutions of tensions proceeded, if not always smoothly, yet directly and firmly."[12] This was done in an environment of public opinion and pressure groups where the government could not always do at the time what it thought necessary. Although in retrospect people may now say that "they should have done something about it more rapidly," the actual fact is that many things were done about as fast administratively and in terms of public opinion as possible.

In line with the general ideas of the government's Industrial Mobilization Plans, but not following them specifically, the President, on May 28, 1940, established the National Defense Advisory Commission to the Council of National Defense to formulate economic plans for the defense program. During the defense period of 1940 and 1941 limited voluntary economic controls were imposed. These included the use of informal price controls, first through a semiadvisory Price Stabilization Division, and later by an executive agency called the Office of Price Administration and Civilian Supply (OPACS). This voluntary method of economic controls proved to be unsuccessful, largely because of the absence of enforcement powers, and shortly after Pearl Harbor the government was granted statutory powers to regulate extensive areas of the productive and distributive phases of our commercial life. The idea was to

[12] *Ibid.*

attack inflation by controls on prices and wages, by allocation and distribution of materials and consumer rationing, and by taxation and increased saving through the purchase of war bonds and through credit controls. All of these measures were to be part of an integrated program.

Thus were developed such agencies as the Office of Price Administration (OPA) in February, 1942, the War Production Board, and the War Labor Board. The War Production Board regulated many phases of industrial allocation and production. The War Labor Board was created to stabilize wages. The job of the Office of Price Administration was to regulate prices of practically all civilian products and most, but not all, military supplies, to control rents, and, through delegation from other agencies, to maintain an equitable distribution of materials through the rationing of such scarce commodities as gasoline, tires, meat, coffee, and sugar. Eventually the planning of the economic programs of the various agencies was coordinated through the Office of Economic Stabilization. The President, in a message to Congress on April 23, 1942, set forth the government's comprehensive program to prevent inflation:

1. . . . tax heavily, and in that process keep personal and corporate profits at a reasonable rate, the word "reasonable" being defined at a low level.

2. . . . *fix ceilings on the prices which consumers, retailers, wholesalers, and manufacturers pay for the things they buy; and ceilings on rents for dwellings in all areas affected by war industries.*

3. . . . stabilize the remuneration received by individuals for their work.

4. . . . stabilize the prices received by growers for the products of their lands.

5. . . . we must encourage all citizens to contribute to the cost of winning this war by purchasing war bonds with their earn-

ings instead of using those earnings to buy articles which are not essential.

6. . . . *we must ration all essential commodities of which there is a scarcity, so that they may be distributed fairly among consumers and not merely in accordance with financial ability to pay high prices for them.*

7. . . . we must discourage credit and installment buying, and encourage the paying off of debts, mortgages, and other obligations. . . .[13]

Subsequently the Office of Price Administration issued over 600 price and rent regulations, regulating the prices of over 8,000,000 articles and 20 categories of rationed commodities and controlling the distribution of numerous essential products. Thus practically every person engaged in any business activity was governed by one or more of the specific trade regulations, and the behavior of each consumer in the United States was affected. This meant that the regulations issued by this one governmental agency exercised some measure of control over 130,000,000 people, exclusive of the armed services, including the owners of several million rental dwellings and 3,000,000 business establishments, of which 380,000 were wholesale and manufacturing, 650,000 service establishments, and the balance retail stores, including 600,000 food stores and 250,000 gasoline stations.

Despite the realities of the war situation few people realized in 1940, 1941, and part of 1942 that with our large stockpiles of surplus agricultural commodities, deflation in prices of most manufactured items, and considerable unemployment we would later encounter the shortages in wide areas that we did by 1943 and through the remainder of the war.

---

[13] *House Document No. 716,* Seventy-seventh Congress, Second Session, p. 3. (Italics mine.)

In the middle of 1942 we still had our usual two years' supply of wheat, corn, and cotton which had been increased by the loss of a considerable part of our export market for these commodities after the outbreak of war in 1939. Most other commodities were in similar large supply. In 1941 we still had 4 million unemployed and our total national income was 96 billion dollars. Inflation in the national defense period, however, was beginning to indicate what was to come, for from September, 1939, to December, 1941, there was an increase of almost one fourth in the price of 28 basic commodities affecting manufacturing and living costs. During 1941 we spent 6.7 billion dollars on defense preparations. By December we were spending almost 2 billion dollars a month. While a large part of this production was being exported to our future allies, at the time of Pearl Harbor our army and navy exceeded 2 million men. During 1941 the cost of living increased almost 1 per cent a month and the wholesale price index slightly more. In this same year farm prices went up approximately one fourth and wages, salaries, and income payment by a fifth.

After Pearl Harbor there was even greater realization of increased inflationary pressures when the President announced what were then considered fantastic annual production goals of 60,000 planes, 45,000 tanks, 20,000 antiaircraft guns, and 8,000,000 tons of new shipping. Our various economic hedges such as agricultural and manpower surpluses disappeared rapidly in 1942. Military operations were under way in North Africa, Guadalcanal, and El Alamein, and were being planned for Italy, Western Europe, and the Japanese-held islands. The loss of control of the western Pacific had meant shortages of rubber, vegetable oils, fruit, and other foodstuffs. Rubber tires, coffee, and sugar were already being rationed and there were shortages of meats, fats, oils, dairy products, and many canned foods. The rationing of gasoline had been started because of the depletion of stocks on the eastern seaboard through submarine destruction of several hundred tankers off the eastern coast, heavy diversion of military supplies for overseas, and the need to conserve rubber in tires. The basic ration for most civilians was three or four gallons a week. Supplies of steel, copper, nylon, and other materials were on strict allocation. The manpower situation was critical and was being controlled by desperate but sometimes futile attempts to channel it into critical areas and by imposing wage controls. The number of persons employed and in the armed services rose from 51.6 million in December, 1941, to 60.3 million two years later. Despite these efforts inflationary pressures were terrific, with the annual wartime national income eventually to go to 180 billion dollars, or double that of 1941, and war expenditures eventually to reach over 90 billion dollars annually.

By April, 1942, the prices of all uncontrolled commodities had been frozen, and rent ceilings were established in many defense areas where the population pressures were great on available housing. Later rent controls were extended almost throughout the country. Still more was to come, for by March, 1943, and for the following two years, consumer rationing was to be in effect for a long list of commodities. Only limited supplies were available through certificates of necessity or ration coupons. During the war, for example, it generally took a person's entire week's ration of meats, fats, and oils to buy even half a pound of butter. Consumer rationing was in effect during World War II for such varied commodities as automobiles, tires, gasoline, typewriters, stoves, fuel oils, meat, cheese, butter, coffee, sugar, canned milk, fish and meats, and most other canned goods. Shoes were rationed, and even clothing rationing was contemplated but never put into effect. The effects of rationing came to permeate the entire economy during World War II. Increases or decreases in the ration of a commodity were of particular interest to almost every family in the land as well as to industry, trade, and the banks who handled the ration currency. The intense interest in rationing was reflected in the amount of newspaper and magazine space and radio comment devoted to it. News articles with headlines such as "Gasoline Ration to Be Reduced," "Less Meat to Be Available," "Larger Butter Ration Possible" were carefully read.

These drastic compulsory controls which were imposed for the first time on our economic system were followed by the immediate development of certain attitudes among parts of the population conducive to noncompliance with government economic regulations. Hardly were the regulations in effect than violations began to occur, particularly in the area of price, rent, and, later, rationing controls. At first those persons engaging in these "black market" activities were looked upon as bootleggers, and "bootlegging" was actually the first term in reference to price and rationing violations. In general it was erroneously believed that violators were drawn from the same underworld as in the Prohibition Era. In May, 1942, *Time* stated: "Wartime price and priority controls have already brought back an old U.S. institution: bootlegging. . . . As long as there is more cash to spend than there are things to spend it on, and prices are not allowed to rise openly, they will rise privately. . . . The U.S. bootleg business is already more diversified, if not bigger, than it was in Prohibition's peephole days." Somewhat later the term "black market" came into more general use as largely referring to the "organized stealthy" diversion of commodities at illegal prices, primarily by racketeers. Even as late as February, 1944, this misapprehension about the restricted nature of the black market was encouraged by the government in its attempts to arouse public awareness of the extent of the problem and the importance of the efforts to combat violations.

Literally, "black market" means illegal business conducted in the dark. . . . safe from the light of day or, more loosely, the light of public gaze. This would include the *out-and-out* thieves who steal cattle off the range at night, slaughter them by the side of the road and sneak them into market to sell above ceiling prices. It would include the *professional burglars* who steal gasoline ration coupons from War Price and Rationing Board safes, to sell for their personal profit. It includes *organized gangs* who work in attics and cellars to print counterfeit ration coupons. It includes the one-time *prohibition racketeers* and *hijackers* who now traffic in nylon stockings and onions and steaks which they deliver surreptitiously up the back alley. And the *unscrupulous businessmen* who will do anything for their own personal profit.[14]

Even at this time, however, the government had ample evidence that violations were widespread and occurred among all segments of our society. Thus as the war progressed the connotation of the black market broadened in scope to include most all violations of businessmen, as well as racketeers, counterfeiters, and other organized gangs.[15] With this awareness of

---

[14] Radio talk of Chester Bowles, OPA Administrator, February 15, 1944, over NBC Network. (Italics mine.)

[15] The *Britannica Book of the Year 1944,* in its first use of the term "black market," broadened it to include "the title bestowed upon those illicit areas of wartime commerce where articles are bought and sold in defiance of official price and rationing controls. . . ."—Page 112. Later in the 1945 edition this concept was even more specifically stated: "It covers all types of profiteering in the sale of war-scarce commodities. Originally the term implied a willingness on the part of the buyer to pay a premium over ceiling prices in order to bid scarce goods away from other buyers or, in the case of rationed goods, in order to get rationed goods without ration currency."—Page 109. Finally, the Britannica of 1946 went one step further to state that the term [black market] "in this broad

the extent of the problem, the government began to inform the public that any violations, willful or not, were a contribution to the black market, as these violations added to the danger of illegal prices or contributed to the diversion of rationed commodities. Numerous articles appeared referring to the black market as any violation of the price, rationing, or rent regulations, rather than confining such terms to organized criminal activities. By 1945 the term "black market" had become a recognized term to refer to all kinds of violations of OPA regulations,[16] and the OPA Administrator stated that the black market "is really any transaction where a sale is made over a ceiling price. I would say, willfully made over a ceiling price; or where there is a transaction of a rationed product without passing of rationing currency. It can take all kinds of forms."[17]

The black market covered a wide range of activities, with price or rationing violations occurring in almost all commodities, from heavy industrial materials to items such as clothing, gasoline, shoes, sugar, potatoes, onions, cigarettes, and alcoholic beverages, involving mainly manufacturers, wholesalers, and

---

sense, . . . covers all types of profiteering in the sale of commodities under price control and rationing violations during World War II and the post-war period of heavy demand for scarce products. . . . While the term black market was not generally applied to violations of rent and eviction control regulations, extensive violations were uncovered in this field. . . . They may be termed in every sense black markets." The article went on to say that in a more restrictive sense the term "refers to dealings in scarce commodities by organized gangs, a use which as has been indicated was characteristic of the first period of price control."—Pages 128–129.

[16] The argument will be presented later that as the war progressed most violations were by their very nature "willful." After the repeal of price control, dealings in commodities above the customary market price came to be designated as the "gray market." These transactions, as distinguished from black market activities, were, of course, not illegal. See, for example, "The Gray Market in Action," *Life*, January 12, 1948, p. 34. Also see "That Daffy Gray Market," *Fortune*, May, 1948.

[17] *Hearings before the Committee on Banking and Currency*, on House Joint Resolution 101, Seventy-ninth Congress, First Session, p. 26.

retailers, but in the case of rationing sometimes consumers.[18] There were also violations of rent regulations by landlords. Black market violations consisted of several types of activities: (1) over-ceiling price violations, (2) evasive price violations, (3) rationing violations (including the theft and counterfeiting of ration currency), (4) violations of rent ceilings, and (5) record-keeping and reporting violations. In Great Britain there was a similar diversity of violations. For example, violations of the orders issued by the Ministry of Food consisted of (1) offenses against maximum-price orders, (2) imposing condition of sale, (3) failure to display price, (4) illegal slaughter and allied offenses, (5) supplying or obtaining food without proper authority, (6) trading without license, and (7) false declarations.[19]

OVER-CEILING PRICE VIOLATIONS. This type of violation was simply a charge above the legal price. Sometimes it was a small overcharge, and at other times a large sum of money was involved. Although the overcharge might involve only a few cents, this should not minimize the fact that if this overcharge involved several thousand consumers the total overcharge might well represent a large sum of money. While many persons believed that the black market consisted almost entirely of straight selling above ceiling, this was not true. A large part of illegalities consisted of price violations in which various subterfuges were used. For example, from interviews with food

---

[18] The majority of violations of price regulations were by the seller rather than the buyer, for a buyer for ultimate consumption not only could not ordinarily be a violator but a violation ordinarily originated with the seller. Price violations by the buyer, in those regulations prohibiting such behavior, were derivative in the sense that the seller ordinarily, but not always, initiated the transaction. Even assuming the purchaser to be a willing buyer, if he paid a price above ceiling he had to pass on the overcharge, provided he was not the ultimate consumer and did not wish to sell at a loss.

[19] Jules Backman, *Rationing and Price Control in Great Britain* (Washington: The Brookings Institution, 1943) , p. 59.

wholesalers,[20] as well as opinions of enforcement personnel, it appears that while sales above ceiling were important, such violations as will be discussed shortly as tie-in sales, upgrading, and falsification of records were equally if not more important. As enforcement became more strict, straight over-ceiling violations tended to diminish and more devious methods involving indirect violations were invented.

EVASIVE PRICE VIOLATIONS. Evasive violations constituted the bulk of OPA violations, and nearly all of them were subject to criminal prosecution because of the definite element of willfulness. They included "cash-on-the-side" payments, payments for goods which were not delivered, tie-in sales, quantity and quality deterioration. "Cash-on-the-side" payments were not recorded or reported and were often difficult to ascertain unless the buyer "talked," for the invoice was made out at the correct

---

20 "Opinion Survey of Food Wholesalers," National Opinion Research Center (NORC) for the Information and Enforcement Departments of the OPA, 1945. This survey will be referred to frequently in the following chapters. In it a representative national sample of 434 food wholesalers in fifteen cities were interviewed by the National Opinion Research Center. Wholesalers were selected because of their intermediate market position, between retailer and producer, and because the major efforts of OPA enforcement work were then being concentrated at that level. The fifteen sample cities were selected on the basis of their importance in wholesale food distribution, their regional location, and their high or low enforcement activity. The cities included were Boston, Baltimore, Syracuse, New York, Grand Rapids, Cleveland, Nashville, Savannah, Chicago, St. Louis, Omaha, Tulsa, Denver, Sacramento, and Los Angeles. The number of food wholesalers drawn for each city was in the same ratio to the total sample as the number of firms in that city was to the total firms in the country. The sample included also representative proportions of small and large wholesalers in each commodity group. Those interviewed constituted four groups: meat, dairy products and poultry, fresh fruits and vegetables, and groceries. The research purpose of the interviews was clearly indicated by NORC and also by the fact that the names of those interviewed would not be revealed to the OPA. The interview lasted from one to two hours and was recorded verbatim by the interviewer. Care was exercised to question the wholesalers not about their own violations but about those of dealers in general or dealers in their own line, on the assumption that, while they would be unwilling to discuss their own conduct, they would be more willing to talk freely about merchants generally in their own trade.

ceiling price.[21] Comments like the following by some members of the trade indicated that this practice of side payments was widespread:

Take some suppliers for instance. They do everything on the surface legally. He delivers beef to the wholesaler and it is signed for at the ceiling price. About half an hour later an inconspicuous fellow comes along and is handed an envelope that contains money. There are no records and no one is any wiser.—Eastern meat dealer.

A firm needs butter for its trade, so the representative offers a creamery manager, say $50 a week, to let them have 500 pounds of butter each week. The manager gets the money personally and the butter is still bought at ceiling price. When a man has a family and is working for a small salary, it's pretty hard to turn down an offer like that.—Midwestern dairy products and poultry dealer.

Often charges were made for goods not delivered. A meat wholesaler, for example, might overcharge retailers by invoicing fictitious items and collecting for them. Often side payments were treated as "loans" which the seller never repaid to the buyer. In other cases it was disclosed that side payments were concealed by the seller's placing one of his employees on the payroll of the buyer to draw a salary for services not actually rendered. A further evasive method devised to violate price ceilings was through the use of "tie-in" sales,[22] in which the

---

21 In most instances these cases also represented falsification of records of a type which could result not only in prosecution by the OPA but by the United States Bureau of Internal Revenue as well. See Chapter Ten.

22 It was felt by many, and particularly the fresh fruit and vegetable dealers, that this practice was common in peacetime and consequently doubly hard to police. Surveying Chicago retailers in a variety of fields, Katona concluded: "Tie-in sales on the retail level were called not only an equitable method of informal rationing but also a method of reducing waste. Butchers, for example, argued that certain unpopular cuts of meat would have gone to waste if they had not been sold together with scarce but popular cuts, since price reductions would not have stimulated demand for them."—George Katona, *Price Control and Business,* Cowles Commission Monograph 9 (Bloomington: The Principia Press, 1945), p. 179.

seller refused to deliver a desired commodity unless a purchase was made of a product for which there was little or no demand, or upon which the profit margin was high. Tie-in sales were either direct, where a purchaser was specifically advised he could not purchase the wanted commodity without purchasing the less desirable product, or indirect, word being passed out that it was "desirable" for them to purchase products other than those wanted. The following comments were typical:

For instance, a man handles tomatoes and they happen to be cheap—$1.25 a box, with a $3 ceiling. He may go out, pay over-ceiling for a scarce item, potatoes, and sell the retailer both items at ceiling, making more on the tomatoes than he loses on the potatoes.—Western fruit and vegetable dealer.

I've known where big packers have said to a man, "You want beef—well, you'll take our sausage, too." It cost me one of my best accounts. Well, he had to have beef to sell and in order to get it, he had to buy sausage, so I lost out. He was a good friend of mine, too, and had done business with me for twenty years. But he said, "I'm sorry, you know, but I've got to get beef and I can't get it unless I buy their sausage." Another man told me he has enough of a certain beef extract to last him for three years, as the packer forced him to buy some every time he bought other meat. They ask me to get rid of it for them, but I can't, as all my customers have all they can use. I did have to take two dozen jars once to get a piece of bacon and most of it spoiled because I can't go up and down the street and peddle it to my neighbors.—Midwestern meat dealer.

Still another type of evasive practice was that involving quantity or quality violations. Most of the quantity violations involved billing for items in excess of what was actually de-livered and short-weighing items by charging, for example, for one hundred pounds of a commodity and delivering only part of that amount. Quality violations, on the other hand, involved grading violations, such as upgrading, failure to grade, or improper labeling. Commodities customarily labeled as Grade B were labeled Grade A, or potatoes intended for table use, for example, were classified as seed potatoes.[23] In some instances there was reduction in size or inferior composition or construction, such as the use of substitute materials of inferior grade, blending with less expensive grades of materials, reduction in amount of materials used, and decreases in length of guarantee periods. Quality deterioration in the form of upgrading was particularly prevalent in the apparel field.[24] In July, 1944, the OPA Standards Division, at the request of the Senate War Investigating Committee, submitted evidence of quality deterioration in apparel. A number of items represented "gross waste of manpower and materials," among them being a pair of man's shorts made of cheesecloth, with 50 per cent added sizing to give it form until washed; a woman's slip made of practically unwearable coarse, heavily sized muslin; a pair of baby's pants, allegedly water-resistant, which permitted a third of a glass of water to leak through after being laundered once; and a cotton sweater which was too loosely knit to hold its shape. Sample comments about quality deterioration by food wholesalers were:

That is something that does go on, selling a poorer product for the same money. For instance, before a six months' old cheese was

---

[23] One western wholesaler of potatoes successively sorted his original purchase to a higher grade by removing the No. 1 potatoes and selling them as a different type of higher grade potatoes, then continuing this resorting process until nothing was left but culls. The culls were then sold at regular prices to consumers willing to buy any type of potatoes.

[24] See interviews with Chicago businessmen, 1942–1944 in Katona, *op. cit.*, Chap. Seven, "Indirect Price Increases: Quality Deterioration." In another survey quality deterioration in the form of upgrading was considered frequent by 27 per cent of the food wholesalers interviewed.

sold at a certain price. Now the same price is paid for a six weeks' old cheese.—Western grocery dealer.

In our line I think this goes on in about 50 per cent of cases when oranges are not graded correctly. So choice grade is sold for fancy grade prices.—Southwestern fruit and vegetable dealer.

They'll go out and sell ungraded eggs at the Grade A ceiling. They'll sell inferior eggs, eggs that are not fresh at the Grade A ceiling. There is one case that I know of. They sold the eggs at the ceiling, 34 cents a dozen, and charged them 75 cents for two empty cases. This retailer said, "When I return the cases do I get the 75 cents back?" They told him, "No." The egg brokers were paying over the ceiling prices for their eggs so finally the government stepped in and froze their eggs. That means the government will pay them the procurement ceilings and they'll lose money. In a lot of cases they pay the ceiling prices but pay cash on the side. They take the eggs that are current receipts and grade them as standard. You can't tell by looking at an egg what its quality is.— Midwestern poultry and dairy products dealer.

RATIONING VIOLATIONS. The rationing of a large number of essential commodities among 130 million persons was one of the most difficult administrative problems ever undertaken by the government. The mass printing of millions of ration coupons and their distribution among all consumers and dealers was a tremendous project. During a single war year the rationing boards processed an estimated 30,000,000 basic gasoline applications and 68,000,000 supplemental applications for gasoline, 18,000,000 applications for tires, 17,000,000 sugar canning applications, 2,500,000 applications for institutional sugar allotments, and 12,000,000 fuel-oil applications. In addition, war ration books for food and shoes were issued periodically to practically all persons in the United States. Lost ration books had to be replaced, and several hundred thousand new ones were issued to new babies and discharged soldiers. "All of this had to be done under safeguarding and accountability procedures similar to those under which the older and permanent currency of the Nation was handled."[25] Ration coupons were actually a special form of money and required the same type of protection given other United States currency if the solvency of the rationed commodities were to be maintained. The restricted commodity supplies, such as gasoline, tires, sugar, and shoes constituted a bank account against which the nation drew checks when ration coupons were issued. The amounts of these checks were determined by the needs of various users of the supplies, manufacturers, wholesalers, retailers, and consumers, and by the importance of these uses to the war effort and to civilian living.

There were numerous types of rationing violations, including cases where dealers secured more of a rationed commodity than they were entitled to through falsifying amounts of supplies they had previously used or had on hand at a given date.[26] The most common rationing violations occurred in connection with the misuse of ration currency, including the use of invalid currency or the improper transfer of rationed commodities without collecting ration currency.[27] A consumer who transferred his ration book illegally to someone else was also violating the law. Counterfeiting and the protection of coupons from theft and alteration were problems of an entirely different

---

[25] Emmette S. Redford, *Field Administration of Wartime Rationing*, No. 4 of the Historical Reports on War Administration, Office of Price Administration (Washington: Government Printing Office, 1947), p. 5.

[26] In Great Britain water was sometimes added to increase the supply of rationed goods such as meat or butter available to a dealer.—Backman, *op. cit.*, p. 62.

[27] For a time in Great Britain when clothing was rationed the authorities were troubled by a rationing provision which permitted so-called "shopworn" clothing to be sold without coupons.—*Ibid.*

type from others which the government faced in dealing with the extensive black market. Certainly the clever techniques used by professional counterfeiters of ration currency and others who stole ration currency from local boards, and the close association between these criminal elements and dealers who frequently purchased these illegal coupons from them, resulted in an exceedingly difficult enforcement problem.[28] The following case illustrates this problem:

During three months of 1942 on eight or nine different occasions a gasoline dealer purchased gasoline rationing coupons for approximately two thousand gallons of gasoline from two different individuals. At the hearing held in this case evidence of these purchases was given by the testimony of the two individuals who sold the coupons. The sales were denied by the dealer but testimony was introduced that he had attempted to bribe the OPA officials who were originally investigating the case and that in his testimony at the hearing he made statements inconsistent with other statements that he had previously made in writing to OPA investigators.[29]

Professional criminals shifted from counterfeiting money to counterfeiting ration currency, which was not only easier to counterfeit but simpler to distribute. In 1939, $487,019 worth of counterfeit money was detected, and in 1944 this figure had dropped to $47,060, according to the annual reports of the Secretary of the Treasury on the State of the Finances. One can attribute this decline as being due to more wartime law-abiding jobs for professional counterfeiters, to better enforcement, to other openings such as ration currency, or to a combination of these three factors. The number of apprehended professional

---

[28] Since the bulk of these particular black market activities centered around gasoline, they will be discussed in more detail in Chapter Six.

[29] Where no other source for case material is cited it is taken from OPA case records.

counterfeiters of ration currency would indicate, however, that large numbers of professional counterfeiters employed their talents in counterfeiting ration currency during the war. The problem was enhanced by the excellent counterfeiting jobs done by the printers, and it was even more difficult when special government paper used in printing ration currency was occasionally stolen.[30] Furthermore, there were numerous cases of ration board burglaries, the thefts in a few cases even being carried out by local board employees or persons associated with them in this activity. There were also cases of "inside jobs," involving faked burglaries, a situation which might easily throw the government enforcement staff off guard, as was also true of cases where coupons which were to be destroyed failed to undergo the proper treatment and thus started a flood of illegal coupons.

VIOLATIONS OF RENT CEILINGS. The regulations governing wartime rents of dwellings and hotels were violated by landlords not only by means of direct excessive rental charges but through various evasive and indirect means, such as side payments, fictitious services and charges, and rentals conditional upon the purchase or rental of some other commodity. Black market activities in rents also included illegal evictions.

RECORD-KEEPING AND REPORTING VIOLATIONS. The last type of violation, record-keeping and reporting violations, did not in

---

[30] One regional OPA office reported on one or two occasions the theft of 250-pound rolls of genuine ration paper used to print counterfeit A-11 coupons: "The paper was stolen by a truckman who regularly made deliveries to the paper plant. At the time of the theft guards were stationed around the plant and under the very nose of one of the guards the paper was rolled out by the thief onto his truck and taken away without the guard being any the wiser. 215 pounds of the original roll were recovered after the thief and his accomplices were apprehended. The 35 pounds which were missing had been used to print A-11 coupons which were distributed apparently in great volume throughout Massachusetts and Connecticut as appears from our checkup at the verification center."

and of itself directly affect prices or rents charged or received or the illegal sale of a rationed commodity and is, therefore, classified as nonsubstantive. It was quite common, however, as well as being one of the most serious and difficult of all violations with which to deal. This type involved simply failure to comply with records and reports requirements, such as failure to register a rental dwelling, as well as those where there was neglect or intentional refusal to keep accurate records in order to cover up actual violations. Disregard of these requirements made it difficult to detect violations and hampered the public and the OPA in their enforcement activities, since it was often difficult, if not impossible, to tell what the seller's maximum prices were, what his legal rent and services were, or how large a supply of a rationed commodity he was entitled to unless proper records were kept. The following case illustrates the importance of records in detecting violations:

In 1943, during the period of acute shortage of such housewares as garbage pails, water buckets, mop sticks, a medium-sized jobber of housewares began to solicit sales for such items through mail order catalogues distributed throughout the country. Not having previously sold housewares and housefurnishings, the firm was obligated under the general maximum price regulation to apply to the OPA for prices. In disregard of the regulation it established arbitrary prices which were on the average about 100 per cent more than prices being charged by other wholesalers. However, because of the tremendous consumer demand many retailers purchased from this firm, but a few of the more scrupulous retailers complained to the national office of the excessive prices. This matter was referred to the regional office, and an injunction was granted restraining all sales of housewares until the firm had corrected maximum prices established by OPA. Such price orders were issued, and a rollback of prices resulted, affecting approximately 90 per cent of the items sold by the firm. One interesting phase of the enforcement action against this concern was the firm's statement to the courts during the motion for a preliminary injunction that its sales records were lost so that no determination could be made of the amount of the overcharges which would be the basis for the assertion of the administrator's claim for treble damages. On the hearing of this motion the United States District Court judge did not believe this story and included in the injunction a provision that sales of housewares and housefurnishings were not to be resumed in any event until the firm had furnished the alleged "lost records."

Failure to keep, or falsification of, records was a serious violation, since it was sometimes used as an aid in violating, concealing, or avoiding detection of such violations. Violators of this type often concealed actual inventories or base period records upon which determination was made as to the amount of rationed commodities such as sugar to be allowed a manufacturer. Through dishonest books it was difficult to detect side payments, goods not actually delivered, upgrading, and the like. False records were kept with a purpose. One out of every five food wholesalers felt that falsification of records was frequent. That businessmen considered such behavior serious, even though widespread, was indicated by the following statements taken from interviews with them.

Oh, sure, there's a black market. Everyone knows you can't buy potatoes for ceiling prices. It's all black market. It was strawberries awhile back. Any scarce item is in the black market. They send you a bill for something you didn't get. For instance, I buy 150 pounds of potatoes and they send me a bill at ceiling price. They also bill me for so many pounds of onions. Well, I never get the onions. That money goes to pay for the potatoes.—Midwestern fruit and vegetable dealer.

The bill reads right. I'll explain. A man orders two cases of peas and the bill is marked two cases of peas at the ceiling price but they will deliver one case to you, and you have to pay for two cases.—Eastern grocery dealer.

A black market of immense proportions engulfed our country in a relatively short period of time. The very extent of wartime controls permitted latitude for great variety in types of violations, and the evasive nature of many of the violations is indicative of the ingenuity of those businessmen and others who engaged in the black market. The absence of previous experience with such wartime regulatory measures restricting the economic life of the entire population, moreover, indicates that patterns of violation developed in a relatively short period of time, which seriously hampered the government in an effective and immediate control of the black market.

CHAPTER TWO

The Extent of
the Black Market

There was general agreement during the last war that there was an extensive black market in this country. Government agencies and business concerns, as well as congressional committees and the general public, concurred in their alarmed awareness of the great extent of these illegal activities and the enormous cost for the consumers and taxpayers. The actual extent of these violations could never be accurately determined; yet the losses involved certainly totaled not millions but billions of dollars and were as real to consumers as if their houses had been burglarized or their pockets picked by professional thieves. There was, of course, no way of knowing the exact number of violations of price and rationing regulations. The OPA, except for a brief initial period, did not gather statistics on complaints of violations, as they were both incomplete and sometimes unfounded.[1] Some estimates can be made, however, from an analysis of various statements made by public and private organizations,

---

[1] This type of information is partially available for ordinary crime through reports on crimes known to the police. See Federal Bureau of Investigation, United States Department of Justice, *Uniform Crime Reports*. Reports of offenses known to the police purport to show most urban crime committed in the United States. Since almost the entire area of white collar or business crimes such as the black market, with the exception of embezzlement, is not included, the reports are, in terms of a theory of criminology, misleading as to scope.

the actual enforcement activities of the OPA, and the percentage of violations found on investigations. Some of the estimates should be considered rather cautiously because of problems of representative sampling and bias.

Government Estimates of the Black Market

Surveys conducted by the Bureau of Labor Statistics during the war years indicated that anywhere from less than 5 to more than 40 per cent of the items checked in retail food stores in selected cities were in violation.[2] Estimates by the OPA of the black market in retail food alone varied, on the average, from 3 to 5 per cent of the nation's food budget of 27 billion dollars. An OPA survey of 337 Chicago butchers in February, 1944, found that 27 per cent of 7,000 inspected meat items were being sold above ceiling. A report of the Department of Agriculture, made in the spring of 1943 with the cooperation of the OPA and the OWI (Office of War Information), stated that "unofficial figures place as much as 20 per cent of the meat supply going into black markets."[3] Some 5 per cent of all gasoline was estimated by the OPA in 1943 and early 1944 to be passing in illegal channels through the trafficking in counterfeit or stolen gasoline coupons on the part of filling station operators.

Business Estimates of the Black Market

Hearings before congressional committees, as well as trade journals, were replete with the testimony of businessmen in

---

[2] Violations reported by the Bureau of Labor Statistics in "Monthly Survey of Food Prices in Selected Cities," a confidential report to the Office of Price Administration. The names of the stores were never revealed to the OPA. These were "over-the-counter" sales, however, and often did not get at many evasive practices such as tie-ins.

[3] This estimate, as well as the Chicago survey above, is cited in Katona, *op. cit.*, p. 48.

many trades about the extensiveness of the black market. Another source was the actual opinions of members of the trades.
A confidential survey of Chicago dealers, both wholesale and
retail, in 1942–1944 by the Cowles Commission showed extensive direct and indirect price increases.[4] In one survey of 179
gasoline dealers' opinions, 51 per cent (58 per cent of the
eastern and 35 per cent of the midwestern dealers) thought
there was "a lot" of gasoline being sold in their cities without
coupons.[5] In 1945 the Greater Cincinnati Meat Packers' Association estimated that 50 to 75 per cent of all civilian meat
was passing in black market channels. In 1946 the American
Meat Institute, after a survey of eleven major cities, estimated
that five out of six stores were in the meat black market. Food
wholesalers' opinions were obtained in an OPA survey in the
late spring of 1945 prior to V–J Day. There was some variation
in the statements of 434 food wholesalers about compliance,
but a large number felt that there was an extensive black
market.[6] Some even expressed opinions such as the following:

Everyone is crooked including myself. They're all crooked in
one way or another. With some it's just minor violations. Others
do everything. Someone is always thinking of a new way to get
around the ceilings. I want to tell you about something that happened. One of our wholesalers went out into the country to buy
some chickens. There was an OPA man at the farm where he
stopped. The OPA man watched the farmer weigh up the chickens.
He watched the wholesaler pay the farmer and get a receipt. Every-

---

[4] Katona, *op. cit.,* pp. 31–95.

[5] "Opinions of Filling Station Proprietors about Gasoline Rationing," an
opinion survey of 179 operators of gasoline filling stations in ten eastern and
midwestern cities conducted by the NORC for the OPA in November, 1944, p. 4.
Clyde W. Hart, OPA Special Assistant to the Administrator, in charge of public
opinion, was in technical charge of this and other opinion surveys for the OPA,
all of which were done by private public opinion agencies.

[6] "Opinion Survey of Food Wholesalers," cited above.

one was on the up and up so far. Then just before leaving the wholesaler said, "Here's that $100 I owe you." The OPA man watched him give the hundred dollars to the farmer, and couldn't stop it.—Poultry dealer in the Midwest.

At least one fifth (21 per cent) of a random sample group of 145 food retailers interviewed in Washington, D.C., in March, 1944, believed that wholesalers did not observe their ceilings.[7] If one included the 23 per cent who expressed no opinion, and which undoubtedly included many who were unwilling to report wholesalers' violations, the figures would increase to one out of two who believed that wholesalers did not stick to their ceilings.

Enforcement Actions

The actual enforcement case load of the OPA represented the minimum figure of the extent of the black market. These figures represented a minimum not only because of the limited size of the enforcement staff, but also because sanctions were instituted only in a small proportion of cases where violations were detected. On the other hand, there is the possibility that some of the figures might not be entirely representative of violations in all industries, since the fields of business selected for investigation were likely to be those with more evidences of violations. It should be noted also that a violation charged against a concern might, and usually did, consist of several counts, or incidents disclosing violation, as it was not the general procedure for the OPA to take action on the basis of a single isolated offense unless it was particularly serious. The volume of violations was so great, in terms of the personnel

---

[7] "Grocer Experiences with the Price Control System," Special Memorandum No. 113, Surveys Division, Bureau of Special Services, Office of War Information, May 10, 1944, p. 11 (Mimeographed).

available to process them, that the enforcement staff had to be selective in their actions.

From the beginning of the OPA in 1942 until its termination on May 31, 1947, a period slightly over five years, the government investigative staff consisted, on the average, of less than 3,000 investigators and some 600 attorneys. During this period this limited staff conducted over a million investigations and turned up 259,966 cases which resulted in the institution of some action leading to possible serious punishment. (See Table 1.) By March 31, 1947, action had been completed on 170,708 of these cases, of which only 8,465 were lost by the government, while 31,469 were withdrawn. (See Table 2.) The large number of cases withdrawn for the most part constituted those in which the defendants made a settlement or adopted some other compromise action, or cases in which the government suspended action in the closing days of price and rationing controls. In Canada, from the beginning of price, rationing, and rent controls in 1939 through July, 1946, the total number of prosecutions for black market violations was 26,250.[8] In the year 1944 Canada, for example, prosecuted 7,718 persons for price, rationing, and rent violations, of whom 2,493 were for price violations. While total figures are difficult to obtain for Great Britian, from October, 1939 until January, 1943, the Ministry of Food instituted 73,738 proceedings against business concerns. Although comparable data are not available for violations in other fields, they were probably not as extensive.[9]

The figures on formal sanctions by the OPA, however, tell only part of the story. Between 1943 and 1945, for example,

---

[8] "Prosecutions September 1, 1939, to July 31, 1946," Report of the Enforcement Administration, the Wartime Prices and Trade Board, Canada (Mimeographed).

[9] Backman, op. cit., pp. 59–61.

Table 1

Sanctions Instituted by the OPA Enforcement Department
for Price, Rationing, and Rent Violations,
February 11, 1942—May 31, 1947

Total sanctions instituted	259,966
Suspension order proceedings	52,297
Determination proceedings	165
Rescission of veterans' housing sale	1
Restitutions of sales control overcharges	10
Revocations of dealers' authorization	27
Voluntary contributions	8,213
Administrator's consumers' treble damage claims:	
Settlements:	
Refund	4,016
Payment to United States Treasury	29,596
Suits filed	26,094
Administrator's own treble damage claims:	
Settlements	28,125
Suits filed	12,638
Injunction suits	78,081
License suspension suits	1,013
Local criminal prosecutions by OPA agents	5,127
Federal criminal prosecutions	13,999
Contempt proceedings	564
Total proceedings closed	167,774

SOURCE: Office of Price Administration, *Twenty-second Quarterly Report*, for the period ending May 31, 1947, p. 17. Excludes 20,758 consumer revocations. Figures do not include most OPA price panel and informal rent violation settlements, debiting of dealers' rations, prosecutions by state and local governments where there were anti-black market laws or ordinances, or actions brought by other federal agencies and private individuals. For definitions of terms used in this table, see Chapter Nine.

volunteer citizen price panels held 623,503 conferences with retail violators. These conferences were the outgrowths of 1,375,-380 reported violations. The price panels during this period negotiated settlements for 71,050 administrators' claims and

Table 2

Administrative, Civil, and Criminal Proceedings Closed by the
OPA Enforcement Department, February 11, 1942—
May 31, 1947

Total proceedings closed *170,708*
   Won 130,774
   Lost 8,465
   Withdrawn 31,469
Suspension order proceedings closed *52,391*
   Won 41,784
   Lost 4,743
   Withdrawn 5,864
Determination proceedings closed *133*
   Won 112
   Lost 7
   Withdrawn 14
Administrator's consumers' treble damage suits closed *19,370*
   Won 13,869
   Lost 605
   Withdrawn 4,896
Administrator's own treble damage suits closed *8,537*
   Won 6,303
   Lost 334
   Withdrawn 1,900
Injunction suits closed *69,864*
   Preliminary 2,970
   Won (permanent) 48,899
   Lost 1,606
   Withdrawn 16,389
License suspension suits closed *836*
   Won 328
   Lost 66
   Withdrawn 442
Local criminal prosecutions by OPA agents closed *5,161*
   Won 4,553
   Lost 216

Table 2 (Continued)

Withdrawn 392
Federal criminal prosecutions closed *13,915*
  Convicted and sentenced:
    Imprisonment only 1,629
    Imprisonment and fine 1,341
    Fine only 5,312
    Probation or suspended sentence 3,318
  Lost 815
  Withdrawn 1,500
Contempt proceedings *501*
  Won 356
  Lost 73
  Withdrawn 72

SOURCE: Office of Price Administration, *Twenty-second Quarterly Report,* for the period ending May 31, 1947, p. 17. Terms defined in Chapter Nine. Differences between total figures in Tables 1 and 2 are due to exclusion from Table 2 of cases which were still pending action.

refunds to 18,133 customers. In addition there were tens of thousands of actions under local anti-black market ordinances in the five states and seventy-five municipalities which had them. In New York City alone there were 18,875 prosecutions of retailers and 4,000 wholesale prosecutions in 1944. Moreover, uncounted black market cases were dealt with by other federal agencies,[10] and in thousands of instances suits by consumers were instituted under the provisions of the law which provided for such suits against dealers. During the three years from June, 1942, to June, 1945, the OPA received a total of 784,147 tenant complaints which resulted in adjustments and settlements of some form, many, of course, being minor difficulties. A total of 6,855 serious rent cases were referred to the Enforcement Department for formal action in 1944 alone.[11]

---

[10] See Chapter Ten.

[11] The estimated 1944 annual grand total of all OPA violations, including consumer, rent, retail, and wholesale and manufacturing, which is approximately

Approximately one in every fifteen of the three million business concerns in the country were punished by some serious sanction.[12] Altogether there were instituted 52,297 suspension order proceedings, a total of 67,919 monetary payments or suits at the retail level, and 40,763 monetary payments or suits for payment at the manufacturing or wholesale level. In addition, there were 78,081 suits for injunction and federal criminal prosecution in 13,999 cases. (See Table 1.) The government collected some 73 million dollars in damages and fines. Some idea of the volume of these court cases can be seen in Table 3. Civil cases begun by the OPA between 1943 and 1947 ranged annually from 7.9 per cent to 54.2 per cent of all cases in the federal courts. Criminal cases during this same period were as high as 12.8 per cent.

These figures, large as they are, scarcely scratch the surface of total violations, being largely cases involving more serious action. In general, less than one fourth of the cases where the government found violation resulted in any serious action. Others were simply warned or sent license warning notices, informal adjustments were made, or the case was dismissed with no action. Consequently, a conservative figure of serious violations during the five-year OPA period, instead of being 259,966 cases, should probably be at least three times that figure, or about 810,000 violations. If an estimate is based on

---

900,000, is equal to the total ordinary crimes known to the police which was also approximately 900,000.—*Uniform Crime Reports.* Semiannual Bulletin, Vol. XV, No. 1, Federal Bureau of Investigation, United States Department of Justice, Washington, D.C.

[12] This estimate is based on 200,000 sanctions for the following reasons. While the sanction figures relate almost entirely to businessmen, they do include a minor number of criminal cases involving ordinary individual criminals such as thieves and counterfeiters, in which, however, a business concern might have been indirectly involved. An undetermined but probably small proportion of rent cases are also included. Some concerns were repeaters and are, therefore, duplicated in this estimate.

200,000 business sanctions, since an undetermined but small proportion of rent and other cases are included in the total of all enforcement activities, there were at least 600,000 business concerns against whom some action was taken, or one in every five.

Percentage of Violation Found by Investigation

Estimates of about one out of five business concerns in violation during the five-year period are also undoubtedly too low, because not all concerns were investigated. The year 1944 is a reasonably satisfactory one for estimates because the war was at its height and controls had been in effect for two or three years. In that year, for example, of those business firms investigated, approximately 57 per cent were found in violation which, if applied to the total of all concerns, would be approximately 1,710,000 violations. This figure may be too high for the five-year period, however, because of some duplication of business concerns in these figures. Noncomplaint or program investigations revealed 48.6 per cent in violation; violations were also found in 68.1 per cent of the complaint investigations. These data do not reveal what proportion were substantive and how many were record-keeping violations, but the importance of the latter to the evasive nature of business violations makes this distinction largely irrelevant. If our comparison is restricted to large concerns, namely, manufacturing and wholesale, approximately 70 per cent of those concerns, or two out of three concerns, investigated during 1944 were found to be in violation. During the first six months of 1945, 9,066 such cases of violation were found. Approximately 30 per cent of all injunctions, and 18 per cent of all criminal cases, were instituted in 1945 against manufacturing and wholesale concerns.

Table 3

OPA and Other Cases, Civil and Criminal, Commenced in 84 United States District Courts, 1943–1947

TYPE OF CASE	1943		1944		1945		1946		1947	
	NUM-BER	PER-CENTAGE	NUM-BER	PER-CENTAGE	NUM-BER	PER-CENTAGE	NUM-BER	PER-CENTAGE	NUM-BER	PER-CENTAGE
All civil cases....	28,166	100.0	29,742	100.0	52,144	100.0	57,512	100.0	48,809	100.0
OPA cases .	2,219	7.9	6,524	22.0	28,283	54.2	31,094	54.1	15,169	31.1
Other U.S. cases.....	15,686	55.7	13,325	44.8	13,804	26.5	13,837	24.0	13,990	28.7
Private cases....	10,261	36.4	9,893	33.2	10,057	19.3	12,581	21.9	19,650	40.2
All criminal cases....			37,063	100.0	37,070	100.0	30,665	100.0	31,114	100.0
OPA cases.	2,791*		4,524	12.2	4,753	12.8	2,520	8.2	1,454	4.7
Others......			32,539	87.8	32,317	87.2	28,145	91.8	29,660	95.3

* Number of criminal defendants larger than number of cases.

SOURCE: Annual Reports of the Director of the Administrative Office of the United States Courts, Fiscal Years Ending June 30. Because of different procedures in the tabulations, these figures will not agree with Tables 1 and 2.

Violations by Commodity

Extensive black market violations occurred in a large number of commodities at the producing, wholesaling, and retailing levels. Likewise, extensive violations occurred in a variety of commodities, indicating the pervasiveness of the black market and contradicting claims that violations were confined to any particular industry. Although there was black marketing in other trade lines,[13] it was particularly flagrant in the following:[14]

coffee	liquor	used cars
meat	apparel	tires
poultry	lumber	building materials
potatoes	waste paper	industrial materials
onions	consumer dur-	scrap metal
sugar	ables	rent
grains	gasoline	
cigarettes	fuel oil	

While commodities such as gasoline and meat were fairly essential, one might venture to speculate what might have been the problems of the American government if it had been necessary, because of limited supplies, to regulate strictly the rationing of bread, eggs, or similar essential foodstuffs, or of essential clothing as in Great Britain. There was much black market activity in these basic items in other countries.[15] Fortunately,

---

13 For example, extensive violations occurred in such commodities as walnuts, honey, shrimp, frozen and dried eggs. See analysis of these black markets in Frank E. Hartung, "A Study in Law and Social Differentiation," unpublished Ph. D. dissertation, University of Michigan, Ann Arbor, 1949, pp. 137–141.

14 Information derived from various congressional hearings and from OPA quarterly reports.

15 Marquis Childs, returning in 1945 after a trip to Europe where black markets existed in commodities where life and death often hinged on acquiring them, had some acid things to say about the meat black market in a comparatively well-fed America.

fairly adequate supplies made it unnecessary for the American government to force a drastic showdown by rationing those commodities as well. There were violations exceeding 40 per cent in program investigations in all but one of thirteen major commodity groups in 1944. (See Table 4.) One in two inves-

Table 4

Percentage of Violations on Noncomplaint (Program) and Complaint Investigations by Major Commodity Groups, 1944*

COMMODITY GROUP	NONCOMPLAINT	COMPLAINT
All commodities................	48.6	68.1
Food........................	45.6	71.2
Meat and dairy..............	43.1	74.5
Groceries...................	46.2	70.1
Apparel......................	49.1	64.1
Textiles and leather............	40.4	63.2
Industrial materials............	40.5	66.2
Industrial manufacturing........	44.8	67.0
Gasoline.....................	60.9	65.8
Automotive supplies...........	42.0	60.7
Heating fuels.................	23.7	60.2
Consumer durables.............	48.7	61.6
Services.....................	53.6	62.8
Rent.........................	52.8	77.5

* For the distinction between these terms, see Chapter Three.
SOURCE: Compiled from unpublished OPA Enforcement Department reports.

tigations of apparel and consumer durables revealed a violation. In complaint investigations, because they were screened, an even higher percentage of violations was found.

Although it is likely that black market violations were fairly persistent in most commodities, certain ones achieved prominence during particular periods of time. It is difficult to say whether this changing picture was actually due to an increase in violations, to wartime shortages, or to the shifting attention of enforcement activities, the press, and the public. The first extensive violations of the OPA regulations occurred in connection with the sale of scrap metal, which was then in great demand for the armed services, since most steel ingots contain a certain proportion of scrap materials.[16] Much of the scrap sold during this period was, contrary to regulations, ungraded; it included inferior scrap mixed with the best grades. During the summer of 1942, when such an event as the Battle of Midway was taking place and Rommel was chasing the British into Egypt, there was a black market in rationed tires. In several cases thousands of tires were moved without ration certificates and at above-ceiling prices.[17] In the spring of 1943 illegal profiteering became extensive in meat and potatoes. Large military purchases, crop failures, and an unprecedented increase in consumer demands drastically reduced the supply of potatoes available for shipment to normal civilian markets. In the summer of 1943, gasoline rationing, which had already been a difficult problem, became particularly serious. One of the worst black markets occurred in the spring and summer of 1943 when there were such extensive poultry violations that some army food programs were being affected. During these months President Roosevelt issued his "Hold-the-Line" order on inflation, the United States forces landed on Attu, and Allied troops invaded Sicily. So serious did the black market in poultry become that the army was finally forced to requisition poultry trucks in the Delmarva area (Delaware, Maryland, and Virginia),

[16] Office of Price Administration, *First Quarterly Report,* for the period ending April 30, 1942, p. 194.

[17] Office of Price Administration, *Second Quarterly Report,* for the period ending July 31, 1942, p. 54.

which was the East's largest producing area.[18] The OPA Administrator, in defending this requisition, said: "The only man who can suffer is the black market supplier who has a truck load of poultry for which he may have paid 6 or 7 cents a pound above the legal ceiling, and this man will suffer to the extent that he has violated . . . ."[19] In the winter of 1944 serious violations occurred in connection with the sale of alcoholic beverages.[20] There were acute shortages of alcohol in this period, which was just prior to the reopening of distilleries for limited civilian alcoholic production. The extensive over-ceiling sales which took place, as well as upgrading and tie-in sales, finally resulted in a congressional investigation.

The black market in lumber and waste paper, in the fall of 1943 at about the time our forces were invading Tarawa and the spring and summer of 1944, consisted of extensive upgrading in these two important commodities. During the spring of 1944, despite strenuous enforcement efforts, the gasoline black market had become not only a menace to civilian transportation but to the entire war effort. Early in the spring of 1944, live cattle prices and fraudulent cash-on-the-side transactions increased, threatening a return to the serious black market conditions of early 1943. This situation continued through the summer of 1944 and resulted in several congressional investigations. Sugar shortages, too, had been getting progressively worse during 1944, with the result that there were serious violations occurring in this commodity.[21] A survey

---

[18] Office of Price Administration, *Seventh Quarterly Report,* for the period ending September 30, 1943, pp. 85–86.

[19] *Ibid.*

[20] Office of Price Administration, *Eighth Quarterly Report,* for the period ending December 31, 1943, p. 64, and *Ninth Quarterly Report,* for the period ending March 31, 1944, pp. 74–75.

[21] Office of Price Administration, *Twelfth Quarterly Report,* for the period ending December 31, 1944, pp. 68–69.

in one region in May, 1944, found that practically every wholesaler was violating the sugar rationing order almost two years
after its issuance. At the time of these serious black markets
in meat, sugar, and gasoline, the Allied Forces occupied Rome
—on June 4, 1944—and on June 6 they landed in Normandy.

Another major black market appeared late in 1944 and
early 1945, affecting a large proportion of the American people.
This was in cigarettes and cigars and was the result of the fact
that tobacco crops were in short supply and the overseas exports
were large. Black markets in apparel and textiles had always
been bad, but they became acute in the spring and summer
of 1945, about the time of V–E Day, May 8, 1945. Reports of
violations were frequent, especially in the piece goods black
market in New York City, where side payments and false invoices were common, and the OPA and the War Production
Board embarked upon many new control programs. Even
though the complexity of the trade made the enforcement
problem most difficult, the extent of the violations indicated
that the apparel business "ignored Government regulations and,
when discovered in violation, had challenged the OPA to
enforce the law at its peril."[22] From the beginning to the conclusion of price control, prices in excess of ceilings were a
fairly common phenomenon in the apparel business, according
to all investigative reports, and quality deterioration was so
clever and extensive that investigators could not deal effectively
with the situation.[23] In the spring of 1943, for example, an
investigation of 20 per cent of the manufacturers of women's,
girls', and children's outerwear had revealed that one third

---

[22] Wilfred Carsel, *Wartime Apparel Price Control*, General Publication
No. 3 of the Historical Reports on War Administration, Office of Price Administration (Washington: Government Printing Office, 1947), p. 97.
[23] See OPA quarterly reports and Carsel, *op. cit.*, p. 170.

were in violation.[24] In the middle of 1944 there was almost universal noncompliance by retailers with the ceiling prices on women's outerwear garments, and sanctions were imposed or license warning notices sent in almost 2,000 of the most serious cases.[25] One study of conditions at the time stated: "It is the writer's opinion, formed on the basis of the OPA quarterly reports, congressional hearings, Carsel's study, and OPA enforcement activity, that the retail apparel industry in large part, not completely, refused even to attempt to comply with certain OPA regulations."[26] In the fall of 1945 and into 1946 there were widespread violations of the used-car regulations, quality deterioration in clothing, and a black market in textile piece goods. In the immediate postwar period, during the days of reconversion, extensive violations took place in rent, meat, clothing, lumber, building materials, used cars, and grains. These postwar violations appear to have been more extensive than during the war period. Testimony by leaders in the lumber industry in 1946 indicated that from 60 to 90 per cent of lumber, particularly southern pine, was moving in the black market, the most common violation being the mixing of green with cured lumber.[27] A journal of the day, reporting a survey of conditions, stated that these practices were common in the lumber industry. This article also pointed out that there was collaboration among the dealers in violating the regulations.

Retailers assure themselves of a supply of lumber to sell by transferring an interest in their business to a mill operator. They

---

[24] Office of Price Administration, *Fifth Quarterly Report,* for the period ending April 30, 1943, p. 58.

[25] Office of Price Administration, *Tenth Quarterly Report,* for the period ending June 30, 1944, p. 69.

[26] Hartung, *op. cit.,* p. 123.

[27] See *Hearings before the Senate Committee on Banking and Currency,* on Senate Resolution 2,028, Seventy-ninth Congress, First Session, pp. 2108–2176.

may agree to pay him stipulated dividends, which are in fact a bonus payment for the lumber supplied. Overbilling, as in delivering 4,000 feet of lumber and charging for 6,000, is prevalent. So is upgrading, whereby run-of-the-mill lumber is billed as the highest grade. Buyers co-operate by notifying sellers whether shipments have been inspected by OPA. In the case of rail shipments, the broken seal indicates which were inspected. The sellers submit invoices for top-grade lumber only after assurance there has been no inspection.[28]

By the end of 1946 black markets were so extensive in a wide variety of commodities that *Fortune* had this to say:

In the U. S. in 1946, the historians will write, it was possible to get anything you could imagine—for a price. The black-market quotations were fairly level across the land, too; for $7.50 you could get a pair of nylon stockings in any city; for $1 to $1.50 you could buy a pound of butter. It was said and not denied that if OPA really enforced the law, all the building-materials business men in Boston would be in jail. In the South, 1,250,000 pounds of black-market sugar went to the highest bidders—the moonshiners. Throughout the U. S. trucks were cold by "tie-ins"; for as much as $1,000 over the ceiling price the customer got some extra piston rings or two front fenders. Carpenters' nails were scarce, with the ceiling at $5 a keg in twenty-five keg lots, they were selling at two or three times the ceiling price. . . . The black market in farm machinery was one of the wildest: used tractors, OPA-priced at $2,000, sold at $3,400. Lumber got around the OPA everywhere by a variety of new grading methods; one lumber buyer grumbled: "If you can pick a board up by both ends without breaking it in the middle, it's No. 1 Select."[29]

---

[28] *United States News*, September 13, 1946, p. 14. Reprinted from *U. S. News & World Report*, an independent weekly news magazine published at Washington. Copyright 1946 United States News Publishing Corporation.

[29] "The Boom," *Fortune*, June, 1946, pp. 258–260.

Extent of Counterfeiting and Theft of Ration Currency

Ration currency violations, while primarily concentrated in gasoline,[30] also occurred extensively in meat, tires, sugar, and shoes and, to a certain extent, in all other rationed commodities.

Table 5

Counterfeit and Stolen Ration Currency Recovered before Use and after Use, July 1, 1944—March 30, 1945

COMMODITY	TOTAL	CURRENCY RE-COVERED BEFORE USE BY CURRENCY PROTECTION BRANCH	CURRENCY DIS-COVERED AFTER USE AT VERIFICATION CENTERS
Gasoline (gal.).	87,762,813	68,595,866	19,166,947
Sugar (lb.)	3,570,575	751,035	2,819,540
Meat (pt.)	339,051,310	334,099,060	4,952,250
Fuel oil (gal.). .		415,505	

SOURCE: Enforcement Department unpublished field reports. The verification centers were places to which used ration currency was sent by dealers to be checked for their accounts. At these centers the currency was verified as to whether it was genuine and whether it was stolen from issuing centers. The findings of the centers were not a complete picture of how much illegitimate currency was actually used, since, except for gasoline counterfeits, there was no complete screening.

During a nine-month period in 1944–1945 counterfeit and stolen ration currency which was discovered amounted to 87,762,813 gallons of gasoline, 3,570,575 pounds of sugar, and 339,051,310 meat points. (See Table 5.) This was not all, for counterfeit stamps for 49,583 pairs of shoes were uncovered at verification centers in a three-month period in 1945. In a nine-month period the OPA arrested over 400 persons engaged in

---

[30] See Chapter Six for a more detailed study of the black market in gasoline.

the illegal traffic in ration currency. These arrests included persons responsible for thefts at local boards, verification and distribution centers, as well as counterfeiters and distributors of stolen and counterfeit currency.[31] By June of 1944 there had been over 650 robberies of local boards involving 300,000,000 gallons of coupons, and about the same time a campaign against counterfeit coupons enabled the identification of over 132 different types of gasoline counterfeits and yielded 13 printing presses used to print counterfeits. One such press was running an order for 15,000,000 counterfeit A gas coupons and for 1,500,000 counterfeit shoe coupons when found.[32] In one case a racketeer with a prison record for robbery was found illegally in possession of 38,000 gallons of counterfeit gasoline coupons, 25,000 gallons of genuine fuel oil coupons, and 437 counterfeit shoe coupons, as well as a loaded automatic, two shotguns, and burglary tools.

During the last three months of 1944 the circulation of counterfeit gasoline coupons averaged 1,533,943 gallons a month. Although the heaviest black market trade was in gasoline ration currency, it increased rapidly in other commodities when supplies became short. In the fall of 1944, for example, when the sugar supply situation grew progressively worse, it was necessary to prevent persons who transferred sugar illegally from replenishing stocks with counterfeit sugar stamps. The most important single area of pressure was the industrial user on an allotment basis, particularly bottlers, packers, and candy manufacturers. In a survey of the inventories and accounts of sugar wholesalers, well over 1,000 establishments were inves-

---

[31] To cope with this problem of counterfeit currency and extensive thefts, from small "inside jobs" to armed robberies of verification centers, many protective methods were developed. For an account of some of these measures see Chapter Six.

[32] Office of Price Administration, *Tenth Quarterly Report*, p. 68.

tigated and more than 750 actions were brought under the sugar rationing regulation. The following report was typical:

> The reports, to date, of the sugar survey reveal a surprising situation. Almost every wholesale dealer in sugar had been found in violation. The percentage of violations is extremely, in fact, alarmingly high. Shortages are predominant, but a goodly number of overages exist. The survey has not been completed, but the reports which will come in hereafter are not expected to reduce materially the estimated high percentage of violations among the dealers.[33]

Later, when meat replaced gasoline as the OPA's gravest black market problem, counterfeiting of ration currency and trade in stolen and counterfeit coupons for meats, fats, and oils became fairly widespread. This development was due, first, to the increased severity of meat rationing and, second, to the success of the campaign against the gasoline black market which forced those trafficking in counterfeit and stolen gasoline coupons to look for a new and more lucrative field. Counterfeit meat currency, along with sugar stamp currency, was a troublesome problem throughout 1945. For example, the number of counterfeit "red" points uncovered at OPA verification centers rose from 2,234,213 during the period from April through June, 1945, to 4,061,616 during the July through September period of the same year.

Comparison with Ordinary Crimes in Wartime

Although the foregoing accounts of the widespread nature of the black market show considerable variation, there can be no question that it extended throughout the entire nation, among all classes of society, from the thief and counterfeiter

---

[33] From an OPA Enforcement Department unpublished field report.

to the businessman, at all levels of our economic structure, from consumer to large manufacturer, and in numerous commodities. The extensive nature of these violations might indicate an over-all increase in crimes throughout the country in a war situation. Such was not the case, however, for ordinary criminal statistics show an exactly opposite trend, with a marked decrease in property crime which is commonly associated with the lower socioeconomic groups. After examining the evidence during the last war, Merrill concluded that, compared with the average of the prewar years, 1939–1941, "crimes against property tended to decrease, with robbery, burglary, and larceny showing varied declines during the war years."[34] Robbery showed a net decline of 13.2 per cent, burglary 8.9 per cent, and larceny 13.3 per cent. This decline can partially be explained by the decrease in civilian population in the younger age groups, an age range from which most ordinary criminals are recruited, while those engaging in business offenses, such as the black market, were of an older age group. Merrill maintained that the withdrawal of large numbers of young men "does not negate the basic fact, however, of the statistical decrease in most forms of crime [lower socioeconomic crimes] during the peak years of the conflict."[35]

The evidence, then, indicates that there were extensive black market violations at the producing, wholesaling, and retailing levels in nearly all major commodities, and in many minor ones as well. Whether one uses government sources, testimony before congressional committees, or actual interviews with businessmen, the results are approximately the same. The belief of some that the black market was confined to certain

---

[34] Frances E. Merrill, *Social Problems on the Home Front* (New York: Harper & Brothers, 1948), p. 189.

[35] *Ibid.*, p. 199.

commodities where there were peculiar regulation difficulties appears to be unsubstantiated. It would be impossible to discuss, therefore, black market activities in all commodities. Instead, certain areas representing somewhat different problems intrinsic in the commodity have been selected for detailed discussion, namely, food, rationing, and rent. A subsequent chapter will deal with the meat black market and will be followed by others dealing with illegal activities in gasoline rationing and in rent. The meat and gasoline black markets were probably as serious as any that arose during the war.

CHAPTER THREE

Attacking the Black Market

After examining the nature and extent of the black market which swept this country during the last war it is not surprising that the government encountered such tremendous difficulties in its attempts to control it. Some have sought to explain this extensiveness as being the result of a "do nothing" policy by the government. When one looks at the problem in the light of the history of the government's enforcement efforts one is impressed with the efforts that were made by the government in its attack upon the black market. A lack of previous experience with controls of this type, however, and an initial period of unsuccessful voluntary controls in this national emergency resulted in a rather weak beginning to what should have been a strong enforcement approach. Successive changes in enforcement policies, directed at a situation rapidly getting out of hand, were like plugging up dikes that had begun to leak, as will be seen on examining the development of the government's control program.

Voluntary Methods of Control

National defense appropriations by April, 1941, had amounted to 35 billion dollars, and expenditures at that time were close to 1 billion dollars a month. To deal with the problem of inflation, the President, by executive order, on April 11, 1941, created the Office of Price Administration and

Civilian Supply (OPACS), with an original staff of eighty-five persons. On May 27 the President proclaimed a state of unlimited national emergency, and on June 22 Germany attacked the Soviet Union. On August 28, 1941, while hearings were in progress on the statutory enactment of a price control measure, the President created, again by executive order, the Office of Price Administration with Leon Henderson as administrator. Only voluntary methods of control were available, however, as these controls were not made into law by Congress until January 30, 1942, shortly after Pearl Harbor. During this voluntary prestatutory period approximately 50 per cent of wholesale prices were brought under price control and there were 120 voluntary price agreements, all of them on a selective basis.[1] When industries were thought to be getting out of line they were asked to adhere voluntarily to price regulations that had been issued, as well as to informal industry agreements. This program of voluntary controls was somewhat similar to the efforts of the Food and Fuel Administrations and the War Industries Board of World War I.

Trade associations and the pressure of public opinion were relied upon to keep industries within designated prices, and the government leaned over backward to avoid any intimation of strong enforcement activities against business. This was clearly indicated by statements made later with reference to enforcement work.[2] Wherever possible, conferences were called to encourage businessmen to stabilize their own prices by collective action. Since these conferences were not always effective

---

[1] *Chronology of the Office of Price Administration,* Miscellaneous Publication No. 1 of the Historical Reports on War Administration, Office of Price Administration (Washington: Government Printing Office, 1946).

[2] See George R. Taylor, "Selective Price Control," in *The Beginnings of OPA,* General Publication No. 1 of the Historical Reports on War Administration, Office of Price Administration (Washington: Government Printing Office, 1947), pp. 215–218.

in discouraging price increases, other methods of informal action were open, as illustrated in the following excerpt:

> The first of the informal types of control took the form of suggestions and warnings. An industry or its individual members were notified that stabilization of prices was expected and that unless such stabilization was obtained more drastic action would be taken. The second type of informal control was the fair price request, which made public a list of prices deemed to be fair and requested the industry to adhere to such prices. The third type of informal control was the "freeze" letter, directed to the members of an entire industry or to those members whose prices were out of line, calling upon them to hold their prices to the level of a specified date. Voluntary agreements constituted a fourth technique. The members of an industry voluntarily agreed not to exceed the price level of a specified date. In some cases the industry merely agreed not to raise its prices without prior notification to the Office. . . . In addition to these informal actions it was found necessary . . . to issue . . . formal ceiling schedules.[3]

In this voluntary period the government lacked formal enforcement measures. The only direct enforcement sanctions available were for the President, under certain conditions, to withhold essential supplies from an offender or take over and operate plants needed for the war effort. While these measures could have been used for violations, they were far too drastic at a time when defense production was essential. Almost up to the time of Pearl Harbor the little attention given to enforcement came primarily from the national office in Washington, as there were no enforcement field staffs prior to that time. No enforcement drives against the black market were conducted, and enforcement activities arose entirely out of complaints, as had been the custom in most other government

---

[3] Office of Price Administration, *First Quarterly Report*, p. 9.

agencies. When publicity failed, the government could do no more about the situation. With tens of thousands of business concerns to cover, the prestatutory OPA had a staff of less than 200 investigators. Prior to Pearl Harbor only about 100 cases were handled; from that date until February, 1942, there were 519 cases, most of these violators simply being warned.[4]

The degree of compliance first achieved by these cumbersome methods was surprising, but the situation in general at the beginning of this period was not too serious. There were unused industrial potentialities, sufficient industrial manpower, and few shortages. In addition, the government, at first, was coping largely with manufacturing and wholesale concerns in selected industrial areas. As inflationary pressures increased, however, such methods met with less and less success. The consumer price index increased from 102.2 in April, 1941, to 112 in January, 1942. At the time of the congressional hearings on the enactment of the Emergency Price Control Act in the fall of 1941 compliance was critical in scrap metals, cotton textiles, and other products where the marketing structure was complex and the products sold were of varied form and heterogeneous quality. The following testimony is typical of the situation which existed at this time.

In the scrap metal markets the same kinds of ingenious devices which were once employed to evade minimum-price schedules under the National Recovery Administration codes are now being used in reverse to evade the Price Division's ceiling schedules. Failure to comply on the part of the unscrupulous minority tends to become contagious in such large trades and to demoralize the

---

[4] There was restitution or payment to the Treasury, usually after a compliance conference, in 103 cases; warning notices in 53; informal conferences in 45. In 173 cases either no action was taken or no violation was disclosed. The remaining cases were pending at the time of the statutory enactment.—*Ibid.*, p. 195.

whole group, as well as to disrupt the healthy operation of the trade in the interests of national defense. Under such circumstances, something more persuasive than mere suggestions, requests, and warnings in the press is obviously necessary to achieve price stability. Urgent pleas for vigorous enforcement action have come in large numbers from the numerous members of trades who sympathize with the government's price objectives and yet find themselves severely pinched by the behavior of unscrupulous competitors. The volume of such complaints has become increasingly large.[5]

During this initial period many businessmen, in sharp contrast to their later pleas to do away with the OPA, were anxious to have enforceable ceilings. This trend of developments was clearly demonstrated by press reports, correspondence, and other communications received by the Price Division officials which fell largely into three types: (1) reports on violations of existing price ceilings; (2) complaints of injury to trade members by unscrupulous violators and urgent pleas for the government to take vigorous action to enforce present schedules; and (3) indications that inflationary price movements were spreading rapidly to new areas, along with emphatic requests that the government do something about it. One example of the flagrant violations of existing ceiling schedules was the "bootlegging" of scrap metals at prices substantially above ceiling levels, practically cutting off the supply of such materials from many regular dealers. Complainants against violators, as well as editors of trade publications, advocated greater price control powers and more vigorous enforcement. Not infrequently they proposed specific programs of enforcement which usually entailed actions beyond the government's

---

[5] *Hearings before the House Committee on Banking and Currency*, on House Resolution 5,479, Seventy-seventh Congress, First Session, Pt. 1, p. 285.

powers at that time. Daily processions of businessmen visited the Price Division of the OPACS in Washington with reports of violations, of which the following are typical.

The disorder created by chiselers in the scrap industry is becoming too acute, and remedies must be found immediately to solve this situation.

The automobile dealers do not support the principle of a price stabilization and refuse cooperation necessitated by the creation of your new price schedule.

We wish to inform you that Wall Street brokers are using the speculative purchase of hides and other commodities. They are pointing out laughingly that, in spite of your and other government officials' statements, commodity prices are continuing to rise to new high levels. They try to impress us and the public that steps so far taken by your good office are ineffective.

The general conclusions about the voluntary methods of OPACS were summed up in the plea for a statutory Price Control Act:

Efforts to achieve desired results on a voluntary basis, even where the number of sellers is small, have been marked by failure in some important instances. Requests from the Price Division for cooperation have been explicitly refused or ignored by certain members of the automobile, gypsum, paper board, petroleum, and plywood industries, for example.[6]

There were numerous instances of firms promising to comply with fixed prices, only to ignore them with unannounced price increases, resulting, of course, in their taking unfair advantage of competitors. Compliance was particularly poor in the iron and steel-scrap industries where all efforts to stabilize prices

---

[6] *Ibid.*, p. 286. The quotations immediately preceding are also from the *Hearings*, p. 300.

on a voluntary basis proved futile. There was a general appeal for strong enforcement to back up price control. This was regarded as particularly urgent before prices got out of hand, as this excerpt points out:

> One major tool of effective price control is woefully lacking: adequate power to secure compliance with ceiling schedules. Without such power the price situation will soon be dangerously out of hand. Time is of the essence. Price increases must be prevented before they occur. Any widespread scaling down of prices once they have risen is impossible.[7]

Statutory Enforcement Provisions

This, then, was the situation generally as the price law was passed and signed by the President. (He had had power to control rationing under the First War Powers Act of December 18, 1941.) From the beginning there had been some recognition that the enforcement of the regulations would be one of the crucial tasks of this new governmental agency, and considerable testimony at the initial congressional hearings on the law was devoted to this problem. The Emergency Price Control Act contained definite powers for enforcing the price, rationing, and rent regulations,[8] and there were specific sections under "Enforcement" devoted to the types of sanctions

---

[7] *Ibid.*, p. 301.

[8] "It shall be unlawful, regardless of any contract, agreement, lease, or other obligation heretofore or hereafter entered into, for any person to sell or deliver any commodity, or in the course of trade or business to buy or receive any commodity, or to demand or receive any rent for any defense-area housing accommodations, or otherwise to do or omit to do any act, in violation of any regulation or order under section 2, or of any price schedule effective in accordance with the provisions of section 206, or of any regulation, order, or requirement under section 202 (b) or section 205 (c), or to offer, solicit, or agree to do any of the foregoing."—*Emergency Price Control Act of 1942 and Stabilization Act of 1942 as Amended by Stabilization Extension Act of 1944,* Section 4 (a), Office of Price Administration, July 1, 1944, p. 8.

provided, including the use of injunctions, criminal prosecution, treble damage actions, and license suspension suits. This complement of enforcement tools with which the administrator was armed was "in marked contrast to the circumscribed and unwieldy sanctions available to secure observance of price schedules issued during the pre-statutory period."[9]

The Issue of Strong Enforcement against the Black Market

Even with these specific statutory powers, however, the first stage of enforcement policy development after statutory enactment might well be characterized by a relatively weak attitude toward the use of these enforcement tools. Even though these formal measures were provided, and there had been a great deal of agitation for including them in the act, the agency itself proceeded to deal with business as a whole with a "kid gloves" policy. What moderate emphasis there was on enforcement, or the "big stick," during the first four months of the new agency was largely reserved for what was thought to be a small minority of "bootleggers" and other violators. Statements by the administrator indicated that the government was confident that

the attitude, the fear of inflation and the desire to abide by the law on the part of the preponderance of people, both buyers and sellers, will operate to police that provision. If you get compliance on the part of the great majority of buyers and sellers, and that covers 90 per cent of all the transactions, you cannot have inflation. You cannot have inflation if 90 per cent are kept within the bounds of the requirement, and that is the important thing about price regulation. . . . I have no difficulty in thinking that as

---

[9] David Ginsburg, "The Emergency Price Control Act of 1942: Basic Authority and Sanctions," *Law and Contemporary Problems,* School of Law, Duke University, IX, No. 1 (Winter, 1942), p. 55. Copyright, 1942, by Duke University.

far as bootlegging and violations are concerned it can be handled. I have no fear at all of the sporadic violations that a regulation of any kind gets. I know that its importance rests upon the basic commodity lines, on maintaining a proper margin, that you can reach the largest part of the transactions, and that will keep the price somewhere near what it should be, and if that is done you will prevent inflation.[10]

In the meantime the public and business had been developing an attitude that the OPA did not mean business, that violations would be followed with only minor actions, usually simply a warning letter, and that the penalties described in the regulations were virtually meaningless. New types of violations were rapidly being devised and spreading from business concern to business concern and from consumer to consumer, while statements were made by the administrator to the effect that only a small percentage of persons were violating the regulations. Great emphasis was put on issuing regulations and ration orders, while a relatively small proportion of personnel was delegated even to ascertain the extent of violations or the general attitudes of businessmen toward methods of controlling violations. The agency continued its policy of selective control, as in the prestatutory period, issuing regulations whenever there appeared to be danger of a price rise.

As the economy was rapidly getting out of hand with this slow hit-and-miss method of price control, the government on April 28, 1942, froze the prices of nearly all uncontrolled commodities by issuing the General Maximum Price Regulation (GMPR) which, up to that time, was probably one of the most comprehensive government orders ever issued in the United States. This regulation provided: "Persons violating

---

[10] Statement of Leon Henderson on price control in *Hearings before the House Committee on Banking and Currency,* on House Resolution 5,479, p. 765.

any provision of this Regulation are subject to the criminal penalties, civil enforcement actions, and suits for treble damages provided by the Emergency Price Control Act of 1942 and proceedings for the suspension of licenses." While eventually many of the commodities under its control were transferred to separate formula or dollar-and-cents regulations, for many months the GMPR continued to govern a large part of the country's economy.

From the time this regulation was issued the problems confronting the enforcement work of the agency became even more difficult. A series of experiments were begun, with resulting successes and errors, but on the whole the attitude of the agency after the issuance of GMPR continued to be primarily one of "pussyfooting" toward violations.[11] Surveys conducted by the OPA indicated that businessmen were not responding to patriotic appeals, and more drastic steps seemed necessary. Finally, the administrator[12] called upon the legal department to take serious steps against violators. He pointed out that GMPR had been in effect two months and that this initial phase was characterized by an intensive educational program[13] designed to inform the general public about the nature and purposes of the regulation and especially to advise businessmen of their responsibilities. Although Henderson's memorandum

---

[11] Despite the fact that several million concerns were covered from May 1 to July 31, 1942, only 1,556 investigation reports were completed in the entire country, of which 607 were GMPR cases. The total number of civil suits to July 1, 1942, was only 62.

[12] Memorandum from Leon Henderson to all deputy administrators and regional administrators of the Office of Price Administration, on the subject of "Enforcement of the GMPR," July 26, 1942.

[13] Extensive use was made of the press, radio, screen, and other means of communication. Meetings and conferences were held with retailers. Two million copies of bulletins and an official "flyer" outlining requirements were distributed through post offices, and thousands of retailers received personal visits.

stated that "as a result of this unusually extensive educational campaign to date, OPA is prepared to take the position that in the overwhelming majority of cases failure of retailers to comply can no longer be justified on the basis of inadequate information about OPA regulations," he went on to caution that "it cannot be too strongly emphasized that this second phase [enforcement] of the general price control program must be guided and conducted with the utmost care in order to strengthen public confidence and to avoid widespread unfavorable reactions."

In spite of these early indications of the need for strong enforcement, it was not until some two years after the original statutory enactment of the OPA that anything like really full support within the agency itself was thrown behind enforcement. During much of this period the attitude of the operating departments, such as price and rationing, as well as that of those dealing with enforcement, was one of leniency toward violators, keeping enforcement activities at a minimum. Another significant factor in the loss of valuable time in establishing effective enforcement of the price and rationing regulations was the initial separation of the legal and investigative work of the OPA into separate divisions. In the spring of 1942 investigators and attorneys were placed in the Legal Department, but each was under separate administrative control.[14] This divided authority and technical responsibility, extending down through the regional and district offices, resulted in considerable confusion and interfered with the operating efficiency of the OPA enforcement activities.

Still another important factor influencing the enforcement

---

[14] It was not until a year later that all enforcement was recognized as a function important enough to be made a separate department.

program was the frequent attacks made by members of Congress who attacked the OPA for having investigators who dared investigate cases and lawyers who dared bring severe punitive measures against business violators. There were frequent references in congressional debates to the maintenance of a large staff of investigators and the expenditure of considerable money to enforce regulations. Congress was repeatedly requested to increase the number of investigators, who were pitifully few for their task, but only inadequate increases were made. It is difficult to know how much of this attack by certain legislators was a failure to appreciate the direct relationship between the success of an agency and its enforcement staff, and how much was rather a covert maneuver to destroy the objectives of the agency by recognition of such a relationship. Some congressmen were heartily in favor of continued price and rationing controls, yet opposed the maintenance of anything but a relatively small enforcement staff because they did not want businessmen they knew prosecuted as violators:

Congressional disapproval of OPA's request to double its present roster of 2,000 snoopers may be one of the biggest boosts the black market ever had. Experience in other nations has shown that only a steady barrage of publicity, coupled with the vigilance of paid policemen, can stamp out this kind of wartime lawlessness. Yet Congress seems in no mood to supply either of these weapons. . . . Nobody can say for sure how big the black market really is or whether it is getting bigger or smaller. Best guess, however, is that the market has not yet reached disastrous proportions, and that it is still largely cyclical (i.e., it rises and falls against the rise and fall in commodity supplies). The cyclical aspect is heartening. For if a genuine syndicate of the type described in Sunday feature stories were in existence, the market would be more steady. The syndicate would see to that in order to assure an even flow of gravy. . . . The big trouble in foods is that black markets are usually operated by regular merchants through regular channels of trade.[15]

This real problem of the limited size of the enforcement staff was undoubtedly the most consistently serious threat to any effort to deal successfully with the black market. During the war there was a maximum OPA investigative staff of only 3,100[16] (with some supplemental assistance from other agencies and private citizens) which was expected to keep under surveillance the activities of millions of individuals and hundreds of thousands of business establishments, with millions of commodities and billions of transactions involved.[17] (See Table 6.) This staff was distributed among 9 regions, one of which administered the territories, and 96 district field offices. Even with this maximum wartime OPA staff there was, on an average, approximately 1 investigator for a county, and some states, for example, Iowa, Tennessee, and Kentucky in 1944, had less than 50 investigators for the entire state. In the Detroit district office, with twelve counties and a total population of over five million, and in an area of heavy industrial activity, acute labor shortages, and intense inflationary pressures, there was an average of only 50 investigators.[18] Metropolitan Chicago,

---

[15] "Ceiling-Price-Gyps," *Business Week,* June 26, 1943, p. 72.

[16] After the war the number of OPA investigators increased to 3,600.

[17] Canada had about 560 investigators to enforce its regulations for a population of 11,000,000. On an equivalent basis OPA should have had 6,700 investigators. This is even more disproportionate when it is realized that under Canadian law the burden of proof in price control proceedings was on the defendant to show that he did not commit the alleged violation, a means of saving considerable manpower. In Great Britain, where the program of enforcement was distributed among several agencies, the Ministry of Food had about 2,000 food inspectors who, although they had some other duties, were assigned to detect black market violations. Still further comparisons can be drawn by the fact that the Treasury Department had a staff of approximately 21,000 investigators and other personnel to enforce the tax laws alone.

[18] Of this staff, eighteen worked with food, nine on apparel and industrial materials, fifteen on fuel and consumer goods, six on rents and services, and two were unallocated. In addition, a portion of this investigative staff's work was devoted to supervision.

with its more than three million people and extensive industrial setup, had approximately 100 investigators, and New York
City had 250, which is in marked contrast to the more than
17,000 policemen in the latter alone.[19]

Table 6

Approximate Size of OPA Enforcement Staff

YEAR	INVESTIGATORS	ATTORNEYS
1941 (OPACS and Prestatutory OPA)............	200	
1942.........................	900	300
1943.........................	1,800	350
1944.........................	2,800	600
1945.........................	3,100	700
1946.........................	3,600	800

* The figures in this table do not include clerical and secretarial personnel.
Prepared from unpublished OPA Enforcement Department reports.

The significance of such a limited enforcement staff is
apparent. With a ratio (in 1944) of approximately 1,000 wholesale, manufacturing, and retail and service establishments for
each investigator, it was impossible for him merely to visit, let
alone conduct a thorough investigation, of all these business
concerns in a year, even if he visited three each working day.
Even after the war, during the worst meat black market in the
spring of 1946 the OPA had about 750 investigators charged
with policing thousands of farmers, several thousand slaughtering houses and wholesale meat establishments, and several hundred thousand retail outlets. When there were flagrant side
payments in the used-car business after the war, there were

---

[19] Anti-black market laws in New York State and New York City did help,
however, to supplement the federal government staff in that area.

less than 300 investigators to police this industry throughout the country.

The problem of the legal and investigative staff, however, was not all a question of numbers; it was also a matter of the quality of the personnel. In addition to a general manpower shortage and the difficulties of selective recruiting there was a large turnover in the investigative personnel and to a considerable extent among the attorneys as well. Few of the applicants for the investigative positions had had appropriate experience or any background in accounting, both of which were essential to the job. Similarly, most of the attorneys who applied came from private practice, with relatively little previous experience with government regulations, and hardly any with the OPA; moreover, in many instances, their sympathies, at least initially, were often with the businessmen with whom they were to deal.[20] The great weakness of the enforcement attorneys, however, was the fact that neither their training nor their previous experience had made them familiar with the problems of a large office or of administering the activities of other people such as investigators, and often as much as three fourths of their time was devoted to such duties. The task of transforming attorneys into administrators and managers for the government was probably greater than the difficulties of making raw recruits into trained investigators. The following excerpt from an enforcement manual points out these considerations.

Not every attorney who goes to work for OPA belongs in the Enforcement Division. Many attorneys either in or out of OPA

---

[20] To overcome these limitations a comprehensive training program for these investigators was eventually instituted. It is interesting to note that many young OPA enforcement lawyers successfully opposed counsel who received many times their salary. One national office attorney whose salary was approximately $6,000 once remarked that he had computed the salaries of the opposition staffs of legal counsel which he faced in a New York court at a figure of at least $100,000.

have no taste for enforcement work. We may sympathize with an attorney who is always finding excuses for somebody's violations, and tries to build up in his own mind reasons for *not* taking action, who is forever seeking a justification for the violations which have been found. Some attorneys dislike suing people or taking money from them, subjecting them to criminal proceedings or suspension proceedings. One may conceive his duty more narrowly. *But* he does not belong to the Enforcement Division. . . .

In the OPA, there is no place for an enforcement attorney who has an abhorrence of managerial responsibilities, or a reluctance to apply sanctions on account of violations. We have rendered obsolete the symbol of the attorney shut off from everybody else in his office, surrounded by tomes, seeking, three months after the case has been referred to him showing violations, the last conceivable legal excuse for not applying the least of all possible sanctions. His passing should occasion no sorrow.[21]

Neither the inadequate size or inexperienced nature of the staff nor the particular enforcement difficulties accounted for all of the OPA's difficulties in this respect, however. As in all large aggregations of personnel there were inefficiency, laziness, and stupidity. The war undoubtedly aggravated this situation because the shortage of manpower made many persons reasonably immune to dismissal. The conditions of work during such an emergency were bound to result in a feeling on the part of some that their work had little purpose and in inadequate supervision of others. Certainly similar reports came as frequently from private employers and the military establishments. Some OPA enforcement personnel worked hard and industriously, while others did little more than collect a pay check. At top administrative levels, moreover, there was at

---

[21] John C. Roach, *Manual for Enforcement Attorneys of the Office of Price Administration,* 1946, pp. 35, 36–37 (Multilithed) .

times a failure to see fully the entire scope and magnitude of the task. This was particularly true during the first year when plans were laid on a minuscule basis. Even later, when the task was more fully visualized, scientific procedures and skilled experts were often not utilized in selecting and preparing enforcement programs. Many programs were poorly selected and prepared. All too often key enforcement positions were looked upon as mainly involving legal qualifications instead of knowledge of economic and commodity problems. Persons with broader qualifications might have prevented many of the difficulties.

A really effective, hard-hitting statement in favor of strong enforcement came in a memorandum from Administrator Bowles to the entire staff in January, 1945, which was some three years after the outbreak of war. For the first time the government went on official record as having come to the conclusion that violations were extensive, were not committed primarily by a criminal element nor by a small proportion of businessmen, but by many businessmen actively violating the regulations.[22] Strong action was necessary, and the implication was that those taking such strong action would have the full support of the agency. It was likewise implied that if the agency did not adopt strong measures many businessmen who had been complying would also violate as a matter of self-protection, and that the public would increasingly lose faith in the effectiveness of the price control program. This was a

---

[22] This was in marked contrast to typical statements of previous years: "The great majority of business establishments voluntarily adhere to our regulations if they realize the need for the regulations and understand their obligations under them . . . . Further, we must have strict compliance for the sake of the great majority of businessmen who comply and who are willing to live honestly within our regulations. . . . In general, enforcement action will be necessary only against the small minority who violate."—Memorandum to Staff from Chester Bowles, Office of Price Administration, on Administration and Enforcement of OPA Regulations, October 5, 1943, p. 1.

drastic statement and one which, in terms of the power structure of our society, required great courage:

> One of OPA's greatest weaknesses with the public today is the
> fact that so many violations go on unchecked, and that when
> violations are found the action taken is not strong enough or
> vigorous enough. I have met this criticism every time I have been
> away from Washington, regardless of where I have gone. More
> and more, the public tends to blame OPA for lack of effective
> enforcement. The public expects the Government to step in and
> effectively penalize those who violate price, rent, and rationing
> regulations.
>
> I think our experience over the last year calls for a re-
> examination of the approach to this problem which many of us
> have followed. We have relied on the assumption that 95 per cent
> of businessmen will comply voluntarily; that enforcement is neces-
> sary only against a recalcitrant five per cent. This has proven too
> optimistic. We know now that, in many an industry, considerably
> larger proportions of hitherto reputable businessmen are in sub-
> stantial violation.[23]

Changes in the Government's Methods of Attacking the Black Market

While the government was gradually developing a stronger
over-all approach to the control of black market violations by
businessmen, there were changes in the types of strategy employed as conditions changed or as various approaches proved
to be unsuccessful.

COMPLAINT APPROACH. During the early statutory period of
OPA enforcement some manufacturing and wholesale estab-

---

[23] Memorandum to Regional Administrators, District Directors, and Program Staffs from Chester Bowles, Office of Price Administration, January 31.
1945, p. 1.

lishments were investigated, but efforts were chiefly directed at retail levels with great emphasis on a few commodities such as gasoline and tire violations. In comparison, less attention was directed toward the large business concerns or at what was frequently the fundamental sources of violations like the wholesalers and manufacturers. Most investigative work was the result of complaints, and although complaints as a source of information for enforcement work are customarily utilized by most agencies, they had many disadvantages as a method of ascertaining compliance among business concerns. Such a procedure combined the trivial with the criminal, and there was a tendency that chance would govern the selection of particular types of industries and concerns. An enforcement official thus described the complaint approach:

We started out in the enforcement field by investigating individual complaints. We waited until a complaint came in and sent somebody out to investigate it. That involved two major difficulties. In the first place we soon found that most of these complaints were without foundation. A very surprising proportion, running from 50 to perhaps 85 per cent, depending on the regulation involved, proved upon investigation to be without foundation. Consequently we found we were using a good deal of our manpower in investigations which proved unfruitful. The other difficulty was that there were many sectors of industry where no complaints were filed. That did not mean, however, that there was successful compliance; on the contrary, it might equally well mean that there was no compliance at all. We soon found that we could not sit back and wait until complaints were filed in order to make sure that we were achieving compliance.[24]

24 Thomas I. Emerson, "Enforcement," in *A Manual of Price Control*, Lecture Series Delivered at the Training Program for Price of the Office of Price Administration, December, 1942–March, 1943 (Washington: Government Printing Office, 1943), p. 297.

COMPLIANCE SURVEYS. Compliance surveys or drives were developed as a substitute for the complaint approach. The purpose of the compliance survey was to give enforcement a more even distribution and to ensure a more complete coverage than could be accomplished solely through the investigation of complaints. Critical areas were selected for investigation and some systematic effort was made to ascertain violations. In addition to covering the field more broadly and using manpower more effectively, the drive technique had other advantages. By having almost the entire enforcement staff concentrate its efforts in a given commodity field for a relatively brief period of time and then shifting quickly to another field, it gave the impression of extensive enforcement both to the public and to business. Shifting emphasis from one commodity to another was thought to maintain compliance since the nature of the next drive was not known.[25] There were a number of disadvantages to this enforcement procedure. The commodities selected usually represented those with the most extensive violations, but the choice was dependent chiefly upon the amount of publicity which the violations had been receiving, which was likely to result in an emphasis on retail violations. The selection of most commodities was not based on their importance either to the cost of living or to their strategic relation in the economy. Only a limited number of industries could be investigated, some needed more continuous investigation, some were never reached at all, and many others disclosing violation could not be disposed of in the allotted time. Most important, however, was

---

[25] During a three-month period in 1942 national drives investigated cement manufacturers and the sale of soft drinks, beer, and other commodities by restaurants and taverns in the vicinity of military camps. Drives in the various regions during this period varied from only one in Chicago to ten in New York and covered such commodities as the prophylactic industry, hides, used steel drums, copper, aluminum and ferro alloys, green coffee, fats and oils, canned vegetables, ice, gasoline, and solid fuels.—*Second Quarterly Report,* p. 250.

the fact that neither investigators nor attorneys had an opportunity to gain detailed, specialized knowledge of an industry so that they could become reasonably expert in detecting violations.

COMMODITY SPECIALIZATION. Enforcement was not put on a par with the operating departments of the OPA until early in 1943, a year after the statutory enactment of price control. Shortly after the creation of this separate enforcement department on an equal basis with those dealing with the issuance of price, rationing, and rent regulations, a number of unique steps were taken in reorganizing enforcement work. Most of these changes were dictated by the pressing peculiarities of economic control problems. The growth of extensive regulations had made it imperative for attorneys and investigators to work together and to specialize in certain commodities. Consequently, one of the drastic parts of the reorganization was to combine attorneys and investigators into units dealing with particular commodities such as food, gasoline, apparel, consumer durables, and rent. In this new setup, attorneys and investigators assigned to food became familiar with these regulations and theoretically dealt only with cases involving food. The organization of these enforcement commodity divisions at the national level is shown in Chart 1. As a part of this same policy change, a ceiling was set on the proportion of time spent in enforcing any given group of commodities, with the purpose of diverting the expenditure of manpower from those in which public pressure could be exerted to those where it could be more advantageously used from a national enforcement standpoint. For example, gasoline, which had up to this point consumed anywhere from 40 to 50 per cent of all manpower devoted to enforcement, was restricted to not more than 15 per cent of the work of any given district office.

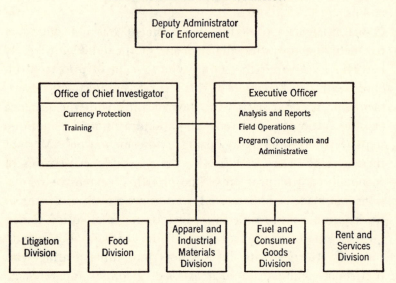

ENFORCEMENT COMMODITY PROGRAMS. A further step was the creation of planned enforcement programs and an almost complete reduction, as far as the general enforcement policy was concerned, in the survey type of enforcement, as well as investigations in response to complaints. Although such a planned program superficially resembled a survey, it was more than that. First, an attempt was made to ascertain those fields in which there were extensive violations. Then manuals were prepared outlining the essential features of the industry, the provisions of the regulations, types of violations, and the plans for enforcement action, including suggested investigative techniques. Some information was derived from working with specialists in the departments such as price, and from industry studies and trade reports. Most of these programs, instead of being of short duration as in the case of a typical survey, were to continue over a considerable period of time, in some cases almost indefinitely, and were also to incorporate into the program any complaints which might have come to the attention of the district office. Some programs called for the nation-wide checking of nearly all firms in a given industry.

Several considerations affected the selection of commodity programs. Some were undoubtedly chosen because of the great extent of violations, but there were other important factors. In some instances it was felt that the failure to enforce strategically unimportant regulations in an area where the black market was being publicized might cause violations to spread to more basic commodities. In other instances, unfortunately, programs were selected without too much recognition of whether the results would be equal to the expenditure of manpower for this purpose.[26] Commodities like meat and gasoline received enforcement emphasis not only because of extensive violations but because of the importance of these two commodities to the general public. This was also the situation in regard to the black market in potatoes and onions. Other commodities like liquor were selected not only because of the extent of violations and the need to keep as much alcohol as possible available for munitions, but because the press, Congress, and others gave much attention to the apparent lack of enforcement in this area. Some programs like lumber and waste paper were necessary because of the importance of these commodities to other indus-

---

[26] As late as 1945, however, a survey by the Bureau of the Budget criticized OPA enforcement efforts in this regard: "First, district commodity chiefs are not conducting their activities on a planned, programmed basis, but rather are working from case to case, and second, the investigators are given inadequate supervision in the course of their daily investigations."

trial concerns. In the consumer durables field, where there was insufficient staff to enforce every regulation, programs were developed to cover a few selected items. Enforcement programs were issued for almost all rationed articles, not only because these commodities were in great demand, but also because of the necessity for close supervision of transactions involving the use of ration currency.

MANUFACTURING AND WHOLESALE EMPHASIS. Instead of dealing primarily with consumer and retail violations, a new strategy was also devised whereby the major attention of enforcement was concentrated at the wholesale and manufacturing level, chiefly on the assumption that violations detected at the lower level could prevent a subsequent spiral of violations. Furthermore, it was generally easier to cover the smaller number of manufacturing and wholesale establishments in a given industry than to police several hundred thousand retail outlets. In conjunction with this new program a revolutionary enforcement procedure called on the assistance of citizen volunteers. To these price panels, as these volunteer groups were called, was delegated a major portion of the work of dealing with retail violations, leaving referrals of the more obstinate cases of retailers and the more complicated wholesale and manufacturing cases to the professional investigators of the enforcement department.[27]

DECENTRALIZATION OF AUTHORITY. Another drastic new procedure was the delegation of authority, with some exceptions, to the ninety-six offices for initiating investigations, disposing of cases, and applying sanctions without referring them to either the national or the regional office. Thus, with the exception of appellate litigation, there was almost complete decen-

---

[27] See Chapter Four.

tralization of operations to the field offices.[28] This new procedure included even the direct referral of criminal cases, with certain limited exceptions, to the local United States attorneys. The adoption of these new procedures broke a serious bottleneck in the national and regional offices and permitted the use of sanctions for the first time on an extensive scale. This delegation of authority over business concerns to so many district offices, at a time when the agency was being sharply criticized for some of its actions, was a hazardous but necessary step.

While this decentralization of authority to take specific legal measures worked quite well, the decentralization of general enforcement authority was a major administrative problem. The nine regional administrators, who were responsible for the direction of all OPA operations in their regions, had full authority, in accordance with established civil service procedures, to appoint and remove all members of the regional office staff. The district director had similar authority at his level, but the deputy administrator in charge of all enforcement at the national level had no method of seeing that the field complied with his instructions. He was without power to hire, fire, or transfer field staff; he could use only persuasion. Consequently, national enforcement policies issued by the OPA in Washington were sometimes carried out immediately by the regional administrators. More likely, however, regional administrators refused for some time to put into effect policies with

---

[28] In order to keep the national and regional offices informed of the enforcement work in the field, individual reports on all cases where sanctions were instituted, except license warning notices and debiting cases, were submitted by the field offices on IBM punch cards and filed. Subsequent cards followed the cases through to completion so that it was thus possible to know the status of practically all cases in the country. These reports, together with statistical reports from the field, were useful in appraising case loads for budgetary estimates as well as in answering inquiries from Congress.

which they disagreed. Similarly, district directors who took exception to the national policies often refused to carry them out unless directed specifically to do so by the regional administrator.

Sometimes the difficulties arose out of the failure of regional administrators and district directors to perceive that the control of the black market was a national problem and could not be conducted entirely on a regional basis.[29] Many national policies such as emphasis on wholesale and manufacturing cases involved a national rather than a sectional approach to enforcement problems. Both regional administrators and district office directors on occasions intervened in cases with the purpose of dictating a type of enforcement action contrary to national policy. Typical of such disputes was that between Daniel P. Woolley, New York Regional Administrator, and Paul L. Ross, the Regional Enforcement Executive, who was finally dismissed by Woolley in June, 1945.[30]

Information Services and Compliance

It has been said by many since the war years that the black market would have been less rampant, and compliance

---

[29] In the United States most goods are not sold where they are produced. This meant that unless products in producing areas were not properly investigated, they would show up in another area either at a higher ceiling or ungraded. It involved the cooperation of OPA districts which were agricultural with those which were manufacturing. This was as true of commodities like lettuce, grapes, and lumber as it was of finished products like apparel, furniture, or heavy industrial equipment.

[30] Ross charged publicly that Woolley diverted enforcement activities from food and clothing to press a "bring-back-the-cigarettes drive," and also interfered with the carrying out of national policies. The New York *Times* of July 19, 1945, stated: "An essential point of disagreement between Mr. Woolley and himself, Mr. Ross said, had been the question of where to put the emphasis on price control. Mr. Ross declared it was national policy to concentrate on the early distribution levels—the producers, manufacturers and wholesalers of price-controlled commodities—but Mr. Woolley insisted that 'we hit the retailers first' because that would be of more interest to the average consumer" (p. 15).

by both the public and business greater, if the government had had a more effective publicity campaign to publicize the regulations and the need for them. An examination of the OPA's strategy in using this type of publicity indicates quite clearly, however, that the government was aware of this need and made every effort to disseminate this type of information. The OPA organized a full-time staff of over five hundred persons into an information department working at the national, regional, and district office levels. The editorial unit of this Information Department not only worked with trade relations, radio, and magazines, but devised enforcement information involving graphics, advertisements, slide films, and motion pictures. In addition, each major commodity group had persons assigned for special coverage. Furthermore, there were thousands of persons on community service panels in the local price and rationing boards where a campaign was directed at the housewife to secure her "home front" pledge of paying no more than ceiling prices and accepting no rationed goods without giving the required coupons. Through this department there were also issued veritable barrages of pamphlets, speeches, and newspaper and magazine articles calling attention to the necessity for price and rationing controls. The radio was used extensively, including a regular weekly nation-wide broadcast by the Price Administrator and talks and interviews with district directors at the local level.[31] In fact, many people complained that this extensive publicity campaign was actually propaganda for the continuance of price control or rationing beyond the time that these controls were necessary. Some even suggested that it was a subtle plan to bring about the "socialization" of our economy. Cer-

---

[31] As early as July, 1942 a radio program, "Neighborhood Call," was started, and a recording of a dramatic show explaining rationing and price control was used by radio stations throughout the country.

tainly it was necessary, however, that the public and the trades be properly informed if they were to be expected to comply. Without this knowledge, falsehoods and rationalizations for noncompliance would have certainly resulted in a much more serious enforcement problem.

To secure further support among the various trades, when the agency prepared a regulation, it asked help of 652 industry advisory committees, which consisted of selected businessmen in the particular industry which would be controlled by the regulation. In general, whenever a new regulation or a ration order was issued, and in the months following, detailed press releases informed the public and the trade of the supply situation, as far as was feasible, and the nature and purpose of the specific regulation. There were innumerable pamphlets, speeches, radio talks, and newspaper and magazine articles. These industry committees were then used as an additional medium for explaining the purposes of the regulation. The OPA also arranged meetings with members of the trades to discuss the regulations, and at times the assistance of the particular trade associations was solicited to increase compliance. In some instances such assistance was even volunteered. It was thus hoped that these cooperative efforts would result in a better understanding between government and business and thus eventually bring about more extensive compliance with the regulations.

After regulations were put into effect attempts were made to continue this working relationship. From time to time, when protests or misunderstandings became extensive or violations were widespread, special conferences were called with trade leaders. Also, OPA representatives appeared before national and regional trade association meetings to go over the regulations and discuss enforcement difficulties.

Enforcement Publicity

In spite of these elaborate plans for publicizing the whole price and rationing program, initially there was little concerted publicity given to OPA's enforcement actions. Undoubtedly the agency was apprehensive of any widespread dissemination of reports of such actions, as any implication that it was attempting to boast of its enforcement work by showing that it was taking extensive and strong measures against violators might react unfavorably. The public might feel that the government was persecuting businessmen; in fact, certain congressmen and certain business interests did accuse the OPA of being a "Gestapo agency."[32] On the other hand, if the OPA as a government agency did not publicize its enforcement actions sufficiently, it gave the impression that there was practically no enforcement; the result, of course, would be even further violations and considerable disrespect for the government on the part of business as well as the public. And thereupon other congressmen then accused the OPA of "pussyfooting."

In spite of this dilemma, which plagued it throughout its existence, the agency later became well aware of the necessity for adequate enforcement publicity. A person engaging in black market activities might be deterred somewhat by fear of possible newspaper publicity if apprehended, the publicity possibly being almost as much a deterrent as a jail sentence or fine. Then, too, any publicity given to actions taken against members of certain trades might help to promote compliance within the trades. Thus, the agency eventually developed a program of enforcement publicity, both in trade journals and in

---

[32] See, for example, Senator Wherry's (R-Nebr.) frequent use of the word "Gestapo" to refer to certain OPA enforcement methods in *Hearings before the Subcommittee of the Senate Appropriations Committee,* Seventy-ninth Congress, Second Session, on H.R. 5458, 1946, pp. 165–176.

newspapers, magazines, and radio. Particularly during the last two years of the OPA an enormous number of stories of black market cases were carried in the press each day. These stories, however, usually contained few details except to emphasize that a certain amount of money was collected as a fine or as the result of a treble damage action, or that a certain length of time was imposed in a suspension order or as a criminal sentence. In general, there was nowhere near the detailed information that is often contained in the story of an ordinary criminal case such as a burglary or robbery. From time to time the OPA sought to enlist public support with fuller human interest stories in magazines and newspapers showing some unusual aspect of enforcement work. These dramatic stories tended to emphasize sensational angles such as those connected with gasoline, particularly counterfeiting, or meat cases, rather than ordinary black market violations by businessmen in all trades. By often giving the impression that the black market consisted of organized criminals, these articles distorted the facts and took much of the stigma away from so-called legitimate business against which the publicity should have been directed. This same criticism could be made of many radio programs and motion-picture shorts.

Publicity about an enforcement case took several forms: releases about local cases which could be played up in local papers, stories about concerns with state or nation-wide reputations, and items describing unusual angles which could be sent out nationally. Information was also often released to the trade press.[33] A single case might receive all of these types of publicity. Cases of interest to the trade press and about which

---

[33] Every OPA district and regional office was instructed to have available a complete list of trade publications and trade associations in the area. The national office also called the attention of national trade papers to articles of national interest.

OPA sent out information were cases of unusual size or involving well-known firms; cases illustrating a particular type of violation in which trade education was necessary; cases which set precedence in court actions, such as the first time a firm was fined; and cases showing that OPA enforcement was taking pressure off a particular trade where black markets were bad. Other releases involved a statistical compilation of a large number of cases or so-called "roundup" stories in which details of particular enforcement cases, as in the case of a drive, might be omitted.[34] One issue of *OPA Food Guide for Retailers,* having a distribution of more than a million copies issued monthly, contained a typical summary of enforcement work against retailers during a preceding month, as well as the following story about the necessity for trimming fats from meats:

Failure to trim excess fats from meat, as required by OPA regulations, is a violation of the Emergency Price Control Act. As excess fat adds as much as 50 per cent to the price, OPA requires that meat be trimmed to specific limits, defined in the regulation, conforming with normal trade practices . . . . Excess fats must be trimmed from the *wholesale* cuts of pork. It is a violation to buy wholesale cuts which have not been properly trimmed. For example, fat on the back of pork loins must not be more than 1/2 inch in thickness. Fat in excess of one inch thickness must be trimmed from sirloin steaks *by the retailer.* When this is not done, consumers are illegally charged both money and points for the excess fat. Another example is loin veal chops, which must have no more than one-half inch of fat on either side.

Different rules apply to the various cuts of meat. If you are

---

[34] One fact that the OPA never seemed to have succeeded in getting across to the trade and to the public was the tremendous total size of enforcement actions, numbering in all over 1,000,000 investigations and over 200,000 sanctions.

not familiar with these requirements, ask your Board for copies of MPRs 336 and 355, or OPA Bulletins 366, 355, 394.[35]

Informational activities were also directed toward changing public opinion about the caliber of the enforcement personnel, as many persons did not have the same respect for the investigative and legal staff of the OPA as they had for the enforcement personnel of some other government agencies such as the FBI, income tax investigators, or postal authorities. This objective was never accomplished, however. The essential difficulty in attempting to give higher status to OPA investigators is revealed in the last sentence of the following quotation from a staff memorandum on this subject.

This can be accomplished by creating a "personality" for our enforcement staff, comparable to the public concept of the FBI or the Northwest Mounted Police. However, our problem is less obviously black-and-white than that of these other law enforcement agencies. The G-men and the Mounties are concerned mainly with bringing to justice professional criminals. But we meet professional criminals only in a few limited areas—notably the gasoline black market. Most of our activity is concerned with violations on the part of hitherto reputable individuals or firms, and with violations that frequently result from indifference or carelessness rather than from criminal intent.[36]

In the 1945 survey among food wholesalers in fifteen cities an attempt was made to determine whether they were getting adequate information about the numerous OPA enforcement

---

[35] Excerpt from July, 1944, *OPA Food Guide for Retailers*, issued by the Department of Information, Office of Price Administration, Washington, D.C., p. 1.

[36] Memorandum to Regional Administrators, District Directors, Program Staffs from Chester Bowles, Office of Price Administration, January 31, 1945.

actions.[37] It was recognized that unless news had been dissem-
inated that the OPA meant business and was taking positive
measures to stop the black market, such activity was almost
worthless. From the survey results it was difficult to conclude
whether satisfactory publicity work had been accomplished or
not. News about enforcement actions appears to have "gotten
around." Eight out of ten (81 per cent) of the food wholesalers
in the survey had heard of such measures as jail sentences,
injunctions, fines, or other monetary penalties imposed against
wholesalers in their localities.[38] About 75 per cent had heard
of sanctions being imposed on retailers. Actions in the cases of
meat dealers and of fresh fruit and vegetable wholesalers were
the most familiar. Of those who reported knowledge of actions
against wholesalers, 53 per cent had heard of "fines" (referring
to all monetary payments whether criminal or not), whereas
only 6 per cent had heard of criminal indictments, which was
not too far from the facts, since there was actually limited use
of the criminal penalty. Three fourths of those interviewed in
the survey (76 per cent) said that such actions were directed
against one or a few firms rather than many. Varied comments
were made, such as that "there should have been more," and
that "most firms are in compliance and only a few were needed."
On the other hand, when questioned about retailers, about
half felt that there had been only a few enforcement actions.
One out of every four said they had never heard of any such
actions at all, indicating that these information services were
not too effective. As to sources of information about enforcement actions, the 1945 survey of wholesalers showed that regu-

---

[37] "Opinion Survey of Food Wholesalers," cited above.
[38] Still the fact that about one out of five (19 per cent) had never heard of
such actions was not encouraging.

lar newspapers were the most important. In order of first mention the percentages were as follows:

Newspapers	57
OPA publications and personnel	13
The "grapevine"	9
Business associates	9
Trade papers	7
Trade meetings	3
Radio	1
No answer	1

The OPA on occasion was criticized for withholding publicity about cases settled out of court. It was implied that this was part of a bargain. In some parts of the country the press complained that it was not given the full information by OPA and felt that the government had hidden reasons for not divulging information. Even the wholesalers interviewed in 1945 shared this opinion. More than a third of them (39 per cent) expressed doubts that the newspapers carried a true picture of enforcement actions, alleging that the government dictated them according to its own bias, and that a suspicious amount of censorship and soft-pedaling was obvious. Late in 1945, however, instructions were issued that full publicity should be given all enforcement actions and such publicity should be regarded as an integral part of enforcement action.

I think you will agree with me that we have no reason for holding back. The public is entitled to know what we do. The over-all purpose of enforcement is to get better compliance. Thus it follows that all sanctions imposed be publicized for better compliance in industry. Without public information on such sanctions, the deterrent effect is lost. Further, it is a basic enforcement policy that no enforcement attorney should ever settle a case on condition that publicity be withheld. On the contrary, every case should be settled on its merits, without reference to how the publicity will be handled.[39]

This program for full publicity had certain limitations, too, for it raised the question of whether violations, rather than being hindered by newspaper publicity, might actually be increased. Since the penalties for flagrant acts were often trivial, an account of such cases may have served as an invitation to violate. Moreover, trade papers sometimes gave details of the violation which, because of the newness of these activities, may have given certain technical knowledge of how to go about violating. In addition, the dissemination of knowledge of the extensiveness of the black market may have encouraged those who were "sitting on the fence" to decide to participate in it. It would be impossible to determine just how important these considerations may have been.

Publishers' Policy toward Enforcement Publicity

It would be unrealistic to leave this presentation of the OPA's publicity of its enforcement activity without some consideration of the role played by the newspapers themselves. It is a well-known fact that the American press of necessity relies heavily upon advertising for its revenues. Consequently, in reporting sanctions against business violators, newspapers found themselves in the position of supporting the war effort on the one hand and of reporting the prosecution of their advertising customers on the other.[40] Some OPA district enforcement attorneys stated that newspapers refused to present a favorable picture of OPA activities or to give sufficient publicity to

[39] Memorandum to All Regional Administrators from James G. Rogers, Jr., Deputy Administrator, Office of Price Administration, on Full Publicity to Lawsuits and Settlements in Civil Cases, September 19, 1945, p. 1.

[40] Except where political influences are occasionally involved there are no such considerations in the reporting of crimes of the lower socioeconomic groups.

prosecuted cases. More frequently, it was charged that when the OPA lost a court case, which rarely occurred, there was great publicity, whereas the reverse was not frequent. Likewise, it was charged that when enforcement activities were improperly handled there was much unwarranted and unfair publicity.

While this treatment of enforcement cases appears to have characterized a number of newspapers, there is evidence that newspapers generally carried numerous accounts of actions against business concerns. Some newspapers who gave such publicity felt, however, that at times the government's actions were unnecessarily unfair to business concerns. They charged that cases were sometimes not followed up after a suit was filed, with consequent stigma without pronouncement of judgment on the business concerns. In one such case a western publisher wrote the OPA stating that on numerous occasions suits were filed for an injunction with no attempt to follow through on them after the original newspaper publicity. Because of his belief that such an unfair policy existed, the publisher advised that his paper henceforth would publicize only those cases in which judgment had been rendered and not cases where court action was begun. The magazine *Editor & Publisher,* in turn, thought this type of selective newspaper publicity unfair and implied that it might be regarded by the general public as biased against the government. It discussed editorially the treatment given OPA charges of ceiling violations against five Philadelphia department stores by the Philadelphia *Enquirer.* According to *Editor & Publisher,* this paper failed to carry a story about these enforcement activities on grounds that in a number of instances injury had been done to some business concerns by such charges when they had to do with "purely technical errors, lack of proper information from the OPA itself, and alleged failure of business houses to file price declarations with the OPA." *Editor & Publisher* acknowledged that what the newspaper had said was true of some OPA cases, as also of some Federal Trade Commission suits, but it stated:

However, we don't believe newspapers should set themselves up as judges on complaints by government agencies deciding that because false charges have been made in the past all charges therefore may be false. Our newspapers carry news of practically all criminal charges. In those cases, as in civil suits, a person or a firm is believed innocent until he or it is proven guilty. We believe the best way to handle OPA and FTC complaints, and charges made by other government agencies, is to print the news in full when they are made together with complete statements by the persons or firms involved.[41]

In summary, the enforcement difficulties in controlling the black market were complicated by a period of almost a year during which voluntary measures were used, the government having no real sanctions to employ against violators. After the passage of the Emergency Price Control Act it took nearly three years of government experience to realize fully the extent and willfulness of violations among business concerns. During this period there was opportunity for the development of thousands of techniques for violating the regulations and a considerable degree of disrespect for the OPA, not only among businessmen but also on the part of the general public. Despite a slow development, the OPA undertook probably the largest piece of enforcement work ever attempted by any government agency in such a brief period of time. The enforcement staff grew from 300 attorneys to 850, and from 900 investigators to about

---

41 *Editor & Publisher,* July 21, 1945, p. 36.

3,600; instead of approximately 20 court cases being filed a month, the figure increased to 4,000; from less than 1 per cent of the civil work before the federal courts it increased to almost 50 per cent; and from less than 1 per cent of the criminal cases it increased to about 10 per cent of all federal cases, including war offenses. It investigated well over 1,000,000 cases and brought serious enforcement actions in over 250,000 cases, figures which far exceeded the enforcement work of most other federal agencies. This was done with a staff pitifully small for the job of controlling the black market, although it was probably one of the largest enforcement staffs ever available to the federal government. To carry out its work the OPA enforcement staff eventually became organized in a somewhat novel fashion, with attorneys and investigators assigned jointly to the enforcement of certain commodity groups. The strict allocation of investigative time to important commodities and to wholesale and manufacturing cases and the development of price panels composed of citizen volunteers to investigate and try retail cases were other important contributions in the control of this largely white collar type of crime. The presence of the black market certainly cannot be explained by a failure to take serious steps to secure voluntary compliance or to publicize regulations and enforcement actions. Although more work could have been done, extensive efforts were made along all these lines, as was indicated in part by the fact that the increase in the Consumer Price Index was only from 112.9 in February, 1942, to 129.3 at the time of V–J Day.[42]

---

[42] This index took into account over-ceiling prices, but not evasive violations or some wartime quality deterioration. See Report of the Technical Committee appointed by the Chairman of the President's Committee on the Cost of Living, June 15, 1944.

CHAPTER FOUR

The Public and
the Black Market

Much has been assumed about the attitudes of the American people toward the black market, many people contending that the situation from the beginning was hopeless because the American people were never really in favor of price and rationing controls. They maintained that everyone was out to get whatever he could, regardless of price or coupons, whether it be clothes, gasoline, meat, housing, or used cars, thus subjecting the businessman to great temptation. In contrast, however, many others believed that most of the public supported controls and that the businessman in the black market had not been tempted there by citizens looking out for their own welfare, but was merely promoting his own.

Public Support of Price Controls

The facts indicate that the public strongly supported price and rationing controls. As early as the spring of 1941 George Gallup (American Institute of Public Opinion) found that two thirds of the public favored price control. In November, 1941, one month before Pearl Harbor and still in the latter period of voluntary controls, this question was asked by Gallup:

"A new law in Canada keeps wage and salary rates from going higher than they are now and also keeps all prices, including prices of farm products, from going higher. Would you approve or disapprove of such a law in the United States?" Sixty-three per cent of the respondents said that they would approve. There was great pressure from the majority of the people for the enactment of a price control law. The National Opinion Research Center in February, 1942, found that 58 per cent of those interviewed saw rising prices as a "bad thing" for the United States. In cities over 100,000 population the figure was 64 per cent; in cities under 100,000, 59 per cent; and among farmers, 46 per cent. In May, 1942, this same research center asked what people thought of the new price control law: "It is now against the law for the prices of some products to go any higher during the war than they were last March. Do you think this is a good idea or a bad idea?" Of those interviewed, 89 per cent thought this was a "good idea," and all groups were in substantial agreement.

Throughout the war there continued to be extensive public support for the law.[1] In 1943 NORC found that 94 per cent of those interviewed were in favor of the government's keeping prices from going higher; by 1945 this figure, instead of declining, had increased to 97 per cent. In fact, the NORC survey in the spring of 1945 found that "support of price control is so strong that only insignificant differences of opinion among groups appear."[2] This NORC survey found that 65 per cent of those interviewed believed that all prices should be frozen,

---

[1] Even if allowance is made for the fact that some of those interviewed were not in favor of OPA, the government agency set up to carry out their wishes, the figures still would have remained high.

[2] *Public Opinion on Control of Prices, Wages, Salaries during War and Reconversion*, NORC Report No. 26, p. 3.

while others were willing to let some prices rise. When interviewed at this time, 84 per cent of the sample thought it would be necessary to continue price control after the war while we were getting back to peacetime conditions. A Gallup poll in 1944 found that 91 per cent of the people interviewed believed that prices should be held at their prevailing levels.

When some Iowa farmers (a group supposedly largely hostile to price control) were interviewed in October, 1943, only one out of five stated that they would dispense with the OPA program entirely.[3] A *Fortune* magazine poll in July, 1945, showed that almost seven out of ten people (68 per cent) thought that without price control prices would go up, and six out of ten (59 per cent) thought that such a price rise would be a bad thing for the country. A September, 1945, report from the Correspondents' Panels of the Bureau of Special Services, Office of War Information, stated that in the correspondents' communities there was overwhelming support for price control. Another survey during that year showed that of a national sample of 2,575 housewives, 79 per cent were in favor of food rationing.[4] In January, 1946, NORC found 83 per cent of the people in favor of continued price control. Gallup found, in March, 1946, that almost eight out of ten (73 per cent) of the people interviewed wanted price control continued.

Where measured, there were differences of opinion by economic groups. In the Gallup survey of the spring of 1941, for example, there was variation in the affirmative answers to the question, "Would you like to see the federal government fix prices so that as long as the war in Europe lasts everything

---

[3] *Ibid.*, p. 13. This poll was conducted by *Wallace's Farmer and Iowa Homestead* of Des Moines.

[4] *Opinion Briefs,* Department of Information, Office of Price Administration, April 6, 1945, p. 3 (Mimeographed).

you buy will cost the same as it does now?" While 68 per cent of those questioned answered in the affirmative, only 53 per cent of the businessmen did so, as compared with 61 per cent of the farmers, 68 per cent of the white collar workers, and 80 per cent of the skilled, semiskilled, and unskilled laborers.[5] Likewise a *Fortune* survey of business executives in September, 1941, found a majority of business leaders in favor of freezing wages, but not wholesale or retail prices. In the fall of 1941 a survey by Gallup found that 62 per cent of the nonfarming population and 55 per cent of the farmers were in favor of regulating prices. A 1945 survey of various economic groups, chosen according to standard of living in each of 123 cities, showed that only 36 per cent of the highest group (Group A) supported price control, while in the lowest economic group (Group B) the support was 61 per cent.[6]

Question: Is it good for America in peacetime for the Government to set top prices which stores and factories may charge for their goods?

REPLIES	TOTAL INTERVIEWS	YES, %	NO, %	DON'T KNOW, %
Total..............	5,000	51	43	6
Group A...........	500	36	61	3
Group B............	1,500	46	49	5
Group C...........	2,000	53	41	6
Group D..........	1,000	61	29	10

[5] *Public Opinion on Control of Prices, Wages, Salaries during War and Reconversion,* p. 3.

[6] A survey by the Psychological Corporation of America, October, 1945. Standard of living meant neighborhood, type of urban residence, and was not simply a dollar income basis. Group A was the highest 10 per cent of the economic groups, Group B the next highest 30 per cent, Group C the next 40 per cent, and Group D the lowest 20 per cent.

Public Opinion and the Black Market

Even discounting some of this high verbal support, the percentage would probably still have been high. Such figures in favor of price control as 63 per cent in 1941, 58 per cent in early 1942, 94 per cent in 1943, 91 per cent in 1944, 97 per cent in 1945, and 83 per cent in 1946 represent such overwhelming support that a small subtraction would still leave a significant percentage remaining. In fact, the tremendous public support for the return of price and rationing controls in late 1947 and early 1948, in some polls running over 80 per cent, lends added weight to this belief.

It would be misleading to imply, however, that public support for the government's efforts against the black market, which seemed strong verbally, was actually this high in practice, except in cases involving the theft or counterfeiting of rationed commodities. The behavior of many persons was often different when the discussion shifted from the general objectives of price and rationing control to actual specifics of everyday life. People receiving black market goods often did not ask further questions, and many were tolerant of black market activity if it involved petty price increases and small quantities of rationed commodities. A Gallup survey in 1945 showed that one person in five would condone black market buying on occasion. If the conditions under which they would patronize the black market were analyzed, however, the situation did not look nearly as serious, the largest number listing emergencies such as illness, others listing unfairness of the rationing board after an appeal.[7]

---

[7] Quoted in *Public Opinion on Control of Prices, Wages, Salaries during War and Reconversion*, p. 15.

Question: Do you think that buying at black market prices is sometimes justified?

REPLIES	YES, SOMETIMES, %	NO, %	UNDECIDED, %
All those interviewed.......	21	74	5
Men.....................	23	71	6
Women..................	18	77	5
In cities over 100,000.......	23	73	4
In towns 10,000 to 100,000..	19	78	3
In towns under 10,000......	21	73	6
Farmers.................	18	73	9

It appears probable that only a relatively small percentage of American consumers participated with full knowledge and volition in the black market.[8] In fact, there is evidence to support the opinion that all too many businessmen either solicited black market business or were willing to violate when the temptation or opportunity presented itself. Had this not been true, the problem of price control and rationing would have been far less acute. In a comparative survey of the attitudes of businessmen and the public in Detroit, Hartung found that the public, in contrast to businessmen, disapproved equally of

---

[8] Marquis Childs maintained in a syndicated column, July 28, 1946, that not only were the majority of the American people in favor of price control but that "a second bit of propaganda, it seems to me, has exaggerated out of all proportion to the truth the black market in such scarce commodities as meat . . . . Moreover, I have made a point in recent months of asking a great many people whether they bought black market meat or if they knew where it could be bought. I have never had anyone say that, through their own first-hand knowledge, they could get rare cuts of meats by paying higher prices. From the propaganda, one would have gathered that most Americans were patronizing the black market. Restaurants and hotels perhaps resorted to under-the-counter sources, which certainly existed in this big, rich country on a large scale. But so far as most householders are concerned, there has been no proof whatsoever that they sought out black markets in the mass."

criminal and civil black market cases. The public was much more harsh in its attitude toward black market cases dealt with by civil actions than were businessmen.[9] As late as the middle of 1946 there was considerable public support for strong efforts to deal with the black market. A representative national survey of chairmen of OPA local board information panels, and their opinions of the community reaction to OPA's enforcement program, revealed that only 7 per cent felt that enforcement was too strict.[10] The replies under "too strict" were not, in general, antagonistic. Rather the opinion of the communities was that the enforcement was too inflexible on small errors. The "other answers" included such statements that "OPA should have more power and personnel," "stricter controls" were needed, and that "controls are removed too quickly." Only a few felt that their communities as a whole were antagonistic toward the OPA.

Volunteer Assistance in the Price and Rationing Program

A further indication not only of the strong public support of the government's price and rationing program but of the attempts to control violations was the nature and extent of volunteer assistance given to the OPA. The government called upon citizens on a wide scale to help administer the rationing and price control regulations, and these volunteers eventually comprised over three fourths of the total staff. At one time there were at least 275,000 volunteers in various capacities, and during the entire war period there were probably altogether

---

[9] Hartung, *op. cit.*, pp. 330–331.

[10] A fourth of them (25 per cent) thought that enforcement was "too lenient," 21 per cent thought it was "about right," 17 per cent had "mixed" opinions, 21 per cent gave various other answers, and 8 per cent gave no answer.—Information Department, Office of Price Administration, Field Reporting Panel No. 3, June 28, 1946.

well over half a million volunteer workers. Men and women of all classes, including many businessmen, served in this volunteer capacity. They performed their functions with little press approval, without benefit of glamour, and often with opposition even from certain parts of the OPA itself. These volunteers in the 5,500 price and rationing boards were of several types. Some were citizens who assisted in the issuance and enforcement of consumer rationing, while others were price panel members and assistants who worked on price violations, making educational and compliance surveys of retailers. Another group of volunteers, working through local organizations, press, and radio, became known as community service members, informing and educating their communities on OPA problems.[11] Still other volunteers served in record-keeping capacities on the local boards. Other citizen volunteers by the hundreds of thousands helped in the actual issuance of food ration books.

This volunteer assistance program had its beginning in

---

[11] To help the volunteer program the Price Administrator gave weekly national "down-to-earth" radio talks in which volunteers often participated. In the fall of 1943 a nation-wide campaign of consumer pledges was conducted. In this pledge it was agreed that "I pay no more than legal prices. I accept no rationed goods without giving up ration stamps." Throughout the nation "retailers displayed the large colored posters in their stores or used the mats provided by Information in their newspaper advertising. In Louisville, 3,000 Boy Scouts called at homes getting the signature and leaving stickers, so that passers-by would know that a home was a 'Home-front Pledge Home.' In Cincinnati, Girl Scouts had pledge booths at the theaters. In dozens of cities school teachers cooperated and thousands of school children carried the pledges home to their parents. In New Orleans where the pledge idea originated, the campaign was carried out by the OCD War Block Service in a 48-hour whirlwind campaign. 250,000 people signed the pledge in those 2 days, and within 1 week the food prices of New Orleans showed a 5 per cent drop. Under the leadership of the community volunteers over 200,000 other volunteers participated actively in getting the pledges signed, and over 20,000,000 people pledged themselves to participate in price control, pledged themselves not to buy above ceiling price and not to accept rationed goods without giving up ration stamps."—Imogene H. Putnam, *Volunteers in OPA,* General Publication No. 14 of the Historical Reports on War Administration, Office of Price Administration (Washington: Government Printing Office, 1947), pp. 88–89.

the prestatutory period shortly after Pearl Harbor when boards were first set up to ration tires. These volunteers had the right to refer a case of improper use of tires to the local district office for such action as it deemed proper. As more commodities were rationed and price controls extended over others, tire rationing boards were reorganized into war price and rationing boards, although the volunteer price phase did not come until almost a year later. The chairman of the former Tire Rationing Board became the chairman of the War Price and Rationing Board and from one to ten rationing panels were organized under his direction, such as those for gasoline, tires, and shoes. Panel members were appointed by the district director from a list of local citizens drawn up by the local Office of Civilian Defense organization and various local groups.

Volunteer Assistance on Rationing Violations

These rationing board members were sworn representatives of the government. They explained rationing orders to tradesmen and consumers, passed on all consumer applications, and dealt with violations. In the case of gasoline the ration boards had authority not only to issue gasoline rations but to revoke the rations after a proper hearing, only the most serious cases of consumer rationing being referred to the OPA office for formal action. Thousands of cases were handled by the local boards as the result of investigations by the professional enforcement staff in connection with violations of the pleasure driving ban which, early in the OPA, was at times part of the gasoline enforcement program. With all the mistakes they made, the assistance of these thousands of local ration board members was of great value in policing the millions of rationed consumers, a task which the formal OPA organization could never have attempted.

The Price Panels

When the prices of almost all commodities were frozen with the issuance of the General Maximum Price Regulation (GMPR) early in 1942, and particularly when the violations of this regulation became quite extensive during that same year, it became evident that it would be increasingly difficult for the relatively small number of OPA investigators to check the large number of retail establishments. Furthermore, it was realized that the direct enlistment of extensive citizen support for price and rationing controls would be of tremendous psychological assistance in promoting compliance. For some time Canada had been using housewives in checking prices, and in this country there were experiments with price volunteers in some states.[12] Still nothing was done nationally along this line. There was considerable opposition from some OPA officials to the use of citizen volunteers to assist in policing price violations, and this initial opposition later had significant repercussions on the recruitment of volunteers. Dexter M. Keezer, OPA Deputy for General Services, gave his opinion about price volunteers: "Self-appointed price policemen should be identified as fifth wheels and trouble makers."[13]   Kenneth Galbraith, Deputy Administrator for Price, spoke of 8,000 to 10,000 paid inspectors and promised retailers that "no Gestapo of volunteer housewives would be used for retail surveys."[14] In fact, Congress at

---

[12] During 1942 a few field offices had experimented with the idea of using price volunteers, among them being certain cities in the New England states, New York, Virginia, North Carolina, Mississippi, and California. Price panels began operating in Rhode Island as a district project as early as 1942 and, according to one contemporary article, they proved somewhat successful even though they had no penalties. See J. Howard Rutledge, "The Little OPA's," *Saturday Evening Post*, May 15, 1943, p. 26.

[13] Speech before congressional wives, June, 1942. Quoted in Putnam, *op. cit.,* p. 32.

[14] Washington *Post,* June 5, 1942.

this time "picked up the name-calling and 'snoopers!' echoed through Capitol Hill. But Congress, no fonder of paid inspectors than it was of volunteer snoopers, made a deep slash in the OPA budget, and thousands of paid inspectors were automatically eliminated from the argument."[15] Thus budget difficulties, as well as the successes of the rationing boards and the increasing seriousness of the black market at the retail level, finally resulted in a proposal by the OPA Legal Division, in August, 1942, that it take over volunteers and local boards to assist in enforcement work. According to this proposal, volunteers were to be trained and supervised by the Legal Division. It was this particular aspect of the suggested program which precipitated an intra-agency argument and nothing immediate came of the proposal, thus further delaying the program for price volunteers.[16]

Although there continued to be difficulties in the enormous amount of work of policing the black market and in making clear the need psychologically for direct citizen participation in the program, several significant events precipitated the issuance of a directive establishing a national volunteer price program: (1) the March, 1943, cost-of-living index showed an increase of 10 points in the first year of price control; (2) the President issued a "Hold-the-Line" order in April, 1943; and (3) dollar-and-cents pricing for many retail commodities, rather than base period and formula pricing, was inaugurated at about this time, with grocery stores throughout the country

---

[15] Putnam, *op. cit.*, p. 32.

[16] Galbraith, Deputy Administrator for Price, writing a memorandum at the time, stated that "the functions of the price wardens should not be restricted to, or even primarily, a matter of enforcement. Neither good public relations nor good administration is served by placing them under the exclusive jurisdiction of the Legal Division . . . . there appears to be some question . . . whether volunteers could be recruited through the Office of Civilian Defense on this basis."—Putnam, *op. cit.*, p. 35.

being divided into four groups.[17] This step made possible the use of volunteers in checking specific prices, whereas the former pricing methods had been too complicated.

Table 7

Composition and Analysis of Board Membership

MEMBERS	NUMBER OF BOARDS	NUMBER OF MEMBERS
Clergymen.....................	1,600	2,269
Consumers.....................	4,131	24,139
Doctors.......................	1,147	1,644
Educators (teachers, etc.)..........	3,335	7,556
Farmers.......................	3,612	11,061
Labor (organized)...............	2,356	5,951
Labor (unorganized).............	1,059	2,392
Lawyers.......................	2,267	3,892
Merchants.....................	4,577	23,648
Negro members.................	197	755
Others........................	4,590	43,768

Total number of boards......................... 5,554
Total number of board members.................. 127,075
Estimated number of hours spent by all
board members............................... 1,510,608

SOURCE: Imogene H. Putnam, *Volunteers in OPA*, General Publication No. 14 of the Historical Reports on War Administration, Office of Price Administration (Washington: Government Printing Office, 1947). District office monthly statistical report on local board operations, continental United States and territories, July 23, 1945, p. 165.

Instructions were finally issued to the field offices in April, 1943, to set up volunteer price panels and to use price panel assistants to check prices, the responsibility for this work eventually being given to the Price Department rather than the

---

[17] See Chapter Eight.

Enforcement Department. These price panels were set up with three objectives: (1) to bolster failing compliance and enforcement; (2) to open a channel for wider dissemination of price control information; and (3) to make the administration of price control more democratic. At first there was usually only a single price panel, but this was soon divided into separate panels for food, services, dry goods, and others as necessitated by the program. In general no panel member, if a businessman, was supposed to deal with problems in his own industry. All price panel members and assistants were to be trained on price operations by liaison representatives of the district office assigned by the price officer from the district price staff.

Each price panel was composed of from three to seven members, appointed in the same manner as members of the rationing panels. These volunteers were picked from lists submitted by the Office of Civilian Defense, the labor unions, women's clubs, citizens' associations, and consumer groups, with an attempt to give proper representation to all groups. The boards themselves, while not entirely representative of the community at large, were a partial cross section of the various occupational divisions of the area. The composition of local price and rationing board members on July 23, 1945, is shown in Table 7.

Recruitment of Price Panel Assistants

Recruitment for this type of volunteer work moved slowly; actually the price panels never had as many volunteers as were needed to carry out the programs. By the end of June, 1943, price panels had been established in 4,700 of the 5,500 local boards and included about 20,000 volunteer members, plus 25,000 volunteer price panel assistants.[18] While the recruitment

---

[18] At about this same time the total professional enforcement staff was less than 4,000, including clerical personnel.

of price panel assistants, exclusive of board members, eventually reached over 40,000, the goal of 125,000 price panel assistants was never reached. This failure was partly due to the fact that the OPA was the last war agency to ask for volunteers, thus giving it a limited supply in an already restricted manpower field. Such a situation might well have been avoided had the price volunteers been appointed at the beginning of the price control program, an action which would also have helped greatly in increasing the prestige of those in the program, for by the time price volunteers were sought the public had already become aware of considerable opposition on the part of some persons to this type of volunteer police work. Finally, the OPA attempted to remedy this situation by suggesting that the position of price checkers be dignified and that checkers be "given training and board membership on an equal footing with rationing, price, and community service members. It was suggested that a national recruiting campaign be undertaken redefining the job and presenting it with the sponsorship of the national women's organizations. These plans came too late in 1946 to be used but should be considered carefully in any future use of volunteers in survey work."[19]

Duties of Price Panel Assistants and Price Panels

Price panels informed retailers and consumers of the reasons for price control and the provisions of the price regulations. They reminded retailers periodically of their duties under price control, and they "persuaded" retailers to comply. These price panels worked on the theory that the average merchant was usually informed about OPA regulations, but that he might become lax in following them, willfully or otherwise. The price

---

[19] Putnam, *op. cit.*, p. 147.

panel assistants, generally volunteer housewives recruited by the price panels, periodically visited all or a large part of the retailers under the jurisdiction of the price panel, furnished the retailer with any information which he might lack, and ascertained from him his selling price on a list of from ten to thirty items of merchandise. A most important part of the work was the investigation of the complaints sent in by shoppers who believed they had been overcharged. If the merchant was charging too much the assistant called his attention to the oversight, and many grocers willingly corrected the price immediately. Later, price panel assistants were given the tremendous job of checking restaurant menus for violations.[20] Price panel assistants were also assigned to check on apparel to see that tags bearing the wool percentage were attached to each article, but this proved a somewhat tedious and rather unfruitful task.

After the price panel assistants had turned over all their information to the price panel, the cases were reviewed and action was taken if indicated. A first violator usually was sent a friendly reminder or warning letter. If he violated again he was notified to appear at the next price panel meeting for a compliance conference with a group of citizens. At this conference the retailer was introduced to the panel members and told that they were volunteers, often neighbors, without legal power to fine or coerce. Then the chairman explained why the retailer had been called to the conference, pointing out the dangers to the country if this type of violation were to continue. If the retailer protested that he had not meant to break the law or had not understood it, the chairman might then carefully explain the regulations. If this were the first summons

---

[20] Because of the magnitude of the job, when a national restaurant survey was conducted in January, 1945, some regions had only 50 per cent coverage, some districts having as low as 29 per cent coverage.—*Washington Letter,* Office of Price Administration, No. 21, March 1, 1945, pp. 14–15 (Mimeographed).

the chairman often dismissed the case, but there were several other courses of action open to these price panels. They could send a warning notice or a license revocation warning notice, they could collect a voluntary contribution to the United States Treasury for the amount of the overcharge, or, after June 30, 1944, they could collect, in the name of the Price Administrator, a settlement of a consumer treble damage suit up to three times the amount of the overcharge, if the consumer did not bring action within thirty days.[21] If the merchant refused to comply with the decision of the price panel, his case was referred to the district enforcement office for possible stronger action. As the volume of violations increased and the enforcement program progressed, procedures were set up in 1945 for the coordination of such referrals between the price department and enforcement.

There was an increased emphasis on the enforcement activities of these price panel volunteers with the introduction of the administrator's consumer claim in 1944, as this represented a decreased emphasis on neighborly persuasion by the price panels. Some industry-minded or industry-dominated panels balked at asserting this stronger sanction. In fact, a

---

[21] Before the adoption of this sanction many price panel chairmen developed a high degree of skill in applying firm yet sympathetic sanctions through more informal methods, but the difficulties in this procedure were great. "It is true that the percentage of repeaters, or persistent violators, was larger than had been anticipated at the inception of the program, and their recurring presence at the conference table was a severe test of the patience of the panel members. The flagrant violator could be referred to the district office but Enforcement was not interested in the retailer with only small violations in posting or price. Although the panels knew that failure to post frequently concealed price violations, and although they knew that continued small price violations added up to alarming amounts, they were helpless at this time to do more than check the stores, keep the tally, and record the promises to comply. The panels fulfilled their purpose in correcting the large number of violations due to ignorance or indifference, but clearly some other method or some increased authority was needed to reach the small persistent violator."—Putnam, *op. cit.*, p. 80.

number of price chairmen and some panels were more concerned with their post-price-control popularity among businessmen in the country than with their obligations as panel members. Price panels did not have the right to file law suits. Their right was limited to that of informing the retailer that he had violated and offering to settle the matter out of court on a local basis rather than sending it to the district office for handling through the usual channels. This action was still a powerful instrument of persuasion. Moreover, it was an extremely significant development in that no other agency had ever given to local, unpaid boards the right to settle damage suits. Many price panels used a surprising amount of ingenuity in accomplishing their purpose.

They [price panel members and assistants] persuaded landlords in areas where rent control was not applicable to hold down rents, they persuaded laundries not to apply for price increases even though legally entitled to do so, they put into effect flat-pricing restaurant price orders that were technically illegal but were so far superior to District and National regulations and were promulgated on such a local, democratic basis that those affected accepted them, they secured refunds for overcharged consumers from sellers who had moved half-way across the nation, they secured both oral and written "agreements to comply" from recalcitrant merchants, and they by and large reduced violations.[22]

From July through September, 1943, alone price panel members made 250,000 recorded visits to retail food stores and handled 60,000 consumer complaints. Over 1,250,000 retail outlets were visited from April through June, 1944, of which

<hr>

[22] Estal E. Sparlin, "The Possible Significance of OPA Price Panels," *Social Forces*, XXIV, No. 2 (December, 1945), 222. The Chicago Area Projects and the Back of the Yards Council in Chicago in delinquency control utilize citizen methods of informal control to supplement formal controls through the police.

Table 8
Price Panel Activity, 1945–1946

	JAN.–JUNE 1945	JULY–DEC. 1945	JAN.–JUNE 1946	TOTAL
Number of reported violations.......	521,887	426,535	426,968	1,375,380
Number of conferences	239,289	184,085	200,129	623,503
Number of consumers receiving refunds.........	29,960	18,521	8,742	57,223
Amount of money refunded	$943,465	$671,708	$511,072	$2,126,245
Administrator's claims: Overcharges	$962,302	$1,008,213	$1,048,176	$3,098,691
Number of settlements....	18,453	18,763	33,834	71,050
Amount to Treasury	$1,444,249	$1,610,293	$2,078,116	$5,132,658
Refunds to customers.....	$107,393	$98,148	$185,806	$391,347
Number receiving refunds.......	4,339	6,211	7,583	18,133

SOURCE: Price Board Management, Statistical Reports, July, 1946. Quoted in Putnam, *op. cit.*, p. 119.

over 300,000 had at least one price or grading violation. In the first six months of 1944 alone the panels successfully mediated 127,529 cases of violation, and during the three years these panel members successfully mediated hundreds of thousands of complaints. In the last two years of price control, for example, there were 1,375,380 violations reported which resulted in 623,503 conferences. (See Table 8.) The price panels negotiated settlements for 71,050 Price Administrator's claims resulting in $5,132,658 in returns to the United States Treasury and $391,347 in refunds to 18,133 customers.

Opposition to Volunteer Price Panels

There was continuous opposition to these enforcement activities of the price panels, since this type of work distinguished these volunteers from those recruited for the other wartime agencies. Probably the OPA was the first federal agency ever to call on large sections of the country's citizens for actual assistance in enforcing regulations.[23] Not only was this agency probably the first to use large numbers of citizen assistants in apprehending law violators; it was also probably the first agency to delegate the responsibility for actually trying the offenders. The work of these thousands of price panel volunteers who assisted directly and indirectly in the enforcement program was a most significant social and governmental innovation which should invite further research on the part of social scientists interested in "grass roots" social control.[24]

Effective as it was in helping to foster compliance and to control the black market, this direct use of citizens was a rather drastic procedure. Had it not worked as successfully as it did

---

[23] The only similar use of citizens is in connection with work of the Bureau of Internal Revenue where citizens are provided with monetary reward for information about tax evasion frauds. This assistance, however, is different from the use of citizens made in price control enforcement where the citizens actually made investigations of violators. Many states also provide for the deputization of citizens where necessary in connection with the enforcement of law, but only rarely has the average man been called upon to enforce laws which are made by his delegated citizens, the legislators.

[24] The success of local, volunteer, easily accessible price panels, using their persuasive influence on people, may offer possibilities in other fields such as juvenile delinquency. In fact, one study has suggested this. See Sparlin, loc. cit., 220–223.

it might well have aroused even greater opposition from the press and from Congress. From the very first use of volunteers a hue and cry was raised about what was termed use of "gestapo" and "drumhead" court martials leveled against "unsuspecting and innocent citizens." The kind of opposition which the government met is shown in the following excerpt from testimony before a congressional committee. Senator Taft had just criticized the volunteer workers as "a group to spy on other people," and the OPA Administrator is replying:

MR. BOWLES: They do not spy on anybody. They go into a store and say, "I am from the OPA." Many of them are local merchants.

THE CHAIRMAN: I think the majority of the members of the committee have regarded that as very courteous and a very fine thing to do.

SENATOR TAFT: I suggest that it is absolutely un-American and contrary to law and contrary to the Constitution. I mean for the Government to go out and get a group of people to work for them for nothing on law violations.

MR. BOWLES: Then do you mean that you would rather have a lot of paid food investigators out spying on these people? I would rather handle it this way.

SENATOR TAFT: I would call it extralegal and an improper thing to do.

MR. BOWLES: We have been doing it for 3 years.

SENATOR TAFT: But it is illegal.

MR. BOWLES: It is the first time I have heard it called illegal.

MR. FIELD: I never assumed there was any requirement that the people had to be paid for giving service to the Government. . . . Certainly many of the endeavors in wartime have been put across only by reason of the disinterested giving of time by citizens to help make the war program a success.

SENATOR TAFT: What you are doing is organizing consumers against business.

MR. BOWLES: These are not consumers any more than paid investigators. And I will say that you are going to have an opportunity to vote on a resolution to compliment these people. There are 200,000 of them. Practically half of them are business people and the rest of them are clergymen, doctors, doctors' wives, and other representative people.

SENATOR TAFT: They are to go out and check up on business on the assumption that business has been violating the law, that business people are necessarily crooks, and are going to get all they can; in other words, stirring up all the feeling you can against these Canton [Ohio] food dealers.

THE CHAIRMAN: I think that is an unfair statement to make about these volunteers. They have come before our committee, and we have commended them for their volunteer work.

SENATOR MURDOCK: Mr. Chairman, may a Democrat ask any questions here this morning, or is this to be considered a field day for those sitting to the right of the Chairman?

THE CHAIRMAN: Go ahead, Senator Murdock.

SENATOR MURDOCK: I should like to call attention to the fact that we have had a few dollar-a-year men in high places all during the war, and they are constantly referred to as very patriotic, outstanding, and leading citizens. If it is a violation to use people one might say in the lower brackets of society who come in and volunteer to do the job there, certainly the same rule should apply to these dollar-a-year men at the top. I have not heard the Senator from Ohio make any complaint about that.

SENATOR TAFT: No; and because the dollar-a-year man who comes here, if he is any good, is representing the interests of the Government, but these other people are employed to represent themselves, so to speak.

MR. BOWLES: They are not employed.

SENATOR TAFT: They are against these businessmen.

Mr. Bowles: The most of them are businessmen.

Senator Taft: The fact of the matter is that OPA goes out and organizes one class of the community, say consumers, and says to them: "Get together and help us enforce the law."

Mr. Bowles: That is completely incorrect. These people are, for the most part, businessmen.

Senator Taft: Many of them are women.

Mr. Bowles: Rarely will you find the chairman of a price panel who is not a businessman.[25]

Difficulties in Keeping Price Panel Assistants

The effect of such opposition upon the recruitment of volunteers has already been mentioned. A Washington, D.C., survey of volunteers who quit and those who stayed showed that the accusation of snooping or policing had much less effect upon quitting than it did upon recruitment. This would indicate that while this attitude played a part in the difficulty of recruiting price panel assistants, it did not play an important part in why they left.

Sometimes as many as one fourth of the volunteers drifted away in a single month, but this does not appear to have been the result of real differences in the attitudes of those who stayed with the program and those who did not. The significant factors in this rapid turnover were typical of volunteer positions rather than due to any opposition to any OPA programs or hostility on the part of retailers. About one fifth quit because of timidity in approaching merchants. Others quit to take paid employment or found it difficult to devote the time necessary away from home. Housewives often had to stay home with sick children, others found that such work as price checking re-

---

[25] *Hearings before the Senate Committee on Banking and Currency,* Inflation Control Program of OPA, Seventy-ninth Congress, First Session, 1945, pp. 30–32.

quired more walking than they could do, but about half of them just drifted away.[26]

The Problem of Using Volunteers in Enforcement Work

Although the price panel assistants discovered many violations, the actions taken by many of the price panels was disappointing. Many apparently settled cases too easily. Almost half of all violations reported resulted in conferences and only 12 per cent of all conferences resulted in settlements of the administrator's consumer treble damage claims. (See Table 8.) They also disposed of too many of their cases at one time through mass, rather than individual, hearings, even though some cases involved second offenders. This situation was sometimes unavoidable, however, for the large-scale surveys uncovered so many violations that many panels were burdened with far more hearing cases than they could effectively handle.

Assuming that a certain minimum percentage of the cases warranted more or less severe action, too few cases were referred to the district office for enforcement action. During one month in 1944 the entire Chicago regional enforcement staff had only 238 cases referred by price panels, one office receiving no referrals. The important Chicago metropolitan area office, serving 4,500,000 people, with thousands of retailers, received a total of only 44 referrals. Some critics felt, and with reason, that volunteers could not be properly supervised and trained in so short a period of time to do such work.

Another difficulty was that some volunteer price panels could not be completely objective in punishing friends with whom they shared common ideas and backgrounds. Moreover, they were likely to feel closer to the local community than to national enforcement policies. "Some panels were unwilling to

<hr>

26 Putnam, *op. cit.*, pp. 101–102.

recommend a treble damage settlement against a member of their own community."[27] These conflicts gave rise to some criticism as to the leniency and uncooperativeness of the citizen panels. The following reports from regional OPA enforcement offices illustrate these difficulties:

They [price panels] feel a marked degree of independence, and a great many of them regard themselves as the specially ordained protectors of the local merchant and the buffer standing between the enforcement department and the hometown grocer. Many of these panels do not believe in enforcement, and particularly in the small rural communities the interests of individual members are more closely identified with the interests of the local merchants than with the interests of the United States government or its agency, the Office of Price Administration. An alarming number of these panels, or members thereof, have betrayed to violators confidential information. They have warned local merchants of forthcoming visits of investigators. In some instances confidential matters sent to price panels have shown up within 48 hours in the hands of attorneys representing violators against whom enforcement actions were pending or imminent. At least half the price panels appear to want nothing whatever to do with enforcement.—San Francisco region.

As we have sat down during the past few weeks with the price panels for a hearing of the cases arising out of the investigations made, many of which panels had had no previous experience in such hearings, we found a general tendency to draw back when it came to suggesting voluntary contributions or the issuance of strong warnings to their local merchants and friends. In a number of instances, panel members indicated in no uncertain terms that if they had understood and known they would be called upon as part of their duties to engage in what they termed "enforcement action" of this type, they would not have accepted appointment

[27] *Ibid.*, p. 146.

to the panel, and if they were required to carry on such a program, they would resign therefrom.—Atlanta region.[28]

Despite all these difficulties, it was reported that in some areas where price panel assistants were effectively used they reduced the grocery store violations from an average of 75 per cent to as low as 4 per cent. Nationally the percentage of food stores in full compliance with the regulations reportedly increased from 41 per cent in March, 1944, to 69 per cent in June of that year.[29] One district office showed the following extensive reduction in violations in part as a result of price panel work. (See Table 9.)

Table 9

Price Panel Results with Food Stores in One OPA District

ITEM	JULY, 1943	JANUARY, 1944	OCTOBER, 1944
Stores in district, number......	7,809	7,299	7,446
Stores surveyed, number.......	3,828	5,577	7,193
Stores in violation,* number...	1,971	2,276	672
Proportion in violation, per cent	51.5	40.8	9.3
Items checked, number.......	28,684	39,633	58,597
Items in violation, number....	4,647	4,220	1,041
Proportion in violation, per cent	16.2	10.6	1.8

* A store is recorded as being in "violation" if one or more of the items surveyed was being sold above the ceiling price.

SOURCE: Estal E. Sparlin, "The Possible Significance of OPA Price Panels," *Social Forces*, XXIV, No. 2 (December, 1945), 223.

Even though they made mistakes and frequently antagonized retailers, perhaps the most important job which price

---

[28] Both cases are from unpublished OPA Enforcement Department field reports.

[29] Office of Price Administration, *Tenth Quarterly Report* for the period ending June 30, 1944, p. 27.

panels accomplished was that of partially relieving the regular enforcement staff of the gigantic task of investigating cases at the retail level. During an eighteen-month period there was a total of 1,375,380 violations reported and conferences were held on 623,503 cases. In all, 71,050 sellers paid $5,132,658 to the United States Treasury. (See Table 8.) Thus the OPA was able eventually to concentrate its professional enforcement staff chiefly on manufacturers and middlemen and on the more flagrant offenders in all ranks of business. Other extremely important accomplishments of the price panels were that they were somewhat successful in increasing public support for the OPA regulations, in distributing information to retailers, and in making communities price conscious. President Roosevelt, on January 4, 1944, paid tribute to the board members and all of the volunteers of the price panels.

High on the list of our Home Front Volunteers are the 276,000 men and women who man our local OPA War Price and Rationing Boards throughout the country. We are the only nation in the world where volunteers are doing this job. In the way it has been done, it's as American as baseball. It has been a difficult job. These boards had to be organized almost overnight. Yet they managed to open for business less than a month after we went to war . . . . I am certain that the overwhelming majority of our citizens have never lost respect and admiration for what these board members and their assistants are doing. In many cases they are friends and neighbors. We shall always remember their devotion and steadfastness to duty because we know that our local boards, by the fair administration of rationing and price control, have been protecting one of the very fundamentals of democracy—"the greatest good of the greatest number". . . .[30]

---

[30] Read by Bowles in a radio program on local boards' secondary anniversary.

CHAPTER FIVE

The Meat Black Market

Experience during the past war indicated that the success not only of a wartime food program but of the entire system of price and rationing controls centers on the effective control of the distribution and price of meat. Several factors make a system of a reasonably equitable distribution of meat at a fair price a "must" in a national emergency. First of all, meat is generally considered an essential part of human diet, not only because our culture emphasizes the eating of meat but, more important still, because it has a high protein content. Meat, particularly beefsteak, is the symbol of good living in American society regardless of economic class or geographic region. In fact, any person in America who does not like beef is likely to become an object of curiosity. Furthermore, without sufficient meat, or substitute protein, our soldiers, shipyard workers, miners, and other workers in heavy industry cannot maintain long working hours with a high degree of efficiency. During World War II the morale of the ordinary American home would have been seriously impaired without some reasonable supply, for Americans are accustomed to eat meat at least once a day. Second, large supplies of meat are needed by our armed forces and our allies, while our own civilian demand increases tremendously because of greatly increased purchasing power. And finally, the great increase in the world demand for grains decreases our supplies available for animal feeding. In spite of all the difficulties attendant upon such a gigantic program, the meat problem cannot be left to fatalistic inaction any more than the production of aircraft, guided missiles, or atomic bombs can be left to chance in the presence of wartime necessity.

Meat Control Program

The comprehensive program which the government eventually worked out over a period of three years for the price control and the rationing of meat involved dealing with the prices of livestock and dressed or processed meat, slaughtering quotas, grading, granting of subsidies to slaughterers in order to guarantee a fair return to them, and rationing.[1] All of these controls were complementary to one another. The rationing of meat, for example, reduced the pressures on price ceilings by giving a fixed supply to each person, thus limiting demand by a method other than bidding up the price and at the same time curbing a black market in over-ceiling prices. The latter important consideration about rationing was seldom realized by the consumer. Quotas on slaughterers resulted in a more even national distribution of supplies among various types of slaughterers such as federally and nonfederally inspected. The price control and distribution program, as eventually worked out, involved:

1. Market control of the price of live cattle and hogs

2. Livestock slaughter and meat distribution controls at the slaughtering levels

3. Wholesale controls involving the price of wholesale cuts, sausages, and edible by-products

---

[1] Judith Russell and Renee Fantin, *Studies in Food Rationing,* General Publication No. 13 of the Historical Reports on War Administration, Office of Price Administration (Washington: Government Printing Office, 1949).

4. Retail controls of price and grading

5. A rationing system which was in effect from the slaughterer through the consumer

6. Apprehension of counterfeiters of ration currency

The Department of Agriculture, largely through the War Food Administration, was given the tasks of assigning allocations and priorities on food including meat, encouraging production, and estimating quantities needed as well as procuring food, including meat, for our armed services, our civilians, and our allies. The Office of Price Administration was given statutory authority to control prices of food, and by authority delegated to it by the Department of Agriculture, was assigned the task of rationing foods such as meat. Thus the determination of what foods should be rationed and when was largely left to the Department of Agriculture, and not to the OPA, a situation not generally realized by the public. In the case of meat, a superadvisory agency, the War Meat Board, was also created to help work out needed supplies and crucial problems. It consisted of representatives of the War Food Administration, the Army, the Navy, the Office of Price Administration, and the meat industry.

The prices of beef and pork at the retail and wholesale levels were first controlled in the spring of 1942, the rationing of meat was instituted in March, 1943, the price of live hogs was controlled beginning in October, 1943, and live cattle in January, 1945. Actually the price of live cattle and hogs should probably have been controlled first in this program. Although meats, fats, and oils were rationed beginning in March, 1943, most of them were removed from rationing the last eight months of 1944 on the expectation of an early termination of hostilities. Full rationing of these commodities was then reimposed at the beginning of 1945 and continued until November of that year. This temporary elimination of meat rationing, which was followed by a recalculation of the length of the war following the disastrous losses at the Battle of the Bulge, did a great deal to discredit the urgency of the program among dealers.

Meats, fats, and oils were rationed on a point basis, in contrast to the unit or equal-quantity basis of so much for each person used in the coffee and sugar rationing programs. So many "red points" were issued in a group, the consumer being allowed a choice of purchases from his total supply of valid ration points. The relative ration points assigned to various kinds and cuts of meats were based on price differentials, the edible portions of the retail cuts, and the quantity that had to be purchased as, for example, in the case of roasts. For the most part point values were kept low on sausage and other meat for which the demand was low. Ration points were the same throughout the nation except in the case of certain emergency disposals of perishable stocks. While ration points were not always manipulated as they should have been to control prices, they actually could have operated that way.[2]

This type of point system was the first plan to be used in rationing major perishable commodities.[3] In England, however, each consumer received a certain meat ration based on a certain total value and had to be registered with, and was permitted to buy from, only one retailer, with each dealer receiving a specified quantity of meat only from specified wholesalers. This arrangement not only aided the enforcement of controls

---

[2] Leon A. Bosch, "Meat Rationing: World War II," Ph. D. Dissertation, Northwestern University, 1948, School of Commerce, Department of Marketing. Bosch was chief of meat rationing for the OPA and later deputy administrator in charge of rationing.

[3] *Ibid.*, p. 175.

but helped the consumer in shopping. The British government was the sole importer of meat and the sole purchaser of home-produced meat,[4] another factor of great importance in controlling the situation. In the United States a close check was kept on the supply situation, and point values were changed as the supply situation changed. Knowledge of supply and demand factors was based not only on data of available supplies, about which there might be a time lag, but also on reports from "Consumer Panels" of 3,000 families representing some 10,000 ration-book holders closely approximating the general population. These families made periodic reports on their food expenditures, including types of meat, to the Bureau of the Census. There were also special surveys of consumers and other efforts to work out consumer preferences.

In our ration program the "primary distributor"[5] of meat was held responsible for (1) the collection of ration points after sale or transfer had taken place, (2) the accounting of such transfers to the central office of large companies, (3) over-all company control of point operations, and (4) preparation and filing of rationing reports. This distributor had to account monthly for his slaughter and purchase of meat, the difference in his beginning and closing inventories, and his sales of the product during this period, thus establishing the number of ration points owed the OPA. Because of the nature of the product such reports were generally allowed a 5 per cent lee-way.[6] An allowable inventory or outright grant of "working capital" was given all establishments involved in the production and distribution of meat to start the rationing program, a grant

---

[4] J. Henry Richardson, "Consumer Rationing in Great Britain," *Canadian Journal of Economics and Political Science,* VIII (February, 1942), 78–79.

[5] A "primary distributor" was the point of origin of the meat supplies and usually was a slaughterer or packer, but might be a wholesaler.

[6] Bosch, *op. cit.,* p. 135.

for which they were held accountable. At the other end of the system were the ration users of meats and fats who were "consumers" such as individuals and families, "pooled book groups" such as rooming houses, restaurants, hotels, and hospitals; and, finally, "industrial users" such as bakers and manufacturers using these commodities in the production of other foods.

Termination of Controls

The government had only a minimum of success with this program designed to ensure a fair distribution, at a reasonable price, of meat, fats, and oils. In fact, it was actually the extensive black market in meat, plus a "strike" to withhold range cattle which, more than any other program, resulted in the final destruction of postwar price control in 1946. When President Truman, on the night of October 14, 1946, dramatically ordered the termination of meat control, he stated that in attempting to deal with the black market and the withholding of range cattle from the packing houses he had considered several alternatives, such as a price control "holiday," further price increases for livestock, importation of dressed meat from foreign countries, and even government seizure of cattle and packing houses for slaughter. All of these solutions had to be rejected. The President denounced selfish interests who "today as in the past are thinking in millions of dollars rather than millions of people," and he also criticized congressmen "who in the service of selfish interests sought to wreck controls no matter what the cost might be to our people." In his radio talk he also said:

. . . . I recognize the hardship that many of you have undergone because of the lack of meat. I sympathize with the millions of housewives who have been hard pressed to provide nourishing meals for their families. I sympathize particularly with our thousands of veterans and other patients in hospitals throughout the country. I know that our children, as well as those persons engaged in manual labor, need meat in their diet.

Many workers have been thrown out of work by meat shortage. The by-products that result from the lawful slaughter of livestock are sorely needed. We depend upon these by-products for insulin and other necessary medicines. We depend upon them also for hides; and already some of our shoe factories are closing and workers are being laid off for lack of leather.

. . . There are reports of widespread disregard and violation of the price-control law. Experience shows that this leads to a tendency to disregard the sanctity of other laws of our country. I need not point out the danger of such a public attitude.

Wartime Production and Consumption of Meat

In examining the difficulties which arose in relation to this vast program for the price control and rationing of meat one is impressed with the tremendous complexities which surrounded it from the beginning and which undoubtedly were basic to the disgraceful black market situation. First of all, there was the problem of the production and consumption of meat in this country. In fact, many persons believed that production was the answer to the meat problem, or, as some dealers put it, supply and demand rather than the OPA would put a stop to the black market in meat. (See Figure 1.) In 1950 after the Korean emergency this same argument was raised again by the American Meat Institute:

Undeniably, the best way to meet an increased demand, if one should develop, is not through restrictions, but through production of quantities of meat adequate to supply the increased demand. The government can promptly encourage stockmen to produce additional quantities of livestock and of meat. Imposition of price ceilings would discourage an expansion in production at the very time increased meat output is most needed.[7]

An examination of the facts on production and consumption during the war years, however, does not bear out this conten-

WOULD YOU LIKE SOME

BUTTER

OR A

ROAST OF BEEF

Well, here's why OPA ceilings make them hard to get—

OPA MEANS LOW PRODUCTION

LOW PRODUCTION MEANS BLACK MARKETS

BLACK MARKETS MEAN NEEDLESSLY HIGH PRICES

NATIONAL ASSOCIATION OF MANUFACTURERS

For a Better Tomorrow for Everybody

FIG. 1

tion. In addition, there is an element of fallacious reasoning about the possibility of unlimited meat production during wartime that will be discussed later.

Actually meat production was greatly increased during World War II. The weight of cattle produced in 1944–1945 was 36 per cent greater than the 1936–1939 average, and farmers received 134 per cent more for their cattle in 1944–1945. (See

[7] *Expanding Livestock Production Makes Controls Unnecessary* (Chicago: American Meat Institute, October, 1950), p. 9.

Table 10.) At a time when the violations were particularly numerous, government reports on the livestock population, January 1, 1945, showed that the number of cattle on farms, both dairy and range, was only exceeded, in the history of the

Table 10

Cattle and Calves: Index of Production, Gross Income, and
Actual Average Price, United States, 1936–1945

(Index: 1936–1939 average = 100)

YEAR	INDEX OF QUANTITY PRODUCED (LIVE WEIGHT)	INDEX OF VALUE OF PRODUC-TION	INDEX OF GROSS INCOME	ACTUAL ANNUAL AVERAGE PRICE PER 100 POUNDS RECEIVED BY FARMERS— CATTLE ONLY
1936–1939 Average	100	100	100	$ 6.63
1940	109	124	114	7.56
1941	119	157	142	8.82
1942	129	207	188	10.70
1943	133	237	213	11.90
1944–1945 Average	136	234	245	11.45

SOURCE: Computed from *Agricultural Statistics, 1948,* United States Department of Agriculture, Table 423, p. 337.

United States, by the record number on January 1, 1944. The number of cattle on farms in the 1944–1945 period was almost 29 per cent greater than the 1936–1939 average, and the number of hogs was 58 per cent greater. The average number of cattle on farms during the two years 1944–1945 was 85,454,000 and hogs 71,536,000. (See Table 11.) In addition, dressed meat production for 1945 exceeded 23 billion pounds, an increase of 42 per cent over the 1936–1939 average but considerably less than the record production of approximately 25 billion pounds in 1944. (See Table 12.) Yet during both years there were extensive violations.

Actually the increase in purchasing power during the war was so great that with the increased demand for the armed services and our allies, together with the decrease in the avail-

Table 11

Estimated Number and Index of Livestock on Farms, Cattle and Hogs, 1936–1947

(*Index: 1936–1939 average = 100; 000 omitted*)

YEAR	ALL CATTLE	INDEX	HOGS	INDEX
1936–1939 Average	66,306	100	45,149	100
1940	68,309	103	61,165	135
1941	71,755	108	54,353	120
1942	76,025	115	60,607	134
1943	81,204	122	73,881	164
1944	85,334	129	83,741	185
1945	85,573	129	59,331	131
1944–1945 Average	85,454	129	71,536	158
1946	82,434	124	61,301	136
1947	81,207	122	56,921	126

Source: *Agricultural Statistics,* 1948, Tables 418 (p. 332) and 439 (p. 350).

ability of various consumer goods, it was virtually impossible for meat production to keep up with consumer demand. Not only was production of livestock greater during the war years; we actually consumed more meat per capita than in previous years. Still we filled orders of millions of pounds of meat for our armed services and our allies, some 35 per cent of all meat supplies in 1945 going to the armed forces. In 1943 the estimated supply of meat for civilians was 140 pounds per capita, which was 14 pounds more than the prewar average, but 24 pounds less than the potential 1943 civilian demand of 164 pounds per capita.[8] This potential civilian demand was, of course, directly related to the purchasing power. National incomes increased from 72.5 billion dollars in 1939 to 181.7

Table 12

Dressed Meats: Production and Index
Total and Per Capita Consumption, United States,
1936–1947

YEAR	PRODUCTION IN MILLION POUNDS, ALL MEATS, LARD NOT INCLUDED	INDEX	CONSUMPTION OF ALL MEATS, LARD NOT INCLUDED	
			TOTAL, MILLION POUNDS	PER CAPITA POUNDS
1936–1939 Average	16,621	100	16,745	129
1940	19,076	115	18,812	142
1941	19,569	118	18,936	143
1942	21,912	132	18,451	140
1943	24,482	147	18,921	146
1944	25,178	151	19,827	154
1945	23,687	143	18,738	144
1944–1945 Average	24,432	147	19,283	149
1946	22,956	138	21,367	153
1947	23,431	141	22,242	155

SOURCE: Computed from Agricultural Statistics, 1948, United States Department of Agriculture, p. 389.

billion dollars in 1944. Without price and rationing controls all available meat could easily have been entirely consumed by the civilian population over a relatively brief period of time. In fact, the temporary relaxation of meat rationing in 1944 resulted in civilian consumption of 2.5 billion pounds of meat

[8] The United States at War, p. 322.

more than had originally been fixed for civilian requirements. Consumption, after removal of point values in May, rose to 160 pounds and "it was estimated that there was purchasing power to support annual consumption of 170 pounds."[9]

The entire argument that if we had produced enough meat to supply all the wartime demand we would not have had a black market problem either in prices or in rationing is built on shortsighted reasoning. In actuality meat production in a time of emergency is directly related to the most judicious use of grains, for one agricultural commodity is related to another. Grains which are not used in livestock production such as for feeder cattle may be made available for other civilian uses and for export. Moreover, meat is a bulky, perishable commodity with a great deal of waste.[10]

Estimates of the Meat Black Market

With this picture of increased production of meat but an even greater demand for it, the stage was set for widespread violation of the meat regulations. Yet probably no one would have predicted the extent to which these violations would eventually engulf the country, involving every aspect of the meat industry from the producer on down to the individual retailer. There was testimony of extensive slaughtering and wholesale violations. A representative of the Joint Livestock Committee stated that, in his opinion, not only were black market violations continuing on an unprecedented scale but

---

[9] *Ibid.,* p. 365.

[10] Bosch has suggested that not only is the possibility of satisfying meat demand impossible but in another emergency we might think of reducing cotton production. Much greater fats and oils production is possible with soybeans and peanuts than from cottonseed oil. We might advantageously ration clothing, as was contemplated in the last war, and divert cotton production to more useful commodities.—Bosch, *op. cit.,* pp. 21–26.

that at least 90 per cent of all meat was being sold in excess of legal ceilings.[11] A vice-president of one of the country's largest packing houses stated that the majority of the slaughterers were in violation: "Our experience has been that there has been no compliance generally with the majority of the slaughtering industry on these government regulations."[12] Similar testimony from the retail meat trade estimated that up to 90 or even 100 per cent were operating in the black market. A spokesman for one New England company estimated that 90 per cent of civilian meat moved in the black market.[13] One New York estimate was that 80 per cent of the meat there was in the black market.[14] The secretary of the Greater Cincinnati Meat Packers' Association estimated that from 50 to 75 per cent of civilian meat was going into the black market and was either sold above ceiling or passing outside of rationing channels. The same paper reporting this item contained an account of furious battles raging in Okinawa, with the Japanese forces making strong counterattacks.

In early 1944 about 85 per cent of the retail meat markets in Richmond, Virginia, were reported as upgrading and selling meat at an average of $9\frac{1}{3}$ cents above the legal ceiling price.[15] The American Meat Institute, in two studies in the spring of 1946, turned up with very high estimates of the black market.

---

[11] *Hearings before the House Committee on Banking and Currency,* on House Resolution 5,270, Seventy-ninth Congress, Second Session, pp. 722–723.

[12] *Hearings before the Senate Committee on Banking and Currency,* on Senate Resolution 2,028, Seventy-ninth Congress, Second Session, p. 1121.

[13] *Hearings before the Special Committee to Investigate Food Shortages,* pursuant to House Resolution 195, Seventy-ninth Congress, First Session, 1945, p. 447.

[14] *Hearings before the Committee on the Judiciary,* on House Concurrent Resolutions 85, 86, 91, House Joint Resolutions 245, 98, Seventy-ninth Congress, First Session, 1945, p. 103.

[15] *Hearings before the Senate Committee on Banking and Currency,* on Senate Resolution 231, Temporary Suspension of Meat and Perishable Meat Products, Seventy-eighth Congress, Second Session, 1944, pp. 23–24.

In these two studies made by the Statistical Research Company and C. C. Chapelle Company buyers made purchases of 3,495 meat cuts in 1,803 independent and chain stores in eleven major cities. As a result of this survey, the American Meat Institute submitted evidence showing that the average housewife was paying about 20 per cent above ceilings for meat. Thus meat was costing the American public over $1,250,000,000 above ceiling prices annually.[16] According to the survey, 83 per cent of the stores (five out of six) in the eleven cities sold at over-ceiling prices. In Providence the figure was 77 per cent, New York City 79 per cent, Newark 85 per cent, Washington 81 per cent, Chicago 91 per cent, Houston 94 per cent, Denver 84 per cent, and Los Angeles 84 per cent.

The OPA challenged these figures. While admitting the extensiveness of the black market at the various trade levels, it was of the opinion that the situation was not as bad as business had maintained. Said the OPA Administrator in 1945: "It is hard for me to believe that black market operations are as extensive as some of the testimony has indicated. I have more confidence in the honesty and patriotism of the American businessman, particularly where wartime price controls are involved."[17] In a District of Columbia survey of 150 retail stores in April, 1946, the OPA found that the overcharge on meat sales, while serious, was only 3.5 per cent, as contrasted with the American Meat Institute's finding in the same city of

---

[16] *New Facts on the Meat Black Market* and *The Meat Black Market— Its Extent and Its Cost to American Consumers* (Chicago: American Meat Institute, 1946), contained in *Hearings before the Committee on Banking and Currency,* on Senate Resolution 2,028, on Extension of the Emergency Price Control and Stabilization Acts of 1942, on Senate Resolution 2,028 as amended, Seventy-ninth Congress, Second Session, 1946, pp. 1104–1113.

[17] *Hearings before the Senate Committee on Currency and Banking,* on Senate Joint Resolution 30, Seventy-ninth Congress, First Session, p. 625.

19 per cent.[18] Another figure submitted in this debate was the report of the Bureau of Labor Statistics that the amount of overcharges in fifty-five cities was, in general, about 12 per cent, although in some cities it was about 5 per cent.

No conclusions can be reached as to which estimate was the most accurate. Both sides had a stake in the situation, business hoping to present evidence of the general breakdown of government controls and thus make possible the termination of the program, while the OPA could not admit the existence of such a breakdown and still survive. There is no evidence that the figures were intentionally untrue, but rather that different methods were employed in securing a representative sample of stores, and in the details of the surveys. Probably the report of the Bureau of Labor Statistics was the most accurate, although certain evasive violations might not have shown up in its figures. While there were these great differences in estimates, even the smaller OPA figures indicate extensive violations.[19]

Regardless of the extent to which meat was actually being illegally distributed throughout the country, enforcement records, though admittedly failing to show all violations, do show

---

[18] *New Facts on the Meat Black Market* and *The Meat Black Market— Its Extent and Its Cost to American Consumers*, American Meat Institute, contained in *Hearings*, cited above, pp. 1884–1885.

[19] The extensiveness of the meat black market was also indicated by the difficulties which the citizen price panels working with retailers encountered: ". . . almost all active panels had held at least one educational 'trade meeting' with meat violators, had referred their most flagrant violators to the district office, and had reported again and again, both that they had a suspiciously high number of consumer complaints on meat, and that meat men when called to conference all claimed overcharges by the wholesalers. In the fall of 1944 the national office sent a special crew of meat investigators into 8 or 10 large eastern cities. They found the panel alarms more than justified. The panels had done their part in reporting this situation, but it cannot be claimed that neighborly persuasion accomplished compliance in the meat trade."—Putnam, *op. cit.*, p. 80.

some of the extent of infractions. During 1944, a typical war year, there were 62,382 cases[20] revealing violations. This figure included wholesale, retail, and restaurant cases dealt with by the Enforcement Department. In the program or survey type of investigation, 11,934 cases of violation were found, or 43.1

Table 13

Formal Sanctions Instituted for Violations of Meat Price Regulations and Ration Orders, 1944

Contributions to the United States Treasury	591
Settlement administrator's consumers' treble damage claims	866
Administrator's consumers' treble damage suits instituted ..	478
Suspension order proceedings instituted	1,425
Settlement administrator's own treble damage claims	662
Administrator's own treble damage suits instituted	506
Injunction suits instituted	1,697
License suspension suits instituted	29
Criminal proceedings instituted	261
Total sanctions instituted	6,515

SOURCE: Table prepared from unpublished OPA Enforcement Department reports. These figures were secured by adding together formal sanctions for violations of all regulations and ration orders dealing with beef, veal, pork, lamb, and mutton.

per cent of the cases investigated; in the complaint investigations, 19,777, or 74.5 per cent, revealed violation. The remainder of the cases represented referrals and debiting that involved rationing violations. During 1944 the OPA levied 6,515 serious penalties, exclusive of license warning notices, against various types of meat concerns. (See Table 13 above.) Over a third of these sanctions were imposed on slaughterers

---

[20] This figure includes a small number of other cases, such as poultry and dairy products which could not be separated statistically.

and wholesalers. These sanctions included 1,168 settlements or suits brought for administrator's own treble damages, part of the 1,697 injunction suits, and 261 cases in which criminal prosecution was instituted.

In the middle of 1945, with what was thought to be a large staff of 750 investigators concentrating on the slaughtering and wholesale distribution levels, the OPA turned up with 2,700 cases of violation in a single month. Despite the fact that this was almost three years since the beginning of the meat program, during April and May of 1945 cases were filed at a rate almost twelve times as great as in the same period in 1944. This increase was not due entirely to an increase in violations, but was partially the result of an increase in enforcement manpower and new programs. A detailed study of wholesale meat violations was made by Hartung in Detroit covering the period between October, 1942, and June 30, 1946. He found that 83 concerns, representing a total of 123 cases, had committed 195 violations and had had 233 sanctions imposed against them.[21] These figures represented "a very conservative picture of violation in Detroit," for they constituted a count of definite violations where a sanction was imposed and did not include cases which were dismissed or closed for any reason.[22]

Price Violations

After the price of live cattle and hogs was regulated, many slaughterers and packers paid more than the regulations permitted. Black market price violations by wholesalers occurred

---

[21] Frank E. Hartung, "White-Collar Offenses in the Wholesale Meat Industry in Detroit," *American Journal of Sociology*, LVI, No. 1 (July, 1950), 25–35. Also see his "A Study in Law and Social Differentiation," previously cited. This article, together with the doctoral dissertation, has been extremely useful in the preparation of certain sections of this chapter.

[22] Hartung, "A Study in Law and Social Differentiation," p. 206.

in connection with (1) requirements set for ceiling prices of all cuts by grades, zones, and classes of purchasers, (2) regulations for cutting, trimming, processing, and labeling, (3) compliance with base-period restrictions and quotas for sales of fabricated cuts, and (4) record-keeping and reporting requirements. Because of the nature of their business, violations by retail markets were usually sales over ceiling, short-weighing, and upgrading, and were frequently the direct result of violations at the wholesale level, often referred to as the "squeeze" on retailers.[23]

The most time-consuming type of investigation and case development was necessary to trace some hidden violations back from the retailer to the go-between and, ultimately, to the responsible large-scale violator. In 1944 one widely publicized indictment against Peter Golas and his confederates for black market activities in meat resulted from the expenditure of more than 1,000 investigative man-days.[24] Industry itself recognized these various types of violations and the tremendous difficulties of apprehending them. For example, Rose Marie Kiefer, secretary-manager of the National Association of Retail Grocers, testified:

In the industry, too, a lot of ridiculous and troublesome problems have grown up, such as (1) short weight, for which the retailer must not complain else he gets no meat; (2) tie-in sales, where needed meat cannot be obtained without the purchase of

[23] The New York State Food Merchants Association reported in 1945 that 57 per cent of its members replied that they could not obtain their meat legitimately. *Hearings before the Special Committee to Investigate Food Shortages,* pursuant to House Resolution 195, Seventy-ninth Congress, First Session, 1945, pp. 622–624.

[24] In this well-known case, which involved several large independent packers, about 10,000,000 pounds of beef were shipped into northern New Jersey and New York City alone in 1943, the meat being sold at an average overcharge of 6½ cents a pound and thus amounting on these sales alone to an illegal profit of $650,000 on $3,000,000 worth of meat.

sausage, shortening, cleansers, and other items; and (3) side payments in cash or other remuneration paid to salesmen, drivers, or
even officials of supplier companies. Sometimes any or all of these
practices must be carried on to get meat into retail outlets. This is
extremely difficult to run down or correct, since it is usually an
individual transaction, and so far no one has been able to clear
it up with patriotic appeal.[25]

Most meat violations, at all levels of distribution, were
evasive in nature, although at the retail level sales over ceiling
were also quite common. There were four main types of these
evasive violations: cash on the side, upgrading, rigged or short
weights, and tie-in sales. "It is indeed a pattern of slyness, of
under-the-counter tactics that would have been abhorred by
even second-rate business houses a few years ago . . ."[26]

As mentioned in an earlier chapter, a common cash-on-the-
side violation was that in which the retail dealers were invoiced at the ceiling prices and were then expected to pay the
wholesaler a prearranged sum in cash on the side. For this cash
the retail dealers were given no receipts, and the wholesaler
made no proper entry in his account books. For example, in
1944, when nonprocessing slaughterers in the East were paying
prices for live cattle far above the legal range, the immediate
results of such transactions were cash-on-the-side deals in dressed
beef and veal with consequent widespread demoralization of
the industry. These transactions were often recorded as "loans"
which the retail dealers were repaying the wholesaler, or as
additional sales of nondelivered meat to the retail dealers in

---

[25] *Hearings before the Special Committee to Investigate Food Shortages
for the House of Representatives,* pursuant to House Resolution 195, Seventy-
ninth Congress, First Session, 1945, Pt. 1, p. 189.

[26] Thomas I. Emerson, Director, Enforcement Division, Office of Price
Administration, "Ration Robbers," *American Magazine,* September, 1943, p. 27.
Also see Anonymous, "Confessions of a Black Market Butcher," *Saturday
Evening Post,* August 24, 1946.

whose names dummy invoices were prepared. Other ways in which the wholesaler attempted to conceal the cash he received was to place one of his employees on the payroll of the retail dealer to draw a salary for his "services," or to require retail dealers to tip his salesmen generously. A novel device was to require retailers to buy stock worth only a fraction of the purchase price in the wholesale corporation, and only those retail dealers elevating themselves to the position of stockholders were plentifully supplied with meat at ceiling prices.

Upgrading of meat was common, Grade A being invoiced as Grade AA to the retailer, thus adding one or two cents a pound to the profit of the wholesaler, who in turn sold the lower quality meat at the Grade AA price in order to preserve his margin of profit. At times the wholesaler invoiced his meat two grades above its actual quality, and the consumer then received even poorer quality for his money. This practice of upgrading was carried on in other ways, one of which was to sell a lower priced cut of meat as a higher priced cut. Sometimes the wholesaler sold illegal cuts, that is, cuts not provided for in the regulations, for which he received considerably higher prices. In the sale of full loins of beef, for example, the wholesaler was required to remove the kidney and a portion of the suet, perhaps 15 per cent of the total weight of the cut. If they were not removed the wholesaler was, in effect, selling the cut about 15 per cent over the ceiling price. The retail butchers then sold their porterhouse steaks over ceiling prices in order to maintain profit margins after trimming the cut. Excessive fat on pork in violation of regulations was a persistent and serious problem, estimated to have cost consumers about $35,000,000 a year.[27]

---

[27] Office of Price Administration, *Tenth Quarterly Report*, for period ending June 30, 1944, p. 64. Also see "Too Much Fat," *Business Week*, June 10,

Rigged or short weights were other methods of evasion in which retail dealers were invoiced for a weight of meat in excess of what they actually received. For example, an invoice would read 125 pounds of chuck beef when the actual weight was 110 pounds. The retailer then either had to charge over ceiling prices or short-weight the customer if he was not to lose money.

Another common practice was the tie-in sale whereby the purchase of one commodity was made the condition for the purchase of another. The wholesaler might refuse to sell beef or smoked hams, for example, unless the retailer also purchased less popular items such as neck bones, bologna, tails, or tripe. This tie-in practice, which permitted the wholesaler to sell meat products ordinarily in small demand, was considered by many dealers to be the most frequent type of violation.

Rationing Violations

Many of these evasive price techniques also frequently involved rationing violations as well. When there was short-weighting by the retailer he was able to build up a surplus of ration points, and when there was upgrading of meat products he was also able to secure more points for the cheaper grades than specified by the regulations. A form of upgrading in relation to rationing was evidenced in the extensive "red market" which developed during the last three months of 1944. This term was used to denote the sale of a lower grade of meat at the ration point value and price of a higher grade. All lower grades of beef and lamb being point-free and upper grades

---

1944. Actually consumers were asked to buy fat at about fifty cents a pound and sell it back to the government for the waste fats program at two cents and two ration points a pound. See Hartung, "A Study in Law and Social Differentiation," p. 252.

being rationed, some merchants operated a "red market" in both points and prices in order to buy and sell more of the rationed meat. To curb this practice the Office of Economic Stabilization ordered slaughterers to mark grade designations two inches apart on all primal cuts, thus assisting customers in identifying grades even when the meat was reduced to retail cuts.

Other practices to get around the ration system included the abuse of ration banking and credit privileges by business firms through overdrafts and point payment defaults; the abuse of ration currency by some business users who allegedly "sold" their establishments to relatives and employees in order to get a fresh start in ration points; and false reports about the amount of meat which was used prior to rationing, as well as false statements about the number of patrons.

. . . the most lamentable defection occurred through the willingness of some commercial users of rationed foods to make false statements to the government when presumably reporting "historical" usage and current volume of patronage or where seeking special relief because the regulations imposed an "undue hardship." There is a limit to which ordinary systems, drawn [for the sake of the] general benefit, can discourage persons out to "beat the system." The number of the latter persons is a function of the extent to which the moral sense of the community holds rationing in serious regard.[28]

Local board officials and other volunteers, while competent to check on ordinary consumers, were not adequate for the task of ascertaining the honesty of institutional and industrial users. As indicated above, stores at the beginning of rationing were allowed a certain inventory of ration points. Later, spokesmen

---

[28] Bosch, *op. cit.*, p. 153.

for the industry maintained that a large number of stores through no fault of their own had spent their inventory. The OPA offered to "bail out" all such legitimate cases, but during a period of three and a half months less than nine hundred such petitions were received. Five times this figure would have been less than 1 per cent of all stores. Bosch has concluded: "In view of the agitation by dealers and their trade associations for point relief, why did so few take advantage of the opportunity? Probably the safest surmise on that score is that those who had consciously engaged in black market operations were reluctant to provide an explanation of losses to OPA."[29]

Primary meat distributors were generally lax in their rationing reports, which were basic to the entire system. In one spot survey of sixty-five hundred reports to twenty-four district offices in seventeen states it was found that few reports were carefully made out regardless of the size of the establishment.[30] Part of the reason for these inaccurate reports was the failure of the OPA to make anything like a complete check of them because of its limited personnel, including meat specialists.

While farm-produced meat was not a large part of the total meat slaughter and most of it was consumed by the farm family itself, only about 9 per cent of that which was sold was exchanged for ration points.[31] Some of this meat was sold to "help out" friends or relatives. The entire situation presented a difficult problem because (1) farmers were often not aware of rationing requirements, (2) this area was difficult to police, (3) the same food ration was given to both producers and nonproducers resulting in surplus points for the producer, and

29 *Ibid.,* pp. 281–282.
30 *Ibid.,* pp. 138–139.
31 *Ibid.,* p. 112.

(4) such black market dealings were highly profitable.[32] The fact that part of this "illegal" meat found its way into frozen food lockers presented quite a problem. Raids on frozen food lockers indicated that patrons had in their possession large quantities of illegal meat which had been purchased from farmer-slaughterers without the payment of red points. One check of a Chicago concern revealed that 87 per cent of the meat contained in the lockers had been illegally acquired.[33] Such evasions would be much more widespread were rationing restored again. In World War II most frozen food storage was in commercial lockers, some three fourths of which were in the hands of farmers. Only about 1 per cent of the civilian meat supply was involved in this type of evasion in the last war. Since then, however, the commercial food locker business has greatly expanded, particularly in urban areas. In addition, thousands of American families now have home freezers, and the possibilities of hoarding meat illegally purchased from farm slaughterers are extremely great. In a future emergency farmers will have to be brought more directly into the meat control situation. Much more could be done to educate farmers about rationing and to enlist their support. Homeowners, commercial lockers, dealers, eating places, and the like, could be made to show that their meat had been legally acquired. We might even be forced to register livestock and report any sales as England did after World War II. From a positive point of view the great expansion of home freezers would enable us legally to stockpile such perishable products rather than have an abundance of meat supplies at one time and a shortage at another, as occurred during the last war. Whether or not this

---

32 *Ibid.,* p. 112–113.
33 "Raid Meat Cache," *Business Week,* May 5, 1945, p. 36.

development would result in hoarding and in emphasizing class differentials through possession of such facilities is another problem which would have to be dealt with by controls.

Many violations of the rationing regulations were covered by the use of stolen or counterfeit ration currency. Butchers, restaurants, and others who distributed meat without receiving ration currency were not always able to cover up such activities in their records; hence they resorted to purchasing counterfeit or stolen currency to turn in to the ration banks. Counterfeit meats-fats stamps recovered at verification centers in a three-months period in 1945 numbered 4,061,616. A well-known Pittsburgh newspaper reporter passed himself off as a meat dealer and had no difficulty purchasing large quantities of meat without coupons.

A gaudy, rustic-looking eccentric, Ray Sprigle, has been wearing a ten-gallon sombrero for 15 years, ever since he went to Arizona to solve a Pittsburgh murder. The ten-gallon hat, a silver-ringed cane, and a fuming corncob pipe are the trademarks of the *Post-Gazette's* 58-year-old star reporter. To disguise himself for his latest assignment—to expose Pittsburgh's lively black market in meat—he gave up hat and cane, but not his pipe.

Sprigle changed his name to Alois Vondich, shaved off his mustache, bought a 69 cent cap, and smoked stogies whenever any black marketeer was looking. He got himself an old truck, and a "partner" who knew something about meat. Within three weeks he had bought from wholesalers (at about double the ceiling prices) nearly 1,300 pounds of beef, 176 pounds of veal, 250 pounds of smoked hams and pork shoulders, 225 pounds of bacon. A ton of meat was his goal, and he made it—without ever having a red point. To show it could be done, he also bought 10,000 red stamps in the black market, at the going price of $6 a thousand.

His three-week spree cost his paper $2,000 (the *Post-Gazette* gave the meat to local hospitals). Out of it came a seven-day-wonder front-page series, featuring names and addresses of the local black marketeers.

After his first two articles appeared, the red-faced OPA subpoenaed Sprigle. (Pittsburgh's OPA had never used its subpoena power to go after a single Pittsburgh black marketeer.) Said the *Post-Gazette's* Sprigle: "We will report the story in our own way and in our own good time. I shall tell you nothing. . . . The record of the OPA is not such as to inspire confidence. . . . And I am quite willing to go to jail—immediately, if necessary."[34]

Federally and Nonfederally Inspected Slaughterers

One particularly significant aspect of the black market which was peculiar to the meat industry was the great growth of the nonfederally inspected slaughterers. Just as some people attributed this meat black market to inadequate production, many persons attributed it exclusively to the nonfederally inspected slaughterer. In many ways these two problems were closely related. "Thus, the problems of meat supply and distribution which aroused so much concern in 1944 and 1945 were due in large part to failure to solve the slaughter control problem in 1943."[35]

In the United States in 1941 there were 365 wholesale slaughtering plants each of which produced more than 2,000,000 pounds of meat, and 3,000 local plants with production of from 300,000 to 2,000,000 pounds, a few operated by retailers but most of them wholesale. In addition, there were about 23,000 butchers who produced less than 300,000 pounds of meat from slaughter. There was also some farm slaughtering, although most of it was for farm use.[36] Nearly all of the large

---

[34] "Meat Makes News, *Time*, April 30, 1945, pp. 61–62.
[35] *The United States at War*, p. 363.
[36] Knute Bjorka, "Marketing Margins and Costs for Livestock and Meat,"

slaughtering plants and some of the local plants were inspected by the Department of Agriculture and thus by law were the only ones allowed to ship their meat in interstate commerce or to sell meat to the government. Department of Agriculture

Table 14

Production of Federally Inspected and Estimated Uninspected Meat, and Percentage of Total, 1941–1946

(In millions of pounds)

YEAR	TOTAL PRODUCTION	FEDERALLY INSPECTED	PER CENT OF TOTAL	ESTIMATED UNINSPECTED	PER CENT OF TOTAL
1941	19,577	13,433	68.6	6,144	31.4
1942	21,917	15,456	70.5	6,461	29.5
1943	24,486	16,833	68.7	7,653	31.3
1944	25,181	17,924	71.2	7,257	28.8
1945	23,691	15,363	64.9	8,328	35.1
1946	22,961	13,800	60.1	9,161	39.9

Source: *Statistical Abstract of the United States, 1948,* Table 767, p. 700. Percentages computed.

personnel inspected the plants which shipped their products in interstate commerce to see that they complied with federal sanitation regulations and grading specifications.

In 1941 meat from federally inspected plants accounted for approximately two thirds (68.6 per cent) of the national meat supply. (See Table 14.) Before the war was over this situation had changed considerably through the growth of non-federally inspected slaughterers who catered not to the government but to local civilian demands. Less meat was therefore available to the large federally inspected concerns which are

Technical Bulletin No. 932, Bureau of Agricultural Economics, United States Department of Agriculture, 1947, p. 36.

the main processing outlets in the country. Since most large urban centers are dependent upon them for supplies, severe civilian meat shortages developed in the heavily populated cities supplied by out-of-state packing firms. The army and navy also had difficulty in obtaining adequate meat supplies.

In the original meat restriction orders issued by the OPA the amount of commercial slaughtering by small nonfederally inspected concerns or farm slaughterers was not mentioned. Later the Department of Agriculture took over this responsibility and issued licenses to the members of this group with the hope of keeping their slaughtering on some sort of quota. These licenses, however, were issued with little investigation, with the result that small slaughterers increased in number. These nonfederally inspected slaughterers found it relatively easy to evade price and rationing regulations. They could more easily pay higher than ceiling prices than the regular packers, and these illegal prices were passed on to wholesalers and retailers, usually without ration currency. Not only did such illegal behavior have direct effects; there were indirect ones as well. Because these products were not federally inspected there was a loss of valuable medicinal by-products such as insulin from the pancreas, livers for liver extract, and so on. A 1946 statement by Parke, Davis & Co. indicated the seriousness of this situation:

You are certainly aware of the fact that the available supplies of animal glands for medicinal use during the past several years have been constantly decreasing. This has variously been attributed to a shortage of labor, a shortage of feed, or a dislocation of animal production on the farms.

At present the situation is perhaps more critical than at any time since the beginning of the war, and we believe that one important cause is diversion of cattle away from the regularly inspected packing houses into black market channels. This, of course,

not only presents a danger from supplying the public with uninspected meats but results in a total waste of all the animal glands,
fats, hides, and other by-products. This is particularly serious to
the manufacturer of medicinal and pharmaceutical products which
are necessary for the maintenance of public health.[37]

It would be an error, however, to presume that either all
nonfederally inspected slaughterers were in the black market
or that all federally inspected ones were not. At the most, and
then not for a long period, nonfederally inspected slaughterers
accounted for an estimated one half as compared with one
third of the prewar total meat slaughter.[38] If we take the published figures of the Department of Agriculture rather than
the somewhat higher unofficial estimates which allowed for a
certain amount of nonreporting by nonfederally inspected
slaughterers, we find that nonfederally inspected slaughter in
1945 had increased by only about 3 per cent of the total over
1941 and in 1946 by about 8 per cent of the total. (See Table
14.) Farm-slaughtered meat was a relatively small part of all
civilian allocated meat amounting to an estimated 9.3 per cent
in 1943, 13.3 in 1944, and 12.6 in 1945.[39] One vice-president
of two of the "Big Four" packers made it clear that the black
market was not necessarily synonymous with nonfederally inspected concerns. He said:

Well, when you talk about black marketing, in the terms I
have used, I haven't meant then just the fellow who kills in un-

---

[37] Letter quoted in *Expanding Livestock Production Makes Controls Unnecessary* (Chicago: American Meat Institute, October 25, 1950), p. 8. This
publication also quoted a telegram from Eli Lilly and Company, Indianapolis,
Indiana, dated April 10, 1946: "If the black market situation continues much
longer someone must be prepared to accept responsibility for shortage of essential drugs such as insulin, and other important drugs such as bile, pituitaries,
thyroid and anti-anemia preparations. Our present procurement is very much
short of minimum needs and appears to be getting worse right along."

[38] Bjorka, *op. cit.*

[39] Bosch, *op. cit.*, pp. 110–111.

sanitary places, but I meant also anyone who operates outside the legal compliance with all the OPA regulations.

Now, I think the OPA would agree with me when I say that the violation of either the OPA live maximum or the OPA dressed ceilings is not confined entirely to the uninspected slaughterer. Both the Government-inspected slaughterer and the noninspected slaughterer, and the state-inspected, and the city-inspected, are, in various proportions, involved in those transactions.[40]

The inroads of the nonfederally inspected slaughterers was serious, however, and the Government took several measures to cope with it. The principal measure was through wartime allocation and priorities to ensure a more adequate distribution of livestock to federally inspected plants. Also there were various restrictions and quotas on livestock that could be purchased to (1) reduce pressures against livestock ceilings through reducing competitive bidding, (2) provide the relative amount of meat which could be distributed to civilians by those slaughterers prepared and organized to distribute meat over wide areas, and (3) support price ceilings on meat in those areas where there was a deficit of locally produced meat.[41] Another measure was taken in February, 1945, when an effort was made to restrict the volume of business done by nonfederally inspected slaughterers. Under this order subsidies were to be withheld when the volume of business exceeded a specified maximum. The Anderson Committee appointed to investigate food shortages pointed out that the subsidy that would be lost, however, was only a small fraction of what could be made by engaging in the black market: "He lost in subsidy 2 cents a pound to slaughter as he pleased and the testimony

---

[40] *Hearings before the Senate Committee on Banking and Currency,* on Senate Resolution 2,028, Seventy-ninth Congress, Second Session, pp. 1142–1143.
[41] Bosch, *op. cit.,* p. 51.

before the Committee was that he could get a minimum of 5 cents to a maximum of 20 cents a pound in wholesale black market channels."[42]

The failure to impose ceilings on live cattle early in the program rather than in 1945 not only facilitated the development of black market activities by nonfederally inspected slaughterers but put a squeeze on the entire meat system. Almost from the beginning the OPA had sought authority to impose live cattle ceilings to prevent any "squeeze" on the large packers. When wholesale meat prices were reduced in the middle of 1943 to bring about a 10 per cent reduction in retail prices, subsidies were granted to meat packers by the Defense Supplies Corporation as compensation for the increased cost of live cattle, which was then unregulated. Prices were to be within a designated range, with less subsidy being given if the average price paid by the slaughterer was outside the designated range. Later even differential subsidies were given to small nonprocessing slaughterers.[43] The annual cost of the subsidy on meats was estimated at 436 million dollars by OPA in 1943 although subsequently the subsidy was increased.[44] By the use of a substantial subsidy on meat, amounting to about one or two cents a live pound, depending upon quality, it was hoped that a squeeze situation on the many federally inspected packers would be avoided and that price violations by federally inspected and later nonfederally inspected con-

---

[42] *House Report No. 504,* Report of the Special Committee to Investigate Food Shortages pursuant to House Resolution 195, Seventy-ninth Congress, First Session, p. 14.

[43] For a discussion of the meat subsidy problem, see Seymour E. Harris and Philip Ritz, *Problems in Price Control: Stabilization Subsidies,* General Publication No. 10 of the Historical Reports on War Administration, Office of Price Administration (Washington: Government Printing Office, 1947).

[44] Jules Backman, *Experience with Wartime Subsidies* (Washington: Citizens National Committee, Inc. October, 1945).

cerns would thus be minimized. Again there was no marked diminution of violations. These subsidies were operating in a virtually impossible situation where the government was not controlling the price of cattle. The problem was further complicated since those slaughterers who did not receive subsidies and even many of those who did bid up the price of cattle and then sold the beef through black market channels. A representative of the Joint Livestock Committee stated:

> Well, the actual subsidy is about $3.00 a hundred [pounds] on your AA grade, $2.95 on the A grade and $1.25 on the T grade. So, what does a man want to take $1.25 as a subsidy for when some black market operator will come out and maybe give him three or four dollars a hundred more for his cattle and hogs?[45]

After a careful study of this problem one observer concluded:

> By December, 1944, it was abundantly clear that a sufficiently large number of slaughterers were prepared to sacrifice subsidy for black market returns so that the subsidy was rapidly becoming an ineffective device for the control of live cattle.[46]

One of the main uses of the subsidy, however, in relation to violations came as a negative factor in the threat of its withdrawal where violations occurred. The Price Administrator in 1944 stated that "denial of the claims of slaughterers who have willfully violated OPA regulations will materially assist in the enforcement of such regulations."[47] Yet a study made this conclusion:

> The fact that loss of subsidy alone was insufficient to dis-

---

[45] *Hearings before the House Banking and Currency Committee,* on House Resolution 5,270, Seventy-ninth Congress, Second Session, p. 728.

[46] Charles M. Elkinton, "The Meat Industry: Economic Characteristics Revealed by Price Control," unpublished Ph.D. dissertation, University of Wisconsin, 1947, p. 178.

[47] Memorandum February 17, 1944, from Chester Bowles, Administrator, to Thomas I. Emerson, Deputy Administrator for Enforcement.

courage payments for cattle exceeding the subsidy maximum is especially significant in view of the fact that the subsidy was greater than the net return realized by packers in normal periods. The average packer profit per hundred pounds of dressed meat over a 16-year period ended with 1940 has been shown to be 19 cents. The subsidy, in contrast, amounted to an average of approximately $2.00 per hundred pounds of dressed carcass of beef, veal, pork, lamb, and mutton.[48]

It was not until January, 1945, however, that the OPA was given the authority to fix maximum prices for live cattle. Much was expected of this program, and the OPA Administrator wrote: "Our entire program of meat price control was in danger of a breakdown. By placing ceilings on live cattle, it will be possible to hold meat prices rigidly to present ceilings."[49] Yet, somehow, even with the assistance presented by this new measure, compliance among packers showed no material increase during the subsequent eighteen months before the demise of the OPA.[50] The explanation probably was that the program of controlling live cattle prices came three years too late and would probably have been much more effective earlier.

The entire problem of this nonfederally inspected meat black market would have been far less serious if the entrance

---

[48] Elkinton, *op. cit.*, p. 178.

[49] Chester Bowles, Administrator, in *Washington Letter*, Office of Price Administration, No. 6, January 16, 1945 (Mimeographed).

[50] See OPA quarterly reports and congressional hearings. One factor in the black market in meat was the black market in field grain. By 1946 Clinton Anderson, Secretary of Agriculture, testified that one of the well-known American manufacturing firms, large users of corn products, made a study through its staff on the extent of the black market in corn. The result of the study revealed that from 80 to 90 per cent of all corn was moving into the black market, running 30 to 40 cents above the general price level. In many instances it was customary to pay a bonus of $500 in cash for a car of shelled corn. During the spring of 1946 OPA government agents took steps to stem the black market operations in grain and corn. In the late spring the Department of Agriculture proposed to subsidize the sale of 50,000,000 bushels of corn by a price increase of 30 cents a bushel, a price which, incidentally, was the over-ceiling black market price of corn.

of this new slaughterer had been prevented in the first place, although admittedly this would have been difficult. As the Anderson Committee reported: "Once legitimate distribution has been disrupted and black market channels are set up it becomes increasingly difficult to reestablish the normal channels of distribution and to make them subject to legal controls."[51] Bosch has suggested that (1) new slaughterers should not have been permitted, (2) nonfederally inspected slaughterers should have been carefully limited, and (3) the output of a plant, after change of ownership, should have been directed by law to customers served by the plant before it was sold.[52]

Problems of Enforcement

Some have stated that the attempts to secure more livestock for federally inspected meat packers by means of various slaughter control regulations generally failed because of lack of proper enforcement. Other persons familiar with the situation have stated that although they would agree that enforcement difficulties entered into the situation and although the relatively large meat enforcement staff available in 1945 could not cope with the problem, a similar strong enforcement staff in 1942, coupled with more centralized control and more vision from the start, would have probably been successful in stopping a large part of the development of a black market in this area.[53] Bosch, who was in charge of meat rationing, has stated in this regard:

While no one better appreciates than does the author the lamentable lack of adequate enforcement machinery, he feels that

---

[51] *House Report No. 504*, p. 5.
[52] Bosch, *op. cit.*, p. 79.
[53] Walter M. Wilcox, *The Farmer in the Second World War* (Ames, Iowa: State College Press, 1946).

it would be a mistake to suggest that even greater enforcement facilities, consistent with all the other demands for manpower, within the annual budget for OPA, could have overcome the inadequacies in the conception and policy management of the slaughter programs. . . . Greater enforcement machinery, if available, could have achieved more than was accomplished.[54]

Despite these extensive violations of the law, meat dealers and even segments of the public were prone to condemn not the criminal but the police. The police, in the guise of the OPA, prepared unfair laws, kept the people from getting all the meat they wanted, and were not doing a good job of controlling the black market. Many statements similar to the following were made by wholesale meat dealers in 1945:

It does not make sense to comply with certain illogical regulations.

The OPA office doesn't know what they are doing. They've just made a bunch of crooks out of honest men.

The overseers are the real saboteurs of this country and Chester Bowles is a traitor.[55]

A prominent meat packer, when interviewed in 1947 about what would happen if there should ever again be an attempt to restore controls, set forth a brash statement of the dilemma:

Without patriotic motives OPA could not survive. Prices are higher now and perhaps keep meat from the lower economic bracket but if controls were restored, the lower income brackets wouldn't get the meat anyhow since it would go into the black market and upper income groups would get it all. Free competition keeps business clean. A dishonest businessman, consistently so, cannot survive under this system. For the sake of our economy it is best to

---

[54] Bosch, *op. cit.,* pp. 97–98.
[55] "Opinion Survey of Food Wholesalers," cited above.

have honest dealings rather than the debasing effects of those under OPA.[56]

Many of these opinions were supported in the newspapers and by certain members of Congress. There were constant attacks on the OPA for its regulations but not necessarily against the violators. Despite the admissions of many businessmen in the hearings before congressional committees, there is no evidence that these committees advised specific action against these admitted violators. Some Congressmen came to the defense of their constituents, as in the following case:

The Georgia slaughterer sold his meat on the books at ceiling prices, but he collected several thousand dollars a week in excess, undeclared profits. On the affidavits of half a dozen of his victims, he was found guilty of price violations, convicted, and fined $2,000, which was only a fraction of his take. On the ground that he had violated his agreement with the government, the Reconstruction Finance Corporation withheld $26,000 in subsidies which had been going to the slaughterer to make it possible for him to keep prices down and still make a reasonable profit. As soon as this occurred, the slaughterer went to his Congressman, who blasted the OPA for picking on a highly respectable citizen who had been doing business in Georgia for thirty years without reproach. The Congressman in this case does not appreciate that the black market, which he wants wiped out, consists of men like his precious slaughterer.[57]

There were cases now and then, however, where the opinions given indicated full realization that food rationing in time of war is a serious matter and that certain practices cannot be condoned. The following excerpt is taken from a decision handed down by an OPA hearing commissioner who ordered

---

[56] From an interview.
[57] Leon Henderson, "How Black Is Our Market?" *Atlantic Monthly*, July, 1946, p. 47.

the suspension of a nationally known restaurant in New York City for the overuse of 100,000 meat ration points. Throughout the war in the meat rationing program one of the most difficult black markets was the over-ceiling purchase of meat and the disregard of ration currency regulations by restaurants seeking choice cuts. The OPA took the position that scarce war supplies should not be unfairly diverted to restaurant owners.

There is no doubt that a difficult problem confronts the so-called steak house in a total war economy suffering a shortage of meat. The commodity in which it specializes can no longer be obtained in unlimited quantity. A choice thus confronts such an establishment: To obey the ration regulation and possibly suffer considerable loss, or to violate the regulation and maintain its business substantially as usual. Such a choice is concededly a cruel one. It cannot be said, however, that such cruelty of choice is confined to high-class steak houses. Many of our sons in their last living hours have been confronted with a choice no less cruel. They, too, have the choice between suffering substantial loss and violating the obligations imposed upon them by war. The casualty lists mounting daily are evidence of the choice made and its unanimity.[58]

The penalties imposed by the courts for flagrant black market activities in meat were extremely inadequate. A large number of wholesale meat dealers, when interviewed, believed that they and others would have been seriously deterred by jail sentences rather than money payments, either fines, settlements, or civil suits, which they thought were inadequate. As one meat dealer, commenting on the effectiveness of jail sentences, put it, "What is the use of doing whatever you did if you have to cool your heels in jail?" There is evidence that

---

[58] The opinion of Mr. Talbot Smith, Acting Hearing Administrator of OPA, in the matter of 51 West 51st Street Corp., operating under the name Toots Shor Restaurant, rendered on August 6, 1943, OPA *Opinions and Decisions,* III, 6114.

jail sentences when used, as in New England in 1945, brought good results. An official of the OPA, commenting on this, wrote: "The suppression of a very threatening black market in meat a year ago was attributed with good reason to this policy of stiff jail sentences." Notwithstanding these beliefs the OPA used the criminal sanction in only 739, or about 8 per cent, of the cases of violation up to January 1, 1945, and obtained imprisonments in only 98, or 1.5 per cent, of the total sanction cases. In 1944 the criminal sanction was instituted in only one in every twenty-five cases of violation where serious action was taken.

A number of instances of light treatment could be cited. A Boston meat dealer who had purchased 70,000 red points from some counterfeiters was suspended from doing business for one month and placed on probation for five. The counterfeiters were criminally prosecuted. In one case a number of meat dealers whose overcharges were shown in court to have exceeded $300,000 were fined a total of less than $40,000. Later members of industry reported that, while the original indictment had induced compliance by other concerns, the lightness of the penalty had the opposite effect. A wholesale meat dealer, when interviewed by a congressional committee, agreed that the penalties imposed on apprehended meat violators were too weak.

MR. SHATTUCK: Well, they are not too afraid of them . . . . I only hear what they are saying in the market, that after anyone has been fined, they consider it more or less as a light fine. . . . Well, they are not too scared about the fine. It is the imprisonment they worry about.

MR. CHAIRMAN: Have there been many?

MR. SHATTUCK: Very few, and very limited.

MR. CHAIRMAN: Do you think some change in the law or in

policy of enforcement that would land more of these people in prison would tend to discourage them from dabbling around in that type of business?

Mr. SHATTUCK: I think you would get much better results. . . . The stiffer the penalty, the less response you would get toward it.[59]

Conclusions

The program of meat price control and rationing was admittedly complex. Unfortunately it was approached in a piecemeal fashion. A more comprehensive and realistic program, which may be needed in the future, should be put into effect early rather than after patterns of violation have been allowed to develop.[60] Specifically, there should be more adequate regulatory coverage of the processes involved in producing and distributing meat, such as the nonfederally inspected and the farm slaughterer. Meat rationing should be used with greater recognition of its usefulness in connection with price control. There should be greater coordination among the government agencies involved and, possibly even better, a central administration for the entire program. There should be stronger and more efficient management of the meat control program with a more adequate budget and adequate manpower for administration and enforcement. On the other hand, so extensive and flagrant was the black market in meat that we should not necessarily assume that these violations would have been materially reduced even with a more adequate control program. Without adequate enforcement and the full support of industry as well as the public no meat control program could hope to succeed.

---

[59] *Hearings before the Special Committee to Investigate Food Shortages,* for the House of Representatives, cited above, p. 626.

[60] See Bosch, *op. cit.,* for details which he suggests for such a program.

CHAPTER SIX

The Gasoline Black Market

Throughout the war the OPA was identified with the entire gasoline rationing program and was blamed almost exclusively for inadequacies in the civilian allotment, maladministration of the program, and the black market. Actually from the beginning, responsibility for the gasoline rationing program was divided among a number of agencies. Although the OPA carried out the program through its local rationing boards all over the country, other agencies were responsible for deciding on actual gasoline supplies available and for giving the ration directives. The shortage problem was the direct concern of the Petroleum Administrator for War, who defined the shortage area, determined civilian gasoline allotments, and issued directives to the OPA to administer the rationing program. For a while in part of the country gasoline rationing was operated by the Office of Price Administration under a directive issued by the Rubber Director, who had over-all policy responsibility. The commercial vehicle rationing situation was the responsibility of the Office of Defense Transportation which determined the allotment of gasoline for commercial vehicles and authorized the OPA to issue rations. As the program got under way, various conflicting and uncoordinated statements of policy issued by the different authorities in charge of the gasoline rationing program often resulted in the failure of the public in general to give the program complete support.

Added to this lack of unified public support were the tremendous complexities encountered in carrying out the rationing measures. These innumerable problems were more than doubled, however, when violators in large numbers throughout the country began to undermine the program. At a time when gasoline meant life or death to many of our soldiers, and there were actual shortages, some people almost everywhere were conniving to obtain "extra" gasoline for non-essential purposes, resulting in one of the most sordid aspects of the entire black market. Gasoline enforcement increasingly consumed investigative manpower until, in July, 1943, it accounted for 37 per cent of all investigative manpower in the eastern shortage area and 25 per cent in the rest of the country. This steady rise in manpower diverted to gasoline enforcement and away from the other commodity fields to which it was allocated was indicative of the extent of gasoline rationing violations. In December, 1944, the director of gasoline enforcement described the gasoline black market situation as being desperate:

A clean, efficient, equitable gasoline rationing program is absolutely vital to prevent a breakdown of the transportation system on which America's war production and civilian living alike depend. Yet this rationing program has been attacked by the most sinister black market that has appeared in the wartime distribution of any commodity, one which threatened, for a time, to make a mockery of the rationing rules. This black market was characterized by the emergence of organizations of professional criminals, who found enormous profit possibilities in supplying the demand for illegal gasoline . . . .

The ugliness of the racket, however, and the fact that it contributes to the enrichment of an unsavory crew of outlaws, is not its greatest danger. Its real threat is that it has set up a rival rationing system, distributing claims against the same restricted supply of gasoline on which the nation is relying to fill essential needs.[1]

Nature of the Gasoline Black Market

This gasoline black market, as well as certain currency violations of the sugar and meat ration orders, was unique as compared with the other black markets in that the illegal activities involved gasoline dealers working closely with ordinary and big-time criminals, including counterfeiters. Professional criminals received full cooperation from many gasoline dealers and suppliers, who, in turn, served the consumers, many of whom could be termed "accomplices" in this racketeering. Even public officials were involved. This alliance between the so-called respectable elements in our society and the underworld, with profit for both, made the gasoline black market one of the most difficult to control.

The usual procedure was for dealers to sell gasoline without coupons at prices often above legal ceilings. Before obtaining more gasoline, then, they had to turn in coupons of an equivalent value. These additional coupons were available from three sources, unissued coupons in the local ration boards, coupons surrendered previously, or stolen or counterfeit coupons. Professional criminals, and some amateurs, would either burglarize local boards, bribe officials of local boards or those responsible for disposing of surrendered coupons, or counterfeit the coupons. Gasoline dealers would then purchase from these criminals sufficient coupons to make up shortages or to secure supplies beyond normal requirements. Operations in illegal coupons could not have existed without large-scale purchasers. One government report stated that all attempts to trace

---

[1] Shad Polier, Director of Fuel and Consumer Goods Enforcement, "The Gasoline Black Market," Memorandum, *circa* December, 1944.

the sources of black market coupons had demonstrated that, contrary to a widely held impression, a very small proportion of black market coupons ever circulated in the hands of the motoring public. Similarly, the filling station operator could not have engaged in black market dealings without the aid of thieves and counterfeiters of ration currency. It was a situation of symbiosis, of mutual benefit to both. A routine account stated:

These Black Markets are being operated for personal profit, sometimes by professional criminals, but more often—much more often—by unscrupulous, unthinking businessmen. They are being supported by thousands of good, loyal, everyday American citizens who patronize them. . . .

Many of the regulations of OPA overlap with the regular criminal statutes. When a Black Marketeer steals ration coupons, for example, he is stealing government property. When a consumer buys stolen coupons he is trafficking in stolen government property. Those are offenses no sane citizen wants to risk.

Yet the fact remains that some of the sanest, most reputable men and women in America are allowing themselves to be drawn into Black Market operations by the lure of big money.[2]

Black market violations in gasoline were not limited to rationing, for there were also price violations, particularly upgrading. This was primarily a distributor violation and even large concerns were eventually prosecuted. One of the upgrading violations consisted simply of the sale of regular grade gasoline as premium grade such as ethyl. The public often assumed that premium gasoline would furnish more miles a gallon and would thus extend ration coupons. In many areas the OPA reported that three out of every four motorists were demanding the premium grade, and gasoline stations apparently

---

[2] Emerson, "Ration Robbers," *op. cit.*, pp. 26–27.

took advantage of this stimulated demand and passed off the
regular gasoline as premium at the higher price. This was
often done by collusion with the driver of the tank wagon who
poured the regular gasoline into the premium tank when a
delivery was made. In Great Britain, where gasoline rationing
was administered by the Ministry of Supply, all gasoline for
civilian use was pooled and consumers could buy only one
quality. In Great Britain the total gasoline ration was based
upon the horsepower of the car, whereas in this country no
allowance was made for such differences.[3]

Supply Shortage Necessitated Rationing Program

There can be no question that from the beginning of the
war the need for gasoline rationing was urgent. The withdrawal
of gasoline and oil stocks for Europe from the eastern states
had made the civilian gasoline supply precariously low. The
use of scarce transport to carry needed fuel oil to the East Coast
also reduced supplies of gasoline, and the torpedoing early in
the war of hundreds of tankers off the eastern coast by German
submarines added enormously to supply difficulties. The "Big
Inch" pipe line which later conveyed oil from Texas to
New York had just been begun. These factors resulted in
abnormally low stocks of civilian and industrial gasoline and
fuel oil, and the only possible way to remedy the situation
was to reduce civilian gasoline consumption. As the situation
became more serious, the OPA, in the spring of 1942, was
instructed to prepare a gasoline rationing program for the
states along the eastern seaboard. This rationing program[4] was

---

[3] Richardson, *loc. cit.*

[4] Under the coupon ration plan a minimum basic ration, the A-book, was
allowed to all passenger car registrants and the limited supply was defended
as a conservation measure of rubber and cars. The A-book represented an administratively practical allotment which would keep such automobiles in

THE GASOLINE BLACK MARKET

extended to the rest of the country in December, 1942, although this action was primarily intended to conserve rubber, as gasoline supplies, except for the East Coast, were fairly ample. As an additional conservation measure, the pleasure driving ban was initiated in January, 1943 on the East Coast. On weekdays and Sundays during this period large numbers of OPA enforcement personnel, aided by state police and local officers, stopped lines of traffic at bridges and other points to inquire the purpose, residence, and destination. In cases of proved pleasure driving, revocation orders of gasoline rations were sent to local boards. There was plenty of business, and where enforcement was lax because of limited manpower, newspapers berated the OPA enforcement officials generally. Up until September, when the new Price Administrator, Chester Bowles, replaced the pleasure driving ban with voluntary cooperation, it had not been enforced for brief periods of time. Although these relaxations had resulted in an average deficit of, for example, 54,000 barrels in June, enforcement personnel could be diverted to more useful work than the impossible task of chasing down tens of thousands of motorists.

In the fall of 1943 the Petroleum Administrator for War assigned a nation-wide quota of only 1,200,000 barrels a day

---

operation; in addition, the A-ration prevented the taxing of public transportation facilities to the point of breakdown. Contrary to widespread belief, there were actually no provisions ever made for pleasure driving in the A-allotment; it was for home necessity and occupational driving. Supplemental rations of gasoline above the basic A-ration of three or four gallons a week were issued on the basis of usage. The B, C, and S-rations were "tailored" to the mileage requirements shown on the application form submitted to and approved by the local boards. A fundamental part of the gasoline conservation program was the "full car" requirement for those who were eligible for supplemental rations. In order to be eligible for the additional gasoline, three people in addition to the driver had to sign the application as members of a bona fide car-sharing plan, unless it could be shown that no adequate alternative transportation was available. The display of a windshield sticker on these cars, showing the ration under which the car was operating, made it easy to identify and check such cars.

for civilian use, and this quota remained about the same for the next two years. In other words, the nation had available just about one third less gasoline than it would use if everyone were doing the same amount of driving as in 1941. With the rationing program, individual passenger car mileage was cut from an estimated prewar annual average of 11,000 miles to about 4,300 miles. It was estimated that in the three months from February through April, 1943, 882,000,000 gallons of gasoline were saved as well as 1,764,000 tires.[5] One wonders, however, if these reductions in our civilian consumption of fuel oil and gasoline were sufficient when the magnitude of our war needs is realized. For example, the terrific cost in manpower and supplies required to invade the Japanese stronghold of Iwo Jima gives some idea of the effect of total war on national resources and the necessity for the rationing program. That operation alone took enough fuel oil to fill a train of tank cars, 10,000 gallons each, 238 miles long; enough gasoline to operate 30,730 automobiles for a full year; enough lubricating oil for one complete oil change in 466,000 automobiles; enough food to feed a city the size of Columbus, Ohio, for 30 days; enough ammunition to fill 483 cars.[6] Yet newspaper accounts reporting some of the worst gasoline rationing violations appeared side by side with reports of fighting at Iwo Jima, Tarawa, Okinawa, Anzio Beach, and Normandy.

Some Difficulties in Gasoline Rationing

The government faced a number of serious difficulties in attempting to ration civilian gasoline adequately and fairly. Thefts of ration currency from local boards, counterfeiting

---

[5] Office of Price Administration, *Fifth Quarterly Report,* for the period ending April 30, 1943, p. 38.

[6] *Washington Letter,* Office of Price Administration, March 26, 1945.

of coupons, overissuance of coupons by local gasoline rationing boards, and a shortage of enforcement personnel complicated an almost impossible task.

THEFT OF RATION CURRENCY. In June, 1943, alone between 31 and 37 million gallons worth of ration coupons were stolen from local boards and sold to filling station dealers to cover sales without coupons. Although frequent instructions for safeguarding supplies were issued and some limited facilities were furnished, these thefts continued at an alarming rate. Actual robberies of ration boards were commonplace: "There have been over 650 robberies of local boards involving 300,000,000 gallons of gasoline in coupons. We have cut that to some extent, as I say, and I think we are beginning to see a little daylight on it, but it is by no means licked yet."[7] The following typical case of a local board robbery from an OPA field report indicates the professional nature of this type of crime. The market for these coupons was filling station operators.

We have just received a report of a board theft on Saturday, May 20 at the Local Board in Tampa, Florida of approximately 1 million gallons of gasoline coupons. On Monday, May 22, our Special Agents, through information obtained from a confidential source, arrested two men who had in their possession over 200,000 gallons of gasoline coupons stolen from the Tampa Board in the Saturday night robbery. One of these men had previously robbed three Local Boards, and at the time of this arrest was out on $6,500 bail for previous robberies. The second man arrested was likewise out on $3,000 bail for a previous Local Board robbery. The latter person was a well-known professional safecracker from Chicago. These two men, were, as we have indicated, arrested and are now under $15,000 bail. This same Tampa Local Board was

---

[7] Testimony of Chester Bowles at *Hearings before the House Subcommittee of the Committee on Appropriations,* Second Deficiency Appropriation Bill for 1944, Seventy-eighth Congress, Second Session, 1944, p. 386.

robbed of over 1 million gallons of gasoline coupons on December 30, 1943.[8]

COUNTERFEITING. Counterfeiting of ration currency was a serious problem in the gasoline rationing program. In sentencing a gang of seven counterfeiters on the West Coast whose chief was fined $20,000 and sent to jail for six years, Federal Judge A. F. St. Sure of San Francisco said: "The acts of these men were akin to treason." Counterfeiters switched from money to this new field, and professional hoodlums from other rackets. Their customers were filling station operators and, in the end, the public. Only a small proportion of coupons was sold directly to motorists, as they were too "hot" for the small amount of monetary return on a few coupons. Selling prices of illicit coupons ranged from eight to fifteen cents a gallon, and a sheaf of five-gallon coupons that could be carried in an overcoat pocket had a selling price of several thousand dollars. The gravity of the tie-up between professional hoodlums and filling station operators at this time is shown by a contemporary item in a news magazine.

As a good, sound and generally bloodless racket, the business of dealing in counterfeit or stolen gasoline ration coupons has bootlegging beat a hundred ways. The risks are fewer, the work is clean and not unpleasant, and the operating costs are not nearly so prohibitive. Moreover, the profits are unbelievably high: $1,000,000,000 a month, by Price Administrator Bowles' estimate.

All this has long been familiar to the underworld. Alarmed at the racket's mushroom growth and possibilities, the OPA last week undertook to give the motoring public an idea of what the counterfeit coupons were costing it. The picture was decidedly gloomy.

It showed most clearly on the map of shame prepared by Shad Polier, the OPA's chief enforcement officer for gasoline. Dark

---

[8] From an unpublished OPA Enforcement Department field report.

color ran down the whole of the Eastern Seaboard. The Pacific Coast states, the eastern shore of the Mississippi, and the Gulf Coast were similarly shaded. All that area, OPA agents believe, is under control of a nation-wide ring of racketeers . . . .

With the situation growing increasingly serious, Polier warned the public that unless it cooperates the whole rationing system will break down, resulting in chaos and a general scrambling for gasoline wherever it can be found.[9]

OVERISSUANCE OF GASOLINE RATIONS. Another difficulty was the overissuance of gasoline rations. One source of this overissuance occurred as part of the ration banking system when used ration currency was deposited by dealers. Persons having excess allotments could deposit them with their dealers who, in turn, deposited them in the bank before the expiration of the ration period and thereby obtained a credit of indefinite validity. Similarly, a dealer would pick up expired coupons from his customers after the coupon validity for sales had expired, but while such coupons were still valid for deposit by the dealer. To cut down these practices as much as possible a large portion of the investigative staff regularly made extensive investigations of coupons in dealers' hands at the end of each validity period. Another source of overissuance stemmed from the requirement that civilian gasoline ration B- and C-books be "tailored" to the needs of the applicant by the removal of certain coupons. Experience showed that some coupons thus taken out of ration books by local board personnel were not destroyed and were later used.

Extent of Gasoline Black Market

While our armed forces were burning an estimated 25,000,000 gallons of gasoline a day, the black market in 1944

---

[9] *Newsweek,* March 27, 1944, p. 46.

siphoned approximately 2,500,000 gallons a day, which if used legitimately could have increased the value of all regular civilian coupons by 25 per cent. From January 1, to June 1 of 1944, 1,362 counterfeiters, peddlers, and gasoline dealers handling stolen and counterfeit coupons were arrested, and 1,538 service station operators who had passed quantities of illegal coupons were suspended from selling gasoline for periods ranging from a few weeks to the duration of the war.[10] In the week ending August 3, 1944, the Detroit OPA office debited 1,500 gasoline stations for counterfeit B-2 coupons alone. The Boston OPA office reported that during February, 1944, six or seven gasoline investigators developed a criminal case a day. These cases from Detroit and Boston were typical of almost all district offices throughout the United States during 1944. Gasoline dealers themselves testified to the widespread nature of the black market. About half the filling station operators in ten urban communities estimated in 1944 that "a lot" of gasoline was bought in their cities without coupons.[11]

At the beginning of the war there were some 250,000 concerns selling gasoline, and up to January 1, 1945, a total of 15,095 of them had suspension orders, injunctions, or criminal prosecutions begun against them by the government, or approximately one in sixteen. These actions included 11,294 proceedings to suspend concerns from doing business for various periods of time and 234 injunction suits. In all, about 3,500 criminal cases were filed under the gasoline regulations, but

---

[10] Chester Bowles, "The Deadly Menace of Black Gasoline," New York *Times Magazine,* July 30, 1944, p. 20.

[11] In the eastern states 58% gave this answer and 35% in the Midwest. "Opinions of Filling Station Proprietors about Gasoline Rationing," an opinion survey of 179 operators of gasoline filling stations in ten eastern and midwestern cities conducted by the NORC for the Office of Price Administration, in November, p. 4 (Mimeographed). Filling station operators were interviewed in Boston, Hartford, New York, Newark, Philadelphia, Charleston, Jacksonville, Memphis, St. Louis, and Tulsa.

how many were against dealers rather than ordinary criminals cannot be determined. These figures greatly underestimate the extent of violations, since the size of the enforcement staff made it necessary to hold down the amount of investigative manpower allocated to gasoline. Moreover, these figures include only cases where serious penalties were imposed and not the cases dismissed even though violations were disclosed. On most surveys violations ran over 60 per cent. If one included the tens of thousands of cases where the gasoline stations were simply debited for counterfeit or stolen coupons which they turned into the OPA willfully or inadvertently, without having serious penalties imposed, the figures would probably vary between one in two to one in five concerns in violation. For example, during 1944 alone there was a total of 124,600 new gasoline cases revealing violation, only a few of which were consumer cases. Of these, 21,232 came from surveys, 25,049 came from complaints, and 78,219 were referrals on ration currency debiting cases. Approximately two out of three of the cases investigated revealed violation—60.9 per cent from the survey and 65.8 per cent from the complaint. These cases of violation resulted in the institution of sanctions in some 8,700 cases, with most of the remainder receiving informal adjustments including debiting, and only 16,100 being dismissed.

There is no question that the majority of the 15,095 gasoline cases in which heavy sanctions were imposed up through January 1, 1945, could have been criminal cases. The difficulty of this procedure, the time element, as well as other considerations, resulted in about one fourth being criminal cases. It is important to note that in these presumably highly selected cases the sentences imposed on those convicted were extremely light. In fact, when one compares the serious effects of these violations on the nation with sentences levied against ordinary property crimes involving individual losses, one sees the illogical nature of the situation. For example, of some 3,400 gasoline criminal cases completed, only approximately one in three received either imprisonment or imprisonment and a fine. Another third got off with a fine, usually only a few hundred dollars, and still another third was placed on probation.

In looking over the distribution of these extensive violations of the gasoline rationing regulations, one notices how general they were. The black market extended from coast to coast.[12] All types of gasoline dealers were involved in the violations—large and small, wholesale and retail, new and old business concerns. While it was true that some filling station operators had not been prewar members of the industry and entered the business primarily for sake of the illegal profits, the evidence indicates that they were a minority and that the majority of the violators were established dealers. Filling station operators interviewed in 1944 about the source of black market gasoline made statements like these: "Some major company has an overflow they don't know what to do with." "I guess it comes from distributors." "Some comes out of refiners and jobbers." This widespread pattern of violation made it impossible for the OPA to concentrate on certain types of dealers. First, the OPA concentrated on trying to bring auto drivers into compliance, particularly by the so-called "pleasure driving ban." When this procedure looked as if it would take the time of the entire investigative staff and many more it was

---

[12] For example, in March of 1944 gangsters from Detroit's "Purple Mob" were captured in Boston while trying to deliver counterfeit gasoline coupons. Hauled off a train in Worcester, Massachusetts, two members of this gang appeared to be innocent, but when they were persuaded to lunch with OPA agents they gave themselves away by refusing to check their topcoats, one even sitting on his. In false interlinings of these topcoats the agents found 26,000 phony A-coupons, which were to have been delivered at a prize fight with the exchange of identical topcoats.—*Chronology of the Office of Price Administration,* cited above.

abandoned. Attention was then shifted to supervising individual retailers, and here, too, violations became so great that this effort was reduced. Eventually, in desperation, the OPA directed its main enforcement efforts at the large distributors.

The OPA found that in many instances distributors and dealers, along with some members of the general public, were uncooperative in attempts to apprehend lawbreakers. As far as the small independent dealer went, part of the explanation might be the question of maintaining supplies. On the other hand, one might reason that because of the individualistic nature of his business, a dealer might have had less reluctance to report a competitor. Certainly many dealers were not organized in anything like the degree of trade associations that prevails in other commodities. Perhaps the most appropriate explanation was that since so many were in violation, it would have been dangerous, for personal reasons, to report a competitor. Public indifference was also involved. In 1943 the OPA Administrator testified before a special Senate committee investigating the gasoline black market:

I might say, also, that there is a great reluctance on the part of the public to give us information as to any violations of rationing. I say this without criticism. I say it to record it as a basis of understanding. Any great amount of bootlegging, or violation of rationing orders, has left us with the necessity of trying to discover that through our own means, and very little has come from the dealers in those products, who have been under great pressure, or from the licensed distributors, or from the industry as to some indication as to where there might have been deviations.[13]

In some chains of gasoline service stations the company

---

[13] Statement of Leon Henderson, Price Administrator, at the *Hearings before the Special Committee to Investigate Gasoline and Fuel Oil Shortages,* Seventy-eighth Congress, First Session, pursuant to Senate Resolution 156, P. 3, 1943, p. 703.

policy made it virtually impossible for the small dealer who rented such a station to conduct an honest business. There were a few cases where black market coupons were sold to gasoline distributors, who then supplied their dealer-customers without collecting coupons. In such instances the role of differential association with criminal norms was strikingly clear. For example, the district sales manager and the salesman of a large oil company in the East were indicted for conspiring with certain of their gasoline dealers in order to build up their volume of sales, inducing them to sell gasoline without coupons and to replace the shortages by purchases of stolen or inventory coupons. The gasoline stations were owned by the company but were leased to gasoline dealers who operated them on a rental basis of a cent a gallon so that a larger volume of sales resulted in higher returns to the company. The employees of the company reportedly urged the dealers to get into the black market and informed them where they could secure supplies of coupons and, furthermore, said that the company, as the supplier, was accepting hundred-gallon inventory coupons purchased by the station operators.

If the government's troubles had been confined only to dishonest dealers, difficult as the situation might have been, enforcement manpower could have been concentrated in one direction. Unfortunately forces had to be deployed in all directions. Ration board officials and clerks sometimes engaged in the illicit sale, usually to professional criminals, of coupons entrusted to them as agents of the federal government. The chief clerk of a Cleveland local board, for example, sold coupons in collusion with a local employee of the Office of Defense Transportation, and in the resulting investigation twelve participants were prosecuted. Employees of the OPA and ODT who were primarily responsible were sentenced to fifteen and twenty months in prison, respectively, and another ODT employee received a fifteen-month suspended sentence. The five peddlers were fined, and three of them also received a jail sentence. It is interesting to note that the four service station operators who bought the coupons were simply fined.

Such operations were not confined to OPA voluntary or paid personnel, but at times reached serious proportions in some banks where coupons were to be destroyed after being recorded. Partly because some coupons were sold by bank clerks to professional hoodlums the government finally assumed responsibility for burning them in disposal centers, although this did not work to perfection. In a few instances even police officers were enlisted by black market gasoline traffickers to dispose of their wares.

Attitudes of Dealers

In view of the fact that the black market permeated a large proportion of the industry, it is interesting to examine the opinions of gasoline dealers regarding this situation. In November, 1944, 179 operators of gasoline filling stations located in ten urban communities were asked a series of questions about their views on gasoline rationing.[14] Despite the wartime situation, only 45 per cent of those interviewed thought that gasoline rationing was necessary, and only 49 per cent thought that other commodities should be rationed. Among those who felt that gasoline rationing was unnecessary the following reasons were given, most of them representing simply rationalizations for the violations which were occurring. (See Table 15.)

There was a relation between opinions about the neces-

[14] For details of this survey, see "Opinions of Filling Station Proprietors about Gasoline Rationing," cited above, pp. 2, 8, 3, 7, 9, and 10.

sity for continued gasoline rationing and estimates as to the amount of black market gasoline being sold. Those who thought gas rationing was unnecessary estimated the black market to be more extensive than those who thought it was necessary. (See Table 16.)

Table 15
Summary of Reasons Given by 179 Dealers for Thinking Gasoline Rationing Unnecessary*

Sufficient gasoline	45%
Black market shows that there must be plenty	31
Doesn't work and don't approve	7
Voluntary rationing is sufficient	5
Politics, graft, humbug	8
Miscellaneous:	8

More would be sold	2%
Contradictory reasons	2
Cut out Sunday driving	2
Too much trouble	2

* Percentages total more than 100 because more than one reason was given by some respondents.

Table 16
Estimates of the Extent of the Gasoline Black Market and Dealers' Opinions of the Necessity for Gasoline Rationing

	THINK GAS RATIONING NECESSARY, PER CENT	THINK GAS RATIONING UNNECESSARY, PER CENT
A lot of black market gas sold....	45	58
Only a little black market gas sold.	38	30
No black market gas sold........	3	5
Don't know or no answer........	14	7

Since few violations could occur without the consent of the dealer, the reasons which filling station operators advanced for some people not obeying the gasoline rationing regulations were significant. Lack of patriotism, as a cause, ranked only in third place. (See Table 17.)

Table 17

Reasons Given by Gasoline Dealers for Noncompliance with Gasoline Regulations*

REASON		PER CENT
Allowance is sufficient......................		27
Think rationing unnecessary.................		22
Not convinced it is necessary, so they chisel...	15	
Ignorance, misinformed, and don't know facts	7	
Selfish and unpatriotic......................		21
Selfish, jealous, greedy, unpatriotic..........	17	
Want pleasure driving—hunting and fishing..	3	
Too lazy to cooperate.....................	1	
Criticism of boards.........................		12
Boards too weak and unfair................	11	
Poor system..............................	1	
Ineffective enforcement.....................		13
Everybody is doing it......................	7	
Law too easily violated....................	5	
Make money in black market..............	1	
Dislike being regimented....................		7
Miscellaneous and "don't know".............		7
People have too much money..............	4	
Rationing makes people dishonest..........	1	
Don't know...............................	2	

*Percentages total more than 100 because some people gave more than one answer.

About 40 per cent thought that the government did a poor job of handling rationing; of the remainder only 27 per

cent thought it was done well. A summary of the reasons is
given in Table 18.

Table 18

Summary of Reasons Given by Dealers Who Believed the
Government Was Doing "Fairly Well" or "Poorly"
in Administering Gasoline Rationing*

REASONS	PER CENT	
Government inefficiency		46
Too much system—checking system all wet...	16	
Boards inefficient and unfair—volunteers ignorant	15	
OPA mismanaged—weak personnel—confusion	13	
Failed to educate the public	2	
Unfair distribution		41
Allotments too little—those who need it don't get it	28	
Allotments too much—some get too much...	13	
Black market		27
Black market fostered	15	
Politics, graft, and corruption in OPA	8	
Law cannot be enforced	2	
Misuse of stove gasoline	2	
Miscellaneous and "don't know"		8
Rationing is a new problem	1	
Ceiling price curtails production	1	
Should have abolished rationing	1	
Don't know and No answer	5	

* Percentages total more than 100 because some dealers gave more than
one answer.

Some of the typical verbatim comments of the filling station operators to specific questions about the black market
situation were factual replies, while others represented simply

confused rationalizations. The number blaming the situation on the government is interesting.

Why dealers thought gas rationing was unnecessary:
"There is plenty of gas and just as many cars on the road."
"There is plenty if you want to pay for it."
"If you do away with it, you will stop the black market."
"More gas would be sold if there was no black market."
"Graft, politicians, waste—I know plenty of it."
"If it wasn't available for the black market, it would be available for the general public."
"First they say it's gas, then it's tires. They say tires are rationed to save cars. Then they say 'Buy a Bond.' If it were really necessary, they'd come out and tell the truth."

Why some people did not obey the gasoline rationing regulations:
"They don't get enough. A lot of them have to have more to make a living. You can't blame them."
"Some feel that gas is plentiful and it is a deliberate attempt to keep them from having it by rationing it."
"Selfishness. They don't care about anyone but themselves."
"Unfair rationing boards that show partiality."
"They think they can get away with it."

What was wrong with the government's handling of gas rationing:
"It is too involved—too much extra work for those short of help."
"The government's intentions are good, but the trouble is with the ration boards."
"The local boards are rotten. Everything depends upon pull."
"Poor management—you can't run a government department with volunteers, they get tired of it and quit; so you have to get in a new bunch."
"If you know anyone at OPA, you don't have any trouble."

"They haven't educated the public well enough to get the wholehearted cooperation they should get from them."

"The right people don't get gas. If it were handled better they would."

"So much black market is being sold I can't sell it."

In another survey of gasoline dealers in March, 1945, 506 filling station proprietors in the Midwest and the East Coast were interviewed on the necessity for continued gasoline rationing.[15] Less than one half (46 per cent) of the filling station operators thought that gasoline rationing was necessary at that time. Beliefs about the supply situation were a factor in dealers' attitudes, 78 per cent of the dealers feeling that gasoline rationing was then unnecessary because the supply situation did not warrant rationing.

One case in particular revealed the callous attitude of some black market gasoline dealers. At an OPA hearing in the East a filling station operator said that he had never read the ration orders on gasoline, so did not know whether or not he was operating his station lawfully. After admitting that he had sold gasoline to many customers without taking coupons he stated that it was impossible to continue to build up or keep a going business and comply with the requirements of the OPA in the administration of the rationing program. The hearing commissioner found that this dealer had accepted hundreds of counterfeit coupons, and a decision was handed down suspending him from the gasoline business for the duration of gas rationing. At about this same time in Paris a similar event occurred:

Five American soldiers who stole "huge quantities" of gasoline from the army, sold it on the Paris black market for as much as

---

[15] *Opinion Briefs*, No. 6, Department of Information, Office of Price Administration, "Need for Continued Gasoline Rationing," March 31, 1945, pp. 1, 2 (Mimeographed).

$60 a gallon and lived in luxury on the profits, have been sentenced
to death, the army announced. Col. Clarence Bran, Staff Judge
Advocate of the Seine Section, said the death sentences—first meted
out in the army black market scandal—were handed down by a
general court martial on specific charges of desertion in time of
war and conspiracy to steal army gasoline.[16]

Controlling the Gasoline Black Market

One can readily see from the foregoing accounts of the
extent and the all-pervasive nature of the black market in gasoline, the insidious link between business and racketeers, and
the general attitudes of dealers and consumers, that the OPA
faced tremendous odds in its attempt to control the situation.
By the middle of 1945, however, the agency had developed a
more comprehensive plan for dealing with this black market.
Its two main attacks involved, first, drying up the market for
illegal coupons and, second, striking at the supply, the counterfeiters, thieves, and peddlers. To carry out such a program the
cooperation of the gasoline industry itself was essential, and
such an appeal was made to the industry, from refineries to
service station operators.

COOPERATION OF PETROLEUM INDUSTRY. The Petroleum Industry War Council, representing oil and gasoline producers in
the United States, helped organize an anti-black market committee and appropriated large sums for newspaper advertising
in aid of the campaign. The industry also loaned OPA 350 of
its own supervisors to reach filling station operators throughout
the country in an attempt to strengthen the campaign in those
crucial outlets. Gasoline distributors agreed to deliver to OPA
illegal coupons which came to them from service stations.

---

[16] Quoted in Weekly Letter No. 59, Fuel and Consumer Goods Enforcement Division, Office of Price Administration, January 26, 1945.

RATION CURRENCY DEBITING PROGRAM. The center of the drive
on the black market was the debiting program, developed to
dry up the market for stolen and counterfeit coupons. The
philosophy of the OPA debiting measures was that there were
tie-ups between dealers and hoodlums. Counterfeits and stolen
coupons were usually "too hot" to sell in the limited quantities
required by an individual. Large quantities had to be sold
at one time. It was based on the principle that a dealer could
buy gasoline to sell only in exchange for valid ration currency.
Thus, if he acquired gasoline from his supplier in exchange
for "phony" or stolen coupons, he remained under an obligation to make up these invalid coupons with valid ones. Until
he had done so, he could not acquire more gasoline from that
supplier or any other supplier who had notice of his default.
Therefore, the dealer who turned in a large quantity of counterfeits soon found himself without sufficient inventory of gasoline and coupons to continue doing business. Or in the language
of the trade, "he was 'debited' out of business."

The dealer had to determine whether the nation's supply
of gasoline was going to be distributed to consumers who held
legitimate coupons or whether it was to go to those who had no
coupons or fraudulent ones. If gasoline was sold to people not
entitled to it the shortage had to be covered by purchases of
counterfeit or stolen coupons. The principle on which the
debiting procedure rested, therefore, was that every dealer who
participated in the distribution of gasoline under rationing
became by virtue of that participation a trustee of a critical
commodity. It was his responsibility to see that the ends of
rationing were served, and that the gasoline he handled was
not dissipated in nonessential uses. The extent of the debiting
activities is indicated by the fact that in three out of ninety-six
OPA district offices during the period from June 1 to Septem-

ber 1, 1944, 31,950 dealers were debited for 6,474,688 gallons of gasoline and that 749 dealers were put out of business as a result of debits. Out of 400 service stations checked in Maine, 223 were found to have accepted counterfeits. These counterfeits were either unendorsed or bore fictitious numbers.

A dealer was not expected to be able to recognize all counterfeit coupons, since this was difficult to do without special equipment. He was, however, expected (1) not to sell gasoline without collecting coupons; (2) to accept no coupons that were out of date or coupons on which the license number was not endorsed on the back;[17] (3) to check the endorsement on each coupon accepted against the license number and state of registration of the car; and (4) to make certain that each coupon accepted was part of a valid ration by inspecting the folder that accompanied it and checking the serial numbers of the coupon against the range of serial numbers shown on the folder.[18] These precautions were all that were necessary to assure that very few coupons which a dealer received would be stolen or counterfeit.

Partly because of pressure from the petroleum industry, and partly because of recognition of the fact that even the most careful operator might by chance accept some bad ration coupons, the OPA allowed a limited type of "bail-out" for debits

---

[17] The filling station operator who bought counterfeits to cover shortages often solved the problem by faking endorsements. One operator was caught in the act of copying down license numbers of passing cars and then writing those numbers on his fake coupons. Another was apprehended when he used registration numbers higher than those issued in his state. This endorsement of coupons, though not a sure check, was an invaluable aid to dealers in checking their validity.

[18] In addition, serially numbered strip coupons were extended to almost all rations in 1944, a fact of major assistance in eradicating the black market, since the serial number gave a permanent identity to every individual coupon from the time it was printed until it was destroyed. If coupons were stolen at any point in the distribution chain, their serial numbers might be flashed to enforcement officers throughout the country.

resulting from invalid coupons to the extent of 1 per cent of each month's volume of sales, to be retroactive to the beginning of the debiting program. A "bail-out" of up to 3 per cent of a month's business was granted once to any dealer, if in the months following it the dealer took warning and mended his ways. Thus each dealer was allowed one big mistake.

There was wide use of an administrative order suspending the dealer from engaging in the sale of gasoline. Thousands of these orders were issued during the war prohibiting the sale for a period of from one day to the duration of the war. During 1944 alone there were over 5,500 such orders involving gasoline dealers. Such cases were tried before an OPA hearing commissioner who served as a neutral judge between the government and the alleged violator. Many dealers who could not continue operations because of a suspension order or a large debit attempted to transfer their stations to a "front man." In a single month in one OPA office nineteen out of thirty-nine requests for new registrations were denied on this ground.

ATTACK ON COUNTERFEITING AND STEALING OF RATION CURRENCY. As indicated elsewhere, the counterfeiting of ration currency was greatest in gasoline, and the government's efforts in combating this aspect of the black market became quite effective. In this work the OPA received valuable assistance from other agencies, particularly the United States Secret Service of the Treasury Department,[19] which loaned personnel to the

---

[19] One might question the government's not turning over entirely such a large and complex problem as ration currency protection to an agency with experience in this type of work, such as the United States Secret Service or the Federal Bureau of Investigation. Even had one of these agencies wished to assume this responsibility, there were a number of reasons against it. In the first place, rationing problems are of a specialized, large-scale nature, involving currency of a unique type, problems of issuance, and others. Second, many of the difficulties of safeguarding currency could only be solved by cooperation among the various departments in the agency concerned with rationing. Such

OPA for investigative work and training, the assistant director in charge of currency protection being loaned to OPA from Secret Service. This type of assistance was invaluable, for prior to January, 1944, work on counterfeiting and theft cases was done by ordinary investigators who had little specialized training, although the work was extremely technical, the offenders were usually professionals, and the counterfeit or stolen currency was often distributed over several states. On a number of occasions, particularly prior to July, 1944, when OPA's special agents were authorized to carry guns, members of the counterfeit specialist squad were physically endangered.

Eventually a Currency Protection Branch was established for the purpose of centralizing all aspects of ration currency protection, and its staff, which grew to one hundred agents, was a professionally trained one, skilled in undercover work. The unique feature about the Currency Protection Branch, however, was the fact that it was the only organization in the OPA Enforcement Department, and practically the only one in the agency whose personnel, even though located in the regional offices, was under the direct supervision of the national office. It was found that effective control of counterfeit activity required more centralized operation and direction from the national office, paralleling the organization of the Secret Service and the FBI.

Various devices were used for detecting counterfeit cou-

cooperation involved understanding of the programs and problems common to the agency and available personnel of other departments. Most important was the need for an over-all authority which could reconcile differences between various departments concerned with the problem. It is unlikely that an agency outside the OPA could have been successful in meeting these requirements. Third, it would have been difficult for an outside agency to take on additional responsibility, particularly of such size. Wartime conditions made it hard to recruit personnel which was, of course, a problem for OPA as well. While OPA later organized special agents for this work, it was always possible to utilize other commodity investigators when necessary.

pons, including special lamps and chemical tests. Several techniques were used for detecting genuine gasoline stamps which
had been stolen from filling stations, distributors, or banks
after they had been pasted onto forms known as "bingo sheets."
Some of the black market gangs then steamed the ration stamps
off sheets which their own men had stolen or bought from free-
lance thieves. These stamps became known as "steam-offs."
Later the shrewder element of the underworld spurned the
steam baths and invented "pop-offs," applying extreme cold to
the sheets to make the stamps come off. Investigators of the
OPA in New York City, however, discovered that the quick
freezing made almost infinitesimal changes in the physical di-
mensions of the ration stamps, and by the use of special delicate weighing and measuring equipment were able to track
down the stolen stamps and seize the equipment. In this particular case the professional criminals were sent to prison. As
counterfeiting techniques improved and as coupons were frequently printed on stolen government safety paper, new devices
had to be developed. Serial numbers for coupon books were
introduced, the issuance of ration books was transferred from
local ration boards to issuing centers, and security sites for
coupons were established throughout the country. Inspections
of local boards had revealed many factors conducive to theft,
such as an amazing oversupply of ration currency in many
local boards, frequently amounting to 5 to 10 years' supply,
often to as much as 40, 80, or 90 years, and in two cases to
about 137 years' supply. Furthermore, ration currency was
inadequately protected, with boxes lying around in easy access
and frequently unwatched, and often improperly transported.
At one local board a 100-year supply of hundred-gallon inventory coupons, which, at a not unusual black market price of

10 cents a gallon, meant coupons worth about $956,420, was being kept in an unlocked garage in a wooden cabinet protected only by a lock which could be opened with a woman's hairpin.

Not only were the local boards, security sites, and mailing centers inspected by special agents, but safeguarding inspections were also made of the paper mills and the printing plants where ration currency was made, as there had been some serious losses from these sources. Later, the United States Government Printing Office contracted with one printing company to produce all OPA ration currency on a continuous schedule basis and arranged also to have the processed paper produced in only one plant. Since the sheer volume of paper involved in rationing was too great to permit the original currency to be handled through all levels of the trade, it was necessary to transform the paper into a form of credit. The government had created the ration banking system for this purpose. The retailer deposited ration evidences, such as tokens, coupons, or certificates in a bank where credits were set up in his favor, against which he drew by check in a manner comparable to regular commercial banking. These banks opened the envelopes on a percentage basis to verify the coupons, and violators often gambled that their envelopes would remain unopened. The banks were also responsible for seeing that the deposited ration currency did not seep back into trade channels. This precaution was not always observed, and there were several cases of this currency being sold by bank employees or other persons responsible for its destruction.

The ration banking supervisory staff of the OPA, which was separate from enforcement, never exceeded a total of 300 persons in Washington and in the 101 field offices, including stenographic and clerical help. This staff was expected to supervise a program involving 14,000 banks and 1,500,000 ration currency depositors.[20] Because of this manpower shortage, OPA could not properly supervise the banks, although it received some help from examiners of the Federal Deposit Insurance Corporation and the Federal Reserve System and from the state and national bank examiners and local bank associations. Even with this help, however, the required annual inspection could not be made, often with serious results. In one case, a district office official made his first call on a bank early in 1945, two years after the program was begun. He found all the deposits lying in boxes in a small room, no checks having been cleared, and no ledger sheets made. The OPA could require the withdrawal of any bank for any reason on thirty days' notice, but this was rarely enforced, and it was unfortunate that some bankers were aware of this fact.

To correct such situations verification centers[21] were established to receive from ration banks all deposited ration evidences, to check the totals of these evidences against the bank reports of transactions, to verify the contents of individual

---

[20] As an interesting sidelight, by the fall of 1943, when ration banking had reached maturity, the 14,000 participating banks were receiving reimbursement from OPA at a rate of $15,500,000 a year, which was one of the largest items in OPA's budget, in fact, equal to the total enforcement budget.

[21] The verification centers were not without their problems, however, for thieves after the lucrative market with filling station dealers struck even there. In spite of armed guards, the Chicago distribution center was successfully entered twice within a month. Although government agents did an excellent job in retrieving most of the loss, the amount stolen was still substantial. In San Francisco an armed daylight holdup of the distribution center which was scheduled for a morning in April, 1945, was only averted when agents arrested one of the gang leaders for several previous board robberies a few hours before the appointed time for the robbery. "Casing" of this center had indicated to the gang that a successful entry could be made when the guard opened the door to admit employees. Often the crimes were committed by ration clerks themselves. In one case a ration board clerk in Massachusetts, involved in the theft of coupons from the local board and disposing of them through confederates on the black market, received a six-months suspended sentence with two years' probation.

deposits, and to detect counterfeit or stolen documents. Weighers counted the contents of envelopes on delicate scales. The center's job involved verifying all coupons with infrared light to detect whether they were printed on genuine paper, examining serial numbers to ascertain if any were stolen, and checking consumer endorsements. Some clerks became so expert that they could finger through several hundred stamps and in a few seconds discover several counterfeits. After being checked the ration currency was destroyed, under supervision, either being put through a macerator or sent, under an armed guard, to a paper mill for reclaiming. All information regarding types of counterfeits and location of use was then forwarded to the national office. These daily reports by the verification centers helped the national office to discover those areas most in need of investigation. A newsletter, commenting on the work of one of the regional verification centers stated:

> They have examined stamps representing countless millions of gallons of gasoline and made debits amounting to 3,212,174 gallons. The debits entered have reduced the inventories of 25,000 filling stations and have put a known 557 operators, who persisted in trafficking in counterfeits, entirely out of business.[22]

With the establishment of verification centers there was a marked increase in the number of counterfeits found and coded. Prior to August, 1944, a total of 121 different types of counterfeits had been coded. During August alone the number of counterfeits coded was 47, and in September the number jumped to 51. In the last two months of 1944 3.3 million counterfeit coupons were turned in to the OPA's eight centers.

The next step in the operation of a verification center was the debiting or charging back of counterfeit, unendorsed, or

---

[22] From an unpublished OPA Enforcement Department field report.

invalid coupons to the account of the distributor. This debiting procedure involved notifying a number of persons, including the dealer who was informed that he had deposited a number of counterfeit, unendorsed, or expired stamps, and that he must furnish his distributor with an equivalent amount of valid coupons. At the same time the distributor was notified that his account was to be debited an amount equivalent to the invalid currency submitted by the dealer, to whom he had supplied the rationed commodity. Finally, the bank was notified to debit the account of the distributor, and the dealer's local OPA board was notified of the invalid stamps. Typical of the manner in which the government handled this problem was a suspension order issued against one licensed distributor in the Midwest who failed to account for 1,331,351 gallons of gasoline. In California a suspension order was issued against one of the ten largest refineries in that area which had been delivering gasoline to some ninety-one stations without obtaining the required exchange of coupons.

While in the last three months of 1944 there were 155 thefts, in the first quarter of 1945 this number was reduced to 94. Total gasoline gallonage lost through these activities was also considerably reduced. Thefts in the first quarter of 1944 amounted to approximately 20,700,000 gallons as compared with 3,250,000 for the last three months of 1944 and only 1,350,000 for the first quarter of 1945. Whereas the average gasoline loss a theft during 1943 was 690,000 gallons, in the first quarter of 1945 the amount was only about 15,000 gallons. Handicapped by the extent and diversity of the violations and by the limited size of the enforcement personnel, the OPA, by using clever techniques and being realistic about the tie-up of gasoline dealers and ordinary criminal elements, was able to bring about a marked reduction in violations by the end of the war.

In the last quarter of 1944 the circulation of counterfeits averaged 1,533,943 a month. In July, 1945, the last month of complete figures, it had dropped 95 per cent. The decline in the use of counterfeits from October, 1944, to August, 1945,

Table 19

Number of Counterfeit Gasoline Coupons Discovered in
Verification Centers, October, 1944—July, 1945

MONTH	NUMBER OF COUNTERFEIT COUPONS
October, 1944	1,264,615
November, 1944	1,357,556
December, 1944	1,981,660
January, 1945	1,087,682
February, 1945	333,851
March, 1945	365,945
April, 1945	327,880
May, 1945	144,638
June, 1945	108,863
July, 1945	78,611

SOURCE: From an unpublished OPA Enforcement Department report.

is apparent in the monthly figures reported by the verification centers. (See Table 19.) Four months before the end of gasoline rationing the chief investigator reported on the program which had been developed to deal with counterfeit and stolen coupons:

It is a fact that counterfeits are now hard to dispose of because of widespread knowledge that they are detected without fail, and that penalties follow. Sales of counterfeits are difficult to consummate without first convincing the prospective customer that they are "genuine." It is also a fact that we have disrupted distribution channels and closed down sources of counterfeits.

This control of the gasoline black market did not come any too soon, for conservation of gasoline for the European offensive was vital. Field Marshal Karl Gerd von Runstedt, German army chief, told Allied correspondents after his capture that the first factor in Germany's defeat was lack of fuel, both oil and gasoline. The German general stated that the superiority of the Allied Air Force in conjunction with the German fuel shortage made defeat certain. The gasoline to power this air fleet was the result of the eventual successful diversion to military purposes of an enormous part of the American civilian supply. How much of the limited civilian supply was diverted into the black market was another question.

CHAPTER SEVEN

Landlords as Violators

Next to food, shelter is the most important single item in the American family budget, comprising at least one fifth and often much more of the total living costs of the average family. Furthermore, it is comparatively inflexible, and a marked increase in rent often means the curtailment of other basic needs. Rent violations were particularly serious in the case of the families of members of the armed forces who had set allotments, but they also caused grave hardships for those in the low-income brackets, particularly salaried employees who were often forced to reduce living standards. As a result illegal rent increases tended to disturb labor-management relations and discouraged workers from going to defense areas where there was generally a shortage of manpower. The presence of rent ceilings, however, and the effective control of violations was a most significant factor in maintaining morale, as the following statement by Price Administrator Bowles indicates:

The contribution it [rent control] has made to the stability of the cost of living and the protection it has afforded to war workers in crowded centers and to the families of servicemen near army camps cannot be overemphasized. In many areas rent control was introduced upon the urgent request of the armed forces and the managers and executives of war industries, harassed by labor turnover. They tell us it is not possible to place a value upon the contribution which rent control has thus made directly to war production.[1]

Development of Rent Control

VOLUNTARY PERIOD. Rent control began as a voluntary program. As early as the fall of 1940 rent surveys were made under the auspices of the Consumer Division of the National Defense Advisory Commission, and the public was warned of the critical rent situation. Appeals were made to the fairness and patriotism of landlords. Somewhat later the government was instrumental in establishing local fair rent committees who represented a cross section of the dominant interests in the community. Using the most recent date when the prevailing rents were generally fair and reasonable, these committees set dates for rent stabilization. Since the impact of the emergency was experienced at different times by different communities, these fair rent dates were not always the same. Rent increases were allowed for a number of reasons, including significant changes in structure or facilities since the fair rent date, and an increase in the cost of maintenance and services or in the cost of fuel or taxes.

The 210 voluntary committees in the thirty-four states where they were set up were also active in preventing evictions, in some communities securing the aid of the local courts to prevent them. The lack of statutory authority was keenly felt, however, and the success of these committees varied throughout the country. They did promote an understanding of the

---

[1] Statement of Chester Bowles, OPA Administrator, at *Hearings before the Senate Committee on Banking and Currency*, Extension of the Emergency Price Control Act of 1942, Senate Resolution 1,764, Seventy-eighth Congress, Second Session, 1944, p. 45.

basic principles essential to rent control administration and demonstrated the need for positive federal action. They also furnished an excellent laboratory for any future rent control programs. As the tempo of the war program increased the dangers of inflation, the federal government recommended legislation to control those situations with which local action and the fair rent committees were unable to deal.

STATUTORY PERIOD. The Emergency Price Control Act of 1942 necessitated major changes in the rent control program.[2] It provided that the Price Administrator could designate war-boom communities as defense rental areas and specify the levels at which rents should be stabilized. A sixty-day waiting period was allowed, during which time the recommended stabilization could be achieved by voluntary action of landlords or by state or local regulations. If the required action was not taken within that time the administrator might establish maximum rents for the area, the OPA designating a maximum rent date which was "generally fair and equitable" and which gave due consideration to rents prevailing on April 1, 1941, or April 1, 1940, if defense activities had inflated rents prior to April, 1941. The act further provided that within approximately sixty days after the designation of the maximum rent date all rental units

---

[2] "Rents have been controlled in Great Britain since 1915 under various Rent Restrictions Acts. Prior to September 1939, about 4.75 out of 12 million houses and apartments—mainly lower-rented working class types—were affected by these acts. Under the Rent and Mortgage Interest Restrictions Act of 1939, which fixed previously uncontrolled rents at the level prevailing September 2, 1939, control was extended to more than 95 per cent of the residential houses and apartments. The only residential rents not fixed are those exceeding about $2000 annually in London and $1500 in the rest of the country. The Ministry of Health administers the acts, which are to remain in effect for the duration plus six months. Rents may be raised to compensate the landlord up to 8 per cent of his annual expenditures on improvements (excluding decorations and repairs) or structural alterations and for increases in local government taxes."— Backman, *Rationing and Price Control in Great Britain,* p. 52.

in a defense rental area were to be registered with the OPA, and that the registered rent then should become the legal maximum rent for the duration of the war unless an increase was approved by the OPA.

The first defense areas in the rent control program were designated in March, 1942. The required sixty-day period elapsed without any local actions, and on June 1, 1942, maximum rent regulations were issued for those areas. Additional areas were designated from time to time, and after the lapse of the sixty-day period they were also brought under federal control. By June 1, 1945, there were 479 areas under rent control, these areas having a combined population of about 94,500,000, or almost three fourths of the population of the United States.[3] In all, 15,650,000 rental dwellings and 514,000 hotels and rooming houses were under rent control.

Two typical maximum rent regulations were issued by the OPA. One covered housing accommodations other than hotels and rooming houses; the other covered hotels, rooming houses, boarding houses, dormitories, auto camps, and trailers.[4] Each of these regulations had five important provisions: (1) maximum rents which landlords could charge; (2) grounds and procedures for adjusting maximum rents in certain cases; (3) minimum services which the landlord must provide; (4) restriction on unwarranted evictions of tenants; and (5) the registration of property by landlords, indicating the rent charged and the accommodations furnished. Since this was done in advance and prior to any violations it frequently made it possible subsequently to check such data with the tenants' statements and discover if a violation had occurred. The rent

---

[3] This figure is based on the 1940 census. Actually the proportion in these areas was higher in 1945 because of the wartime increases in population.

[4] The OPA had no statutory authority regulating commercial rents for offices, stores, and the, like.

control program could not have succeeded if any one of these five provisions had been omitted.

Generally the maximum rent regulation went back to some period before the national emergency caused rents to increase. A base date was selected, and rents were then frozen as of that date. A landlord was automatically required to reduce his rents to the level of the freeze date, but he could petition for, and often got, an adjustment if it could be shown that this level was unfair to him. In January, 1943, analyses of registration statements showed that in 9 per cent of the cases landlords were permitted to establish a maximum rent which was not in effect at the time the rents were regulated. From July, 1944, to April, 1945, for example, 349,549 petitions were received from landlords, and in 173,984, or about one half of the cases, adjustments in rent were granted. The most common reason for granting upward adjustments of rent to landlords was a substantial increase in services, furniture, or equipment. Sometimes the local rent director, upon his own initiative or upon application by a tenant, would order a decrease of the maximum rent if the landlord had allowed his property to run down or had decreased the number or quality of services, or for other special reasons. The landlord had to provide the same essential services, furnishings, furniture, and equipment as were provided on the freeze date, unless he had been granted permission by the rent director to decrease them. The tenant was also protected from unfair eviction. As long as he continued to pay the rent he could not be put off the property unless he himself had violated some important obligation of tenancy, such as permitting the housing accommodations to be used for illegal or immoral purposes, or unless the landlord wanted the property for sale or for his own immediate use.

Extent of Violations

From available evidence there were extensive violations of the rent regulations during the war. During the three years from June, 1942, to June, 1945, the OPA received a total of 2,612,062 tenant adjustments and complaints, many, of course, being unfounded or minor difficulties. Adjustments or settlements of some form, however, were made in 784,147 of the cases, and from 1 to 3 per cent were referred for more severe enforcement action.[5] During 1944, professional investigators of the OPA dealt with 20,150 serious rent violations, sanctions being instituted in 4,665 cases and a total of 282 landlords being criminally prosecuted. In the first six months of 1945 an average of less than 350 rent enforcement investigators turned up 11,485 violations; during this period 9,034 sanctions were instituted against landlords, 101 of them criminal cases. A door-to-door survey of the South Side Negro section of Chicago in 1944 revealed that of 739 units investigated, 310, or over 40 per cent, were not registered, overcharges being found in 125, or in some 17 per cent of the cases. Illegal eviction cases were a particularly serious problem throughout the years of the OPA. It was estimated in 1946 that one out of twenty tenants, or an estimated annual rate of 800,000, faced eviction. While not all such evictions were illegal, a considerable proportion were.

The situation in Norman, Oklahoma, late in 1944, at that time an important naval training center, can be cited as an example of how extensive violations of the rent regulations could be, even in a rather small city. The situation came to the attention of the OPA through the passage of a resolution by

---

[5] Harvey C. Mansfield and Associates, *A Short History of OPA*. General Publication No. 15 of the Historical Reports on War Administration, Office of Price Administration (Washington: Government Printing Office, 1947) , p. 127.

the Norman Chamber of Commerce deploring excessive rental charges to naval personnel and a protest by the United States naval authorities. As a result the OPA dispatched some ten regional and district office investigators into the area. In this city, which had 11,429 persons before the war, the government found over 1,500 violations and as a result filed 53 civil suits amounting to over $5,000 in overcharges.[6] In addition, several landlords were criminally prosecuted. For the most part the charges included failure to register property and falsification of statements of the original rent charged. In most cases there was a 300 to 400 per cent increase in rentals at a time when the families of enlisted naval personnel were living on an average of $80 a month.

Rooming houses also presented a fertile field for violations which were particularly costly to low income groups. In an enforcement survey in Brooklyn, 122 establishments were visited, with 18 cases warranting enforcement action. The violators were prosecuted, and within a week 15 were fined and given suspended jail sentences. In many auto courts throughout the country there was a widespread disregard for weekly and monthly rates. Some idea of the compliance picture in 1944 among large and small hotels can be gained from the following enforcement reports of the New England regional office.

The ———— Hotel Survey, conducted by the regional office, is now completed. It is safe to state that all hotels, with few exceptions, are in serious violation of the rent regulation. Practically all hotels failed to consult their base period records in preparing registration statements for the Office of Price Administration.

In Connecticut, the same situation exists. Certainly, it has

---

[6] Those involved were, for example, a minister, doctors, college professors, and business men. The day after the cases were announced in the local newspaper someone burglarized the rent office records of the local OPA office.

been the case to date, with practically every hotel in Waterbury, Hartford, New London, and New Haven in violation. During the past month the hotels in New Britain and in Danbury were investigated and the same situation prevails.

The Rhode Island enforcement office continued its survey of hotels throughout Rhode Island and of eight hotels investigated by the two district investigators, substantial violations were discovered. It is a fair conclusion that compliance activities have been unavailing in Region I so far as adherence of hotels to the rent regulation is concerned.

Types of Violations

Rent violations generally resembled those of price regulations and hence the problems were similar. Rent violations were committed by the owner or operator, for under the Price Control Act it was virtually impossible for a tenant to be a violator. Rent violations may be classified into the following types:[7] (1) the charging of rent over the registered maximum; (2) charging or demanding rents in excess of the maximum by indirect methods supplemented by evasive practices intended to cover up or hamper the detection of the violations; (3) causing evictions contrary to OPA regulations; and (4) violations of record-keeping and reporting requirements.

DIRECT OVERCHARGES. The first type of rent violations involved simply charging more than the actual legal rent. Since rented dwellings had to be registered and this type of violation was relatively easy to detect, they constituted a minority of rent violations, most cases involving attempts to evade the rent regulations being evasive in nature. Still a straight overcharge in violation of regulations was often willful and such persons

---

[7]In the discussion of types of recent violations much assistance has been derived from a memorandum by Wilfred Carsel, "Rent Enforcement in the Office of Price Administration," undated, *circa* spring, 1945.

could be subject to criminal prosecution. As one judge put it, "Certainly it is not meant only that he willfully charged $35 a month. Of course he willfully charged $35 a month rent. He would hardly do it accidentally. Whatever rent he charges, he charges it willfully."

INDIRECT OVERCHARGES. Indirect or evasive violations were characterized by attempts on the part of the violator to beat the law by covering his tracks and presenting a superficial appearance of scrupulous compliance.[8] These evasive rent violations often consisted of such simple devices as payments of rent in advance which in reality represented actual over-ceiling charges. In other instances security deposits or deposits of sums of money with the landlord, theoretically to guarantee compensation for loss, damage, or breaking of lease, were actually overcharges. Other evasions involved the elimination of customary discounts such as those for prompt payment of rent. More likely the evasive rent violations were not as simple as these. Separate rental of an apartment and the furniture, with the total rent in excess of the legal maximum, was frequent, as were side payments involving cash on the side in addition to the rent. These side payments were not reflected in bills and receipts to tenants or in records maintained for the OPA. In one side payment case of three dollars in Nebraska in 1944 the defendant was fined $200 after pleading guilty to a criminal infraction. The judge stated:

An item of three dollars may not be serious as a single instance, but in the ultimate implications, exacting of excessive rentals will be taken as a disposition to get a little more. On the street they call it chiseling. If this is pursued with respect to apartments, ultimately these will be the worst kind of thievery—

---

[8] Nearly all such cases, as will be discussed in Chapter Nine, were prima-facie criminal cases.

the thievery of inflation. The country is at stake. Lives of our sons and daughters are involved. I, therefore, am not inclined to treat this as a three dollar matter.

Tie-in agreements in rent resembled tie-in sales in price violations. The characteristic feature of this type of violation was that the landlord compelled the rental or purchase of something which the tenant did not want, need, or use, in order to obtain a consideration in addition to the maximum rent. The purchase of furniture at an exorbitant price, as a condition of securing a lease, also became a flagrant and general abuse. Sometimes the furniture was of the "stuffed" variety, i.e., hastily assembled from secondhand stores for disposal to a desperate would-be tenant at exorbitant prices. Even when the furniture was not "stuffed" the chances were that the price would be far above the market price. In many cases the tenant already had his own furniture and did not need more. There were cases where the landlord required the prospective tenant to rent, in addition to the dwelling unit desired, a vacant lot which he neither wanted nor needed, the "rented" lot usually not even being near the dwelling unit. Or there might be a requirement that the tenant subscribe to a magazine, purchase a car or clothing, or purchase or rent something else which was wholly unrelated to the housing accommodations. The following examples represent actual cases of these violations.

The most common dodge is the must-buy-furniture requirement. A prospective tenant in Chicago, to take a somewhat extreme example, found a six-room apartment which he could rent for its proper OPA ceiling of $75 a month. But he was informed that there was one slight detail which had to be arranged before he could sign the lease—the furniture had to be purchased for $1,500. A landlady in Norfolk, showing two Navy officers a moderately priced apartment, announced that to get the apartment, the officers would first have to buy her paintings, a bargain at $300 each. Other forced sales concern kitchen furnishings, bathroom fixtures, supposedly rare plants, and the ubiquitous cat.

A second tie-in trick of the landlord is the requirement that tenants rent or buy other property to get the desired apartment or house. The owner of an apartment house in Connecticut recently asked each of his tenants for $30 extra a month, above their OPA rent ceilings, as payments toward the purchase of some building lots which OPA appraisers found were swamp lots worth at most $50 apiece. The owner was convicted and fined.

There are many other such cases. A government worker in Arlington, Virginia, renting a small cottage, was compelled to pay $25 a month extra to rent the pocket-sized yard which bordered the house. A school teacher in Boston, trying to find a home for herself and for her husband, due back shortly from the Pacific, was asked to rent a vegetable garden plot before she could lease a certain house. The vegetable garden, when she asked to see it, turned out to be a city dump.[9]

Fictitious "sales" to the present or prospective tenant were numerous, different variations turning up practically every week during the enforcement of rent regulations. Often the small down payments were a premium for possession or continued occupancy, and the installments exceeded the maximum ceiling price.[10] Fictitious services or reduction in services were still other types of evasive violations. In many cases there was a claim of major capital improvements. Sometimes utilities, such as electricity, gas, or water were reduced without changing rents. At other times excessive charges were made for separate

---

[9] Henderson, *loc. cit.*, p. 47.

[10] In one, for example, the landlord of a furnished apartment collected $10 a month in addition to the necessary rent on the ground that this represented installments for paintings sold to the tenant. In another case the landlord of a house which rented at a maximum rent of $50 a month hypothetically "sold" the house to the tenant for monthly installments of $150.

services such as a garage or cleaning. In the fictitious service type of violation the landlord collected an additional consideration because of the alleged performance of personal services of various types. For example, landlords claimed that they (or their children) mowed lawns, ran errands, or performed other services, and that the extra money collected was not additional rent but compensation for labor. This type of violation was closely akin to side payments and the same investigative techniques applied. This violation was also worked in reverse, with the landlord claiming considerations other than monetary as part of the maximum rent, such as exacting janitorial services from tenants.[11] A similar practice was that of charging tenants "something extra" for small services or pseudo service and "privileges" for which they had never been charged before such as a charge for basement or storage space, and even for such things as allowing a piano or a dog in the apartment. A variation of this device was to increase the charge for a service.[12]

Since customarily monthly rent rates average less than weekly rates some landlords resorted to shortening the periods of payments as a device for obtaining increased rents. This situation occurred most frequently in hotels and rooming houses but was not infrequent in the rental of furnished apartments. Another form of violation, alteration of rental units, can be illustrated by the case of a dwelling unit composed of six rooms with a maximum rent of sixty-five dollars a month which was subdivided, without OPA authority, into two three-

---

[11] If the rendering of such services by tenants was not specified in the registration statement and was not supported by evidence from the base period tenant, such claims fell of their own weight.

[12] Examples of this were the landlord who stepped up the meter of his washing machines so that a dime had to be inserted every ten minutes instead of every twenty as on the base period date, and the landlord who increased the charge for switchboard service from ten to twelve cents a call.

room apartments, each renting for forty dollars a month.[13] Overcharges also occurred when the landlord fictitiously claimed an exemption from the regulation on the basis that the establishment was used as a business accommodation, a farming operation, or even a clubroom, as in the following case:

In a 1945 case a landlady claimed to operate a club devoted to the selling of war bonds. She had an elaborate system by which she purported to admit persons as special guests to that club and to allow them to participate in an opportunity to secure government victory war bonds through ballots, license plate cards, and other devices. Persons who joined the club were allowed to occupy the premises "without rental," but paid dues averaging $100 a month. The landlady claimed that these persons were members of the club and were not tenants. The judge who heard this case proclaimed it an obvious subterfuge and decided that persons who joined the so-called "club" were tenants; that the arrangements made by the landlord with these persons were rental agreements; and that the payments made under these arrangements were rents and not club dues.[14]

One clever form of evasive violation was the use of bonuses, commissions, rewards, and gratuities. When the housing situation became increasingly acute, landlords and agents were able to collect special bonuses and commissions for obtaining apartments. In many rental areas tenants publicly offered rewards to the person locating an apartment for them. The government found that deposits which landlords demanded of

---

[13] A Los Angeles landlord was sentenced in 1944 to two years' imprisonment for this type of violation. The landlord had evicted the wives and children of soldiers and converted the apartment house into a rooming house simply by placing numbers on rooms within apartments, adding some furniture, and claiming that the living room constituted a lobby with the kitchen a courtesy.

[14] From an unpublished OPA Enforcement Department field report.

prospective tenants were seldom returned when the tenant moved away. In general this practice served as hidden rent or a premium on occupancy.

ILLEGAL EVICTIONS. Not only were illegal evictions one of the most troublesome violations; even a threat of legal eviction after a dwelling was sold often made tenants pay more rent than was required. Illegal evictions, moreover, "had a devastating effect on the morale of war workers and members of the armed forces and their families; if widespread it fostered a sense of insecurity which spread through congested areas and endangered the maintenance of rent ceilings generally."[15] Common types of eviction contrary to OPA regulations were those where a landlord evicted a tenant allegedly in order to gain occupancy of the housing accommodations for his own use, when actually he intended to rerent the premises and, in fact, did rerent them after eviction.[16] Such illegal eviction was ordinarily accompanied by an increase in the rent to the new tenant, although sometimes there were personal reasons as in the following case.

In 1944 a Mr. ——— evicted a tenant from a single housing accommodation in Dayton on the ground of self-occupancy. He did not, however, occupy the accommodation, but immediately rerented it to a new tenant, the real cause of eviction being that the tenant had filed an application for reduction of rent because of decrease of an essential service. After having filed this application the tenant immediately had been served the eviction notice. The violation was discovered when the evicted tenant complained to the

---

[15] Mansfield, *op. cit.*, p. 119.

[16] In Great Britain tenants could not be evicted except for specified reasons, for example, "failure to pay rent, maintaining a nuisance, illegal uses, landlord owned house prior to 1939 Act and requires premises for the use of himself, his family, or in certain cases an employee."—Backman, *Rationing and Price Control in Great Britain,* pp. 52–53.

area office on the landlord's failure to occupy the premises. The landlord pleaded guilty and was fined $250.[17]

RECORD-KEEPING AND REPORTING VIOLATIONS. As in the case of price violations, those landlords who refused to file or falsified their reporting information were usually trying to obtain a higher income for the rental properties. This type of violation seriously interfered with rent enforcement. A Bureau of Labor Statistics survey of living accommodations early in 1945 revealed that between 10 and 20 per cent of the landlords failed to register with the OPA and on the part of those that had been registered there was an average overcharge of 8 or 9 per cent.

Public Support of Rent Control

Although some persons might suggest that these violations indicated a general lack of public support of rent control, numerous public opinion polls showed that this was not the case. The National Opinion Research Center in April, 1946, several months after the end of the war, announced the results of a nation-wide survey in which 85 per cent of those questioned felt that the government should continue rent control. When asked how long a time rent control laws should be kept, 52 per cent said that they should be kept for more than a year beyond June 30, 1946. The April, 1946, survey made by *Fortune* magazine reported that more than eight of every ten persons questioned in its national cross section favored the retention of ceilings on rents.[18]

---

[17] From an unpublished OPA Enforcement Department field report.

[18] In a March, 1946, poll of Iowans, three-fourths of those interviewed were in favor of extending rent control to the state, including ceiling prices on old and new houses and on building lots.—*Opinion Briefs*, No. 14, Department of Information, Office of Price Administration, "Iowans Favor Year's Extension for OPA and Ceiling Prices on Homes," March 19, 1946, p. 4 (Mimeographed).

Common Explanations of Violations

There were many explanations for these extensive violations. Many felt that the ceilings were so unfair that the landlords were losing money. There was no satisfactory standard for measuring the fair value of individual rental units, and it was neither possible nor desirable to determine rent on an individual basis, but both facts and statistics seem to disprove the contention that landlords, in general, faired badly under OPA restrictions. There were exceptions to this general picture, as might be expected in the administration of several million rental units. Generally, while there were some increases in costs, such as fuel, there were substantial decreases in outlays for repairs, maintenance, and redecoration. In a study made by the OPA in 1943, vacancies were shown to have declined from 8 per cent before the war to 1.5 per cent.

The Office of Price Administration took the position that the key to the general fairness and equity of the rent regulations was the net operating position of landlords during the war as compared with the period immediately prior to the war. Its surveys indicated that in 1944 landlords renting housing in pressure areas had increased net operating income between 35 and 40 per cent. A study of thirty-six cities between 1939 and 1944 was reported to show that the actual excess of income over expenses for apartment units was from $116 to $158; for rental units of small structures the comparable figures were $111 to $153.[19] Net operating income on hotels from 1939 through 1944 rose up to 182 per cent, while total income increased 82 per cent and expenses went up only 64 per cent.[20] Altogether

---

[19] Testimony of Chester Bowles on the Extension of Price Control, prepared for Banking and Currency Committees of Congress, about June 30, 1946.
[20] *Ibid.*

over a period of four years the OPA conducted income and expense surveys in 90 different cities covering over 200,000 rental units. Testifying before a congressional committee in 1946 the OPA Administrator reported:

> While individual area results have varied, the most recent data show that the average net operating income for the year ending June 30, 1945, was 38 per cent higher for apartment houses and 37 per cent higher for small structures than it was in 1939. There is no evidence of substantial change in the position of landlords generally since that time.[21]

The condition of the real-estate market since 1939 revealed further evidence of the improved operating position of owners of housing property. In 1944 there were only 18 per cent as many mortgage foreclosures as in 1939. Loans by building and loan associations for home purchases had nearly tripled, while the amount of residential real estate owned by financial institutions had fallen to nearly one tenth of the 1939 value. To the landlord, increased economic activity meant heightened demand for a commodity fixed in supply, and almost complete sale of his product with a minimum of selling expense.

Control of Rent Violations

Despite extensive black market violations in the field of rent control, the government appears to have been reasonably effective in its drive to control rents. The reports of the Bureau of Labor Statistics on wartime rents lend support to the statement that "ceiling violations have not been common enough, however, to destroy the reputation of rent control as the most

---

[21] Statement of Paul Porter, OPA Administrator, at *Hearings before the Senate Committee on Banking and Currency*, 1946 Extension of the Emergency Price Control and Stabilization Acts of 1942, as Amended, on Senate Resolution 2,028, Seventy-ninth Congress, Second Session, 1946, I, 193.

effective of all OPA operations. The very zeal with which the control has been administered is one of the grievances of the rental-property owner."[22]

One of the most significant factors in this record of control was the complete registration of rental charges at the time of the base period, which made it subsequently possible to police the activities of landlords more effectively. An equally important factor appears to have been the role played by the large number of tenants throughout the country. As compared to their number the landlords were on the whole a small and sometimes not too effective minority. Thus there were greater pressures for compliance with the regulations than was true with many other commodities. As a result of this effective public support, rent regulations continued from year to year almost intact. One enforcement official aptly stated:

> Another favorable feature of the matter so far as rent enforcement is concerned is the consoling fact that the rent regulations, standing almost alone, are not amended at the whim or caprice of every Tom, Dick and Harry in the country at frequent intervals and, therefore, we almost always are in a position to prove actual knowledge of the regulations.[23]

Although the price control and rationing of all other commodities terminated shortly after the war, the importance of rent control was recognized by its continuance. So vital was rent control to the general welfare and morale of the people that such controls were still in effect in many areas of the country when, after the beginning of the Korean war in 1950, price controls were reinstated.

---

[22] "Rents and the Real Estate Lobby," *Fortune*, June, 1947, pp. 195–196.
[23] From an unpublished OPA Enforcement Department field report.

CHAPTER EIGHT

Enforceability
of the Regulations

The Office of Price Administration issued almost six hundred regulations and some twenty ration orders covering various commodities. The nature and complexity of these regulations has been offered by some as one of the contributing reasons for the black market. According to this belief the entire regulatory setup was an impossible one with which to comply and served only to antagonize businessmen unnecessarily. These opinions were based on a lack of knowledge of what the regulations represented and an unawareness of the relation of enforcement difficulties to different types of regulations. Actually regulations had to be even more explicit than the legal statutes because the latter are clarified by interpretations by the courts and by previous decisions. A good regulation from the standpoint of enforcement was one that was specific and easily understood, difficult to evade, and readily enforceable.

The complex wording of the regulations was a subject of extensive criticism. It is true that they were generally quite complex. Some of them, even without later amendments, covered as many as twenty-five pages of fine print. But without this detailed technical wording not only could a regulation often be violated; it could even be argued, as was done many times, that it did not apply at all. The commodity or commodities covered by each regulation had to be defined in detail. A regulation could not state simply that it covered the price of certain types of commodities such as given items of clothing. These items had to be specifically defined; otherwise it would have been possible for the manufacturer or dealer to claim that his product actually was not the same as the one described in the regulation.[1] The regulations also had to contain detailed statements as to types of sellers which particular regulations covered. Not only did all of these possible situations have to be covered; they had to be worded in such a way that in the event of a violation enforcement action could be taken. Loopholes in some regulations were prevented more effectively by the wording and construction than in others. The Deputy Administrator for Enforcement stated:

Certainly, from 50 to 75 per cent of our enforcement success depends upon the regulation itself. There are some regulations which no group of attorneys and investigators, no matter how competent, could possibly enforce. There are other regulations which are relatively easy of enforcement and require little manpower. The shape of the regulation has as much bearing as any other single factor upon the success of our enforcement program.[2]

The contention was also frequently made that a businessman often had no recourse but to gamble on the possibility of his being in violation of the regulation, since he could not

---

[1] At times the definitions seemed ridiculous, as, for example, the problem of defining "seed potatoes" so that all potatoes would not be upgraded to this category. Actually any potato which would grow was a seed potato, and the government began designating the type referred to as "certified seed potatoes" and later tried making technical specifications.

[2] Emerson, "Enforcement," *A Manual of Price Control,* cited above, p. 294.

possibly understand its wording.[3] This contention might well have been true in the early days of the agency, but on the whole it is unfair to raise this issue after the forms of the regulations had been more or less standardized and businessmen had had longer experience with them. Certainly two to four years' experience ought to be sufficient in most instances to learn the technicalities. Moreover, businessmen are by no means unfamiliar with legal verbiage in their civil contracts, in ordinary terms of sale, and in the numerous municipal, state, and federal regulations governing the normal course of business.

A business concern could always get an official interpretation of the price and rationing regulation in writing or an informal one orally, although the latter was not binding. Similarly, many newspapers and trade journals carried a digest of explanations of the regulations for particular trades. Many of the major concerns employed legal counsel who would interpret the regulation. In some cases where skilled legal talent was employed "to interpret the regulations," often the primary purpose was to find ways of complying with the letter of the law while violating its spirit. At least there were many stories to this effect, and there is some indication that this practice is fairly common in peacetime. The ability of some businessmen and their legal talent to find loopholes in OPA regulations was indeed a tribute to the shrewdness and ingenuity of the American mind. Many businessmen, however, readily admitted that simple regulations would not fit a broad business operation and

---

[3] Many humorous stories circulated to this effect. Stories were told of how businessmen visited local OPA offices to secure an interpretation, only to find that the field offices could not understand the Washington regulations either. One story told in Washington was of a businessman who called an economist instrumental in framing a regulation for an interpretation, only to have him say that he could no longer understand what he had written after the lawyers had gone over it.

that if the regulations were to be made applicable details were necessary. They had to be because the honest law-abiding merchant or manufacturer had to live with a regulation drawn so as to keep the scheming, conniving seller and buyer within bounds. The difficulties of the problem are illustrated by the statement of a steel man in a case involving resellers of iron and steel products: "I don't see how they [the OPA] ever drafted a regulation which would cover this business. I've been at it thirty-five years. The business has 'growed up' like Topsy. Whoever prepared this regulation really had a job I'd not want to undertake."[4]

The Issue of Nonfamiliarity with the Regulations

Some businessmen maintained that they did not know there was even a regulation affecting them. What truth was there to this statement? In the early days of the OPA there were a few cases in which a person was charged with violating a regulation on the date it was issued.[5] In some instances the actual regulation did not reach the business concern until several weeks after its official issuance, and the contention was raised that there was no knowledge of its existence. In order to take care of these two eventualities the federal law provided that when certain regulations, including those of the OPA, were published in the *Federal Register* all persons by this method should have notice. Most regulations later contained provisions stating that the regulation was to be effective so many days after its issuance, and it became more or less a matter of custom for enforcement action not to be started immediately after the

---

[4] Statement furnished by an OPA enforcement attorney.

[5] One such case involved a consumer's treble damage suit over a pair of nylon hose in the Municipal Court of Washington, D. C. In this case the judge ruled against the plaintiff on the grounds that the issuance of the regulation and the alleged violation occurred on the same day.

issuance of the regulation, allowing an unofficial period of grace. In some instances, time extensions were granted even up to several months in order to be sure of adequate time for compliance. Assumed familiarity with the regulations became later a cardinal principle of government enforcement, and justifiably so.

Two Basic Enforcement Problems in the Regulations

All violations of the price and rationing regulations, in the final analysis, grew out of the fact that shortage situations existed. Those who maintained that the solution to a black market was adequate supply were undoubtedly correct. This, of course, said little more than that the reason for the OPA itself was the cause of violations of its regulations. Still, the difficulties of enforcement were enhanced during the war and the reconversion period by the existence of minor shortages in certain areas and acute shortages in others, thus putting unwarranted enforcement pressures on some areas while leaving others almost unaffected. This situation helped bring about violations, and there was little in the construction of a regulation that could be done about it.[6] The fact that the government would never take steps to regulate by compulsion the channeling of supplies from the manufacturer to the retailer made for enormous complications. Goods were channeled from *suppliers to manufacturers only* insofar as manufacturers could not secure supplies without prior approval of the War Production Board and later the Civilian Production Board. Most retailers received their supplies according to no plan at all or according

---

[6] The Food Enforcement Division of the OPA, for this reason, later developed a detailed system for keeping informed on supply difficulties in various meat distribution centers, with the intention of strengthening enforcement in these areas. Efforts to channel meat into licensed slaughterers located in large cities were also a recognition of this problem. See also Katona, *op. cit.,* p. 141.

to quantities of purchases prior to the war. Moreover, it is likely that many wholesalers and manufacturers kept their distribution costs down by channeling their goods into the areas representing a minimum figure in their production costs since they could readily sell any article they produced. As a result, some non-defense communities which had lost population, received rather plentiful supplies of some commodities, whereas defense areas were short in supplies and presented extremely complex enforcement problems.

Where quality provisions were involved and where there were no standard grading specifications, the regulations were particularly difficult to enforce, regardless of pricing methods. The clothing regulations were probably the most difficult for the government to enforce, not because they were inadequate but rather because the nature of the commodity, without standardization, made it virtually impossible to enforce quality provisions properly. The regulation was not unenforceable as written, but its enforcement meant little because its provisions need not be "evaded"; they could be "avoided." Changes in pricing methods undoubtedly helped to improve enforcement of this type of regulation, but the basic problem of quality provisions, under the existing desire to maintain only limited control over this feature, made enforcement extremely difficult.[7]

Enforceability of Various Types of Price Regulations

From the standpoint of enforcement, the detailed provisions of a particular regulation were probably secondary to the larger question of the type of pricing method, of which

---

[7] Benjamin Caplan (editor), *Problems in Price Control: Changing Production Patterns,* General Publication No. 9, of the Historical Reports on War Administration, Office of Price Administration (Washington: Government Printing Office, 1947).

there were three: freeze pricing, formula pricing, and dollar-and-cents pricing.

FREEZE PRICING. A method whereby commodity prices were "frozen" as of a specific date, or at the highest prices during a certain period, was known as freeze pricing. These prices were designated as the maximum prices of such commodities. Such a regulation based its pricing practices not on particular conditions in the trade but on a specific time factor. This method of pricing was quite common in the early days of the OPA and reached its height of utilization with the issuance of a general freeze, the GMPR, in April, 1942,[8] which set prices on thousands of commodities as the highest charged in March, 1942.[9] In order to work, a freeze regulation assumed, first of all, that reasonably adequate and complete records were maintained by the business concerns involved, and that these records would show the prices charged on a particular date; second, that these records would be filed with the agency or otherwise placed where they could not be changed; and third, that the product frozen was sufficiently standardized so that new styles or forms did not develop.

This type of regulation was particularly useful where the agency had to move rather rapidly into a field without prolonged study. It was also useful where there was little need for preparing detailed regulations. It might be regarded, there-

---

[8] Harris mentions that a successful freeze required the three following conditions: (1) the freeze must be all along the line, (2) a subsidy system must necessarily be a part of a general freeze program, and (3) a general freeze would be likely to break down if, in spite of the freezing of prices, total incomes rose.— Seymour E. Harris, *Price and Related Controls in the United States* (New York: McGraw-Hill Book Company, Inc., 1945), pp. 107–108. Copyright, 1945. Courtesy of McGraw-Hill Book Co.

[9] When GMPR (General Maximum Price Regulation) was issued there were about 120 regulations which provided freeze, dollar-and-cents, or formula pricing. With the reinstitution of price controls after the beginning of the Korean war a general price freeze was reimposed in January, 1951.

fore, either as a form of emergency pricing, or as a simple method where conditions warranted, or both. Regulations in the form of price freezes also had some factors favorable to enforcement. In his interviews with Chicago businessmen, Katona found that the introduction of price freezes tended to make both businessmen and consumers feel, in a dramatic fashion, that price stability had arrived, thus aiding enforcement. Complex regulations did not have this effect.[10] Another element favorable to enforcement was the fact that such regulations were easily understood by most businessmen. Moreover, the method maintained the traditional price differences between various producers and distributors and did not involve the interference of a governmental agency with such practices. Retailers whose prices were generally frozen on a rising market had to replace their goods at the higher wholesale and manufacturing levels at which prices were simultaneously frozen. Provided accurate price records were available, it was generally a fairly easy procedure for an investigator to check them.

The unfavorable aspects of freeze regulations, however, outweighed the favorable ones. First of all, since the ceiling probably varied from firm to firm, as time passed, businessmen had great difficulty in knowing the ceiling prices of their suppliers, and consumers in knowing those of the retailers. There was also the matter of records. If no basic records were available to be used in determining the frozen price, there was little chance of effective enforcement. There had to be records available to check prices, and where the records did not exist it was at times suspected that they had been willfully destroyed. In general, the OPA's experience with this pricing method revealed that the records kept by many business concerns in the United States are woefully inadequate when they are neces-

---

[10] Katona, *op. cit.*, p. 101.

sary in the proper administration of a government regulation.[11]

There was also the problem of the prompt submittal of these records. Even if they were slightly inaccurate they could have furnished a fairly adequate index of correct prices if secured within a relatively short time after the original base period date. However, the task of seeing that pricing statements were submitted promptly was difficult. Every month that elapsed allowed the base period statement to become inflated, consequently more inaccurate, and the dishonest person was thus given an advantage in markings.

These were not the only limitations of the price freeze. This type of regulation served to perpetuate chance differences in prices prevailing during the base period.[12] Such regulations also might have caused an initial squeeze, for by freezing prices at all levels a squeeze was created at certain levels of the economic system which as costs increased could only be eliminated by the granting of subsidy payments or by increasing prices. Increasing prices, however, might make for confusion in the computation of the prices of some commodities which remained according to base period pricing, while others quite similarly related had had their prices increased. The lack of equitability between different production levels in a general freeze might also put tremendous pressures at certain levels to violate the regulations, thus making enforcement difficult. For example,

---

[11] Since federal and local governments must have recourse to such records for taxes, social security, labor legislation, and other similar purposes, the government might find it feasible to establish common methods of bookkeeping for the various concerns of the United States.

[12] As Katona has stated: "A businessman who happened to have raised his prices before the base date was benefited as against one who had not. Rarely did merchants complain that they had been caught with all their prices too low, but frequently they complained about those of a few isolated articles. In this respect many businessmen condemned the practice of the OPA which they described as granting relief only if the profits of the firm and not the profits made on specific items justified price increases. As a result items with relatively low ceiling prices were often discontinued."—Katona, *op. cit.*, p. 101.

if the same base date were used in setting prices for both manufacturers and distributors, the retail prices might be set at a
figure which was based on old purchases and which did not
allow for the fact that the manufacturers' prices might have
risen. In getting more stocks the retailers had to pay more than
the margin appearing in the regulation.

Another major difficulty encountered by those who prepared the regulations was the problem of pricing seasonable
commodities which were, for example, not produced or sold
during March, 1942, the base period for the GMPR. In some
instances this permitted higher prices at certain times during
the year than were warranted. Somewhat related was the problem of working out a price for new or changed commodities,
and this eventually became the chief source of violation. Base
period pricing regulations could be evaded in two ways: (1)
by lowering the quality and claiming it was the same, and
(2) by making minor changes not actually affecting the price
but claiming it to be a new commodity and pricing it by comparison with one known to have a "high" price. Since it was
maintained that it was not the same commodity, either a higher
price could be requested or efforts could be made to find some
comparable commodity sold by a competitor at a higher price.
After the issuance of GMPR there were literally hundreds of
so-called new items. Many of them were new, to be sure, but the
question was difficult to determine and enforcement was practically impossible. Had Congress been willing to pass laws permitting the OPA to establish standard grades for merchandise,
some of these difficulties might have been mitigated. In sum-
marizing the GMPR experience Seymour Harris put great
emphasis on the difficulties of enforcement:

Yet the main conclusion is that the GMPR has been but a
modest success. One has but to study the very large rise in

margins (and profits) in the years 1942–1944 to be convinced. Through deterioration of products, uptrading, and excessive recourse to production and sale of "new" products, businessmen have been able to circumvent the GMPR. These considerations do not entirely explain the large rise of middlemen's profits. A substantial reduction of selling costs and savings on services are relevant.[13]

After the emergency period and the initial enthusiasm for base period pricing, such as GMPR, waned, the method of formula pricing was increasingly utilized. Although freeze pricing covered more commodities than any other type of regulation, in point of numbers there were more formula regulations. It is not to be assumed by this statement, of course, that all three pricing methods did not go on simultaneously almost from the beginning of the agency. In fact, some regulations allowed for a choice of all three methods. On the whole, though, there were trends, with certain types being emphasized more at certain times. These trends actually were in large measure the result of enforcement experience and the fact that more data became available for other types of pricing. The GMPR regulation was scrapped principally because it could not be enforced effectively.

FORMULA PRICING. Sometimes referred to as a cost-plus system, in some ways formula pricing resembled the cost-plus formula used in war contracts. This method of pricing represented the computation of markups on the cost of a commodity according to the price charged in the previous base period. For example, a business firm, under certain OPA formula regulations, might be allowed to charge a specific percentage above the cost of producing a commodity; in other cases the percentage might be added to the price charged on a certain base period date. Frequently the formula was even more complex than this.

---

[13] Harris, *op. cit.,* p. 112. Reprinted by permission.

As compared with freeze pricing, this method had in its favor the fact that its basic procedure was, in general, the same as that used customarily by businessmen. The majority of business concerns have always computed their prices for given commodities by means of a formula allowing for a certain profit. Some, of course, had not previously utilized the same standard methods established by the OPA, having many practices peculiar to their businesses.[14]

There were numerous disadvantages to formula pricing. In the first place, under this type of regulation there was a tendency to lower the incentive to purchase or to produce as cheaply as possible, and there was also a tendency to deal in the more expensive goods where the percentage of markup was greater. This was particularly true in finished piece goods. Likewise, there was a tendency to increase the price by a series of markups as the product passed through several hands, as in the case of the movement of "gray goods" in the mill through to finished textiles. In fact, this type of regulation encouraged, rather than discouraged, higher pricing and therefore a higher total margin over manufactured cost, involving a greater use of manpower and materials in the commodity when there were actually extreme shortages. All of these factors increased enforcement difficulties by inflationary pressures on cheaper goods; moreover, the OPA had to contend with such illegal devices as

---

[14] Interviews with Chicago businessmen showed several different methods of computing the markup: "Some said that, while they could still use margins to determine selling prices, they had to forgo their traditional practice of 'averaging out' prices of different articles in the same line, that is, using higher margins on certain articles and lower ones on others. Many merchants, particularly of produce and of millinery, said that they never used margins but just fixed prices 'intuitively' or according to what 'competition permitted.' Finally, though probably least important, most retailers, especially grocers, were accustomed to calculating margins on selling prices rather than on costs and complained about having to change their traditional methods."—Katona, *op. cit.*, p. 105.

fictitious processors, as in the textile trade, to increase the profit margin.

The most serious difficulty was the actual investigation problem. If previous customary margins were involved it was frequently found that some businessmen either did not maintain adequate records or invented fictitious margins. Most of these regulations assumed the existence of detailed and accurate records as to cost, base period pricing, or some other base of computation. In addition, the records assumed that the formula was applicable to the commodity for which it was computed and that it was worked out accurately. Unfortunately, investigators found that in a large number of cases they could not presume that these prerequisites had been satisfactorily met. If the question was one of cost accounting the formula was usually quite complex, and to ascertain the correctness of any one of these factors required tremendous amounts of investigative time. While it is true that there was a large amount of falsification and deliberate misrepresentation in the preparation of prices using the formula method, part of the difficulty again lay in the rather haphazard way in which records were kept in many business concerns. It later became customary to require business concerns to submit detailed statements of their formula prices and the records from which they were obtained in order to be sure that the formula pricing records would not be changed when some enforcement action seemed possible. These records were then filed in the OPA office for future use. While this aided in the investigation of cases, it still did not aid the investigator materially in computing the correct price and in avoiding the necessity of making separate computations of the correct price, nor did it necessarily guarantee the correctness of the data submitted in the records.

An expert in the field of price control has summarized

these enforcement limitations of formula pricing regulations
as follows:

These ceilings at best offer general instructions for determining
prices. Each seller's price is not easily checked, and it is most
difficult for the buyer to protect himself. Yet, on the whole, this
approach is generally preferable to exclusive reliance on freeze
provisions and is certainly a great improvement over no control at
all. Dollar-and-cents ceilings would be more desirable; but they
may be impractical where standardization is impossible or difficult
of achievement, where thousands of commodities have to be dealt
with, where commodities are produced according to specifications
(in the case of machine tools, for example), or where costs vary
greatly. Undoubtedly, price control cannot be enforced as effectively
by this type of ruling as through the use of dollar-and-cents ceilings. And the more variables included in the formula, the less
precise the regulation and the more difficult of enforcement.[15]

DOLLAR-AND-CENTS PRICING. This type "obviously meets all the
requirements the Enforcement Division would like to impose.
A dollar-and-cents regulation is the ideal that enforcement
attorneys dream about."[16] Such a method, often called "flat
pricing," was simply placing a standard price on all sales of a
commodity. This standard price applied to all sellers and conditions at a given level of business. Sometimes it was a national
price and at other times a community price. Freeze dates and
formulas were omitted. In a sense, this method was similar to
the standard pricing of many nationally advertised products in
peacetime. While this type of regulation was employed from
the beginning of OPA and used nationally in some products
such as rayon hosiery, its widest extension came later in community ceilings for retailers of groceries, meats, fresh fruits,
and vegetables. In the reconversion period it became the gen-

---

[15] Harris, *op. cit.*, p. 118. Reprinted by permission.
[16] Emerson, *A Manual of Price Control*, p. 296.

eral method of pricing durable goods. "It was hoped that the introduction of dollar-and-cents ceilings would make price regulations more comprehensible and more enforceable."[17]

The most useful feature of this type of regulation was that hypothetically it required only the comparison of the author-ized price with the selling price. Being uniform for all sellers in a given area, it made ceilings easy to investigate. They could also be easily checked by consumers and by relatively untrained personnel, such as price panel volunteers. Surveys of consumers indicated that the public was much better informed about ceilings on dollar-and-cents articles than on any others. One survey made for the OPA in December, 1943, showed that most consumers did not know there were ceilings on women's dresses, men's suits, or shoes which were covered by GMPR or formula ceilings, but did know the dollar-and-cents ceilings on meat and sugar. After a survey of compliance in a number of mining communities early in 1943, this conclusion was reached:

It is imperative that the preparations for the issuance of dollars-and-cents ceilings and a simplified retail food regulation be pushed to a conclusion immediately. Retail enforcement will always be difficult, if not impossible, unless every housewife is able to know at the time of a food purchase what the ceiling price for that commodity is. This result can best be secured through the issuance of dollars-and-cents price ceilings at the retail level. Man-power must be made available and kept available for this purpose. Where dollars-and-cents prices cannot be fixed, a single retail food regulation, simple and enforceable in nature, must be issued to cover the entire field. Revision of the regulations along these lines, as has long been recognized, is the basic, and single most important, step in achieving real enforcement.[18]

---

[17] Harris, *op. cit.*, p. 131. Reprinted by permission.
[18] Memorandum to Prentiss M. Brown, Administrator, from Thomas I. Emerson, Associate General Counsel, on "Report on Survey of Compliance with

Such pricing methods gave business and consumers the impression of relative price stability, thus furnishing a more adequate social-psychological situation for enforcement. The price was fixed by the OPA and did not fluctuate with freeze period records, formulas, increased costs, and other items. In fact, since they caused the least amount of work for businessmen, one would anticipate, following some of the rationalizations of the day, that such regulations would be violated least.[19] This was not necessarily true, however, as there was no evidence that any one regulation was more or less conducive to compliance for this reason alone.

Such specific ceilings had their limitations. The chief difficulty was that, in the first place, these regulations affected standardized goods principally, and the government was largely prohibited from standardizing commodities in many areas where they were needed. Also seasonal supply fluctuations required either the procedure of sales below ceiling or numerous price adjustments. Second, as was the case with all pricing methods, it was no guarantee against side payments. During the reconversion period, for example, where automobiles had flat pricing there were extensive sales above ceiling, side payments being the customary method of violation. In some cases the ticket indicating the ceiling price on a commodity was removed or altered. Compared with other forms of regulation, however, "dollar-and-cents ceilings are relatively precise and enforceable."[20]

Regulations Governing Retail Food Prices in Mining Communities, May 6, 1943, p. 5. In all references to this type of regulation we have adopted the spelling "dollar-and-cents" as used by Seymour Harris.

[19] On the other hand, while much paper work was eliminated, some persons felt the harsh hand of government uniformity upon them because variations in type of sellers were eliminated.—Katona, *op. cit.*, p. 110.

[20] See Harris, *op. cit.*, p. 142. Reprinted by permission.

Thus each pricing method had its advantages and disadvantages. Some pricing methods worked well in the enforcement of some regulations for certain types of commodities. The same methods, when applied to other types of commodities, were wholly ineffective. This was particularly true when one compared commodities with little risk of deterioration or price change with those where a good deal of risk was involved. It was also true where quality provisions were involved in contrast to those industries where this was not of prime consideration, and where the circumstances of business enabled one readily to ascertain the correct pricing in comparison with those in which a good deal of investigative work was necessary.

Investigative Techniques

Good regulations and an adequate enforcement staff were not the only important aspects of controlling price violations, for adequate investigative techniques in conjunction with the requirements of the regulations were also significant. Obviously straight over-ceiling charges were rather easy to detect, difficulties in detection being mainly with side payments, tie-in sales, and falsification of records. Many techniques were devised to detect price violations and gather evidence, some of which had been used by other investigative agencies prior to the enactment of the OPA. A large proportion of them represented much ingenuity, but only a few can be mentioned here.

In connection with concealed violations it was found to be a good procedure to scrutinize the books closely for any erasures, longhand entries, and the like, or any other diversion from the subject's customary bookkeeping practices. In other cases it was discovered that a violation might be concealed by incorrectly computing the charges. For example, a bill might read: "5,000 lbs. @ $.50 per lb. = $2,600.00." Computation on invoices was also spot-checked. Sometimes, in order to circumvent a price regulation, a firm might date its sales invoice to a time prior to the effective date of such regulation. In these cases the discovery of large numbers of sales appearing immediately before the issuance of the regulation often led to the discovery of significant information. Similarly, clues to possible violations were found when sales records were numerically or chronologically out of order. To prevent back-dating of sales it was often found feasible to check bills, receipts, and purchase orders on records to determine when the merchandise was actually sold or recorded.

In order to detect false invoices investigators were taught to question any cases where a small invoice continually accompanied a larger invoice from the same company or to the same buyer. One test was to divide the quantity of units on the larger invoice into the amount on the smaller invoice, the result usually being the exact amount of the overcharge per unit. A false invoice was frequently made up on a different bill from that of the legitimate one. The authenticity of such documents was often verified by examining other documents which usually itemized the sale, such as purchase orders. For example, the actual shipment of merchandise might be backed up by a delivery receipt or bill of lading, whereas an invoice representing cash overcharges but no merchandise would have no such documents. In the event of a questionable invoice the documents were often examined. A further method of verifying the authenticity of such an invoice was to determine when it was paid. A legitimate invoice was usually paid under customary terms of time and discount, whereas an invoice representing an overcharge alone was usually paid at the time of, or shortly after, delivery. Payment data were also verified by examining check stubs and cash dispersal books.

The difficult problem of cash-on-the-side payments did not involve the issuance of false invoices. In its place was a legitimate invoice at the correct price for the material delivered, and at about the same time of delivery a cash payment of the overcharge was charged to the buyer. In many cases this type of violation was established by visiting the buyer suspected of making such payments and securing his statements. Frequently the buyer took cash out of his personal funds and then gave it to the seller, who then placed the money in his personal account without depositing it to the business. When the buyer or seller maintained records and the cash payments passed through these records, it was often possible to discover the violation through the following specific procedures:

From the buyer's records.—All checks issued are listed in the cash disbursement book. Examine carefully the "general" column in this book. Each entry here should show the purpose for which payment is made. Some firms have earmarked illegal payments as "advertising, entertainment, bonuses, etc." Secure proof for all questionable expenditures. Examine canceled checks for these payments to see whether the endorsement on the reverse side of the check is that of a firm selling to the subject.

Firms have often used the petty cash fund for making illegal cash payments. For this reason it is also advisable to examine petty cash vouchers.

From the seller's records.—Payments received are recorded in the cash receipts book. Most payments received result from sales that have been made and will usually be listed in the accounts receivable column of this book. Illegal cash receipts are frequently listed in the "general" column. Entries in the "general" column usually show the reason for which money was received in the column marked "account." Illegal receipts have at various times been explained as "cash sale, salary returns, etc." Explanations should be secured for all entries that are questionable.[21]

Upgrading was one of the most difficult violations to detect, particularly where no professional investigator was available who could appraise the grade or where there were no state and federal grades stamped on the commodity. In the case of a commodity of Grade B quality billed as Grade A, the inventory records, where kept, could be checked to determine the inventory of each grade as of a previous date. The purchases of each grade were added, the sales subtracted, and the result was compared with the subject's inventory. It was also found advisable to check purchase records to see if the type of merchandise being bought corresponded to that being sold. For example, a business firm supposedly selling primarily Grade A merchandise, and at the same time purchasing Grade B, was likely to be indulging in upgrading. Where possible, statements were sometimes secured from customers as to what grade they were actually receiving.

Tie-in sales were probably the most difficult of all violations to detect, particularly since it was often hard to prove such a violation without statements by the concern's customers that they were forced to buy additional merchandise. The possibility that they might be cut off from their source of supply made many reluctant to testify. Some of the ways of detecting such violations were to observe the constant sale of one product in combination with another to certain customers where no such combination sales had existed previously. Such facts could often be ascertained by inspection of the invoices.

Regardless of how well trained an investigator might be in

---

[21] *Basic Manual for Enforcement Investigators of the Office of Price Administration,* Prepared by the Training Branch, Office of the Chief Investigator, Enforcement Department, Office of Price Administration, Washington, 1944, p. 29 (multilithed).

investigative techniques, however, there were certain commodity fields so specialized in nature that many an investigator was often unable to detect a violation even after an intensive investigation. Such investigations as those of retail food, particularly where there was a brand specification or some sort of labeling, did not present much difficulty. On the other hand, such commodities as lumber, scrap metal, and textiles were quite difficult to appraise as to quality. Upgrading violations, without the aid of some highly trained specialists, were therefore difficult to detect in many commodities. It was manifestly impossible for the government, during such a short period of time, to train investigators so that they would have such technical skill. This problem was attacked in a number of different ways. In some instances it was possible to borrow specialized personnel from other agencies, such as the Department of Agriculture in the case of meat inspections of black market cases, and members of the Secret Service from the Treasury Department for use in connection with counterfeiting work. In many instances commodity specialists were appointed investigators or borrowed from the Price Department. These men had a background of working knowledge in particular industries and were hired at salaries slightly higher than those paid the ordinary investigator. As the war progressed and as black market violations became more evasive, it was necessary to employ more skilled investigators.

CHAPTER NINE

Black Market Violations

as "Crimes"

Most persons probably would not regard the black market as being primarily "criminal," since only a small proportion of the violators were either imprisoned, fined, or put on probation. Persons who disobeyed the law could also be punished by the government in a variety of ways, some by civil actions and others by administrative. The OPA was authorized to decide what kind of measure should be used for a black market violation. The only specific limitation was that the criminal sanction could be employed only in cases of "willful violation." Since there was no implication that the criminal sanction should be employed in all willful cases, the use of alternative measures was left entirely up to the agency.[1] Actions which could be invoked against violators of price and rationing regulations and orders ranged from admonitory warning letters to criminal prosecutions which might subject the violator to imprisonment up to one year or to a fine of not more than $5,000, or both, for each violation. Between these extremes were administrative actions, such as monetary settlements, and civil actions, such as treble

---

[1] In Canada, on the other hand, where formal action was deemed necessary in the event of a price or rationing violation, all offenses were dealt with by criminal prosecution rather than by such actions as injunction or treble damages, with the exception of a few cases where a license to do business was revoked.

damage suits, injunction suits, and license suspension proceedings. Violations of ration orders might be enforced by local
board and district office revocations at the consumer level, by
administrative proceedings to suspend the privilege of dealing
in rationed commodities, and by injunction actions to enforce
compliance with ration orders at retail and wholesale levels.
The Second War Powers Act provided that willful violations
of ration orders might be punished by imprisonment up to one
year or a fine of not more than $10,000, or both for each
violation.

Contrary to popular thinking, however, the use of a
criminal sanction is not essential for a black market violation of
law to be considered sociologically as a "crime." Viewed from
a sociological approach, although not strictly in terms of the
legal definition, such violations of the law should be included
as part of the subject matter of criminology. Violations of the
law committed primarily by groups such as businessmen, professional men, and politicians in connection with their occu-
pations, although often not strictly designated or treated as
such in the judicial process, have come to be referred to as
"white collar crime."[2] Sutherland has aptly depicted this new

[2] Edwin H. Sutherland, *White Collar Crime* (New York: The Dryden
Press, 1949); his "White Collar Criminality," *American Sociological Review*,
V, No. 1 (February, 1940), 1–12; "Is 'White Collar Crime' Crime?" *American
Sociological Review*, X, No. 2 (April, 1945), 132–140; and his "Crime and
Business," *Annals of the American Academy of Political and Social Science*,
CCXVII (September, 1941), 112–118; Marshall B. Clinard, "Criminological
Theories of Violations of Wartime Regulations," *American Sociological Review*,
XI, No. 3 (June, 1946), 258–270. Also see Hartung, "A Study in Law and
Social Differentiation: As Exemplified in Violations of the Emergency Price
Control Act of 1942 and the Second War Powers Act in the Detroit Whole-
sale Meat Industry," cited above. Marshall B. Clinard, "Sociologists and American
Criminology," *Journal of Criminal Law and Criminology*, XLI, No. 5 (January–
February, 1941), 549–577; and Donald R. Cressey, "Criminological Research and
the Definition of Crimes," *American Journal of Sociology*, XVI, No. 6 (May,
1951), 546–552. In the fields of criminology and law there are persons who
would object to this formulation of the nature of crime so as to include most

emerging emphasis on white collar crime, and has indicated how
violations of law by such groups is dealt with by society through
measures other than the criminal law.

White-collar crime is real crime. It is not ordinarily called
crime, and calling it by this name does not make it worse, just as
refraining from calling it crime does not make it better than it
otherwise would be. It is called crime here in order to bring it
within the scope of criminology, which is justified because it is in
violation of the criminal law. The crucial question in this analysis
is the criterion of violation of the criminal law. Conviction in the
criminal court, which is sometimes suggested as the criterion, is
not adequate because a large proportion of those who commit
crimes are not convicted in criminal courts. This criterion, therefore, needs to be supplemented. When it is supplemented, the
criterion of the crimes of one class must be kept consistent in

---

black market offenses since it does not follow either the conventional or the
common legal views. Tappan, for example, has advanced several criticisms of
such an approach, pointing out that the penal treatment prescribed in the
criminal law is a customary method in our culture, affecting our conception
of crime, and influencing the criminal in his conception of himself, because
crime carries public stigma in its association with a fine, imprisonment, or
probation. According to this argument the inclusion of civil damages, injunctions, and administrative actions results in complete confusion in the nature of
both criminal law and crime. The legal determination of a crime, moreover,
follows careful procedural methods, including the statement of specific acts as
crimes: actual or implied intent must be established, unless the statute excludes
it; guilt is established, except where jury trial is waived, by a unanimous
verdict of a jury; and, finally, there is protection against double jeopardy.
Burgess has similarly objected to the inclusion of white collar crime, including
black market violations in the field of criminology although his argument,
contrary to Tappan's, is based on the fact that the considerations are sociological
rather than legalistic. He maintains that black market offenses cannot be
considered crimes since such white collar violators do not conceive of themselves
as criminals, nor does the public express strong public disapproval. The objec-
tions raised by Tappan and Burgess are contradictory, as Hartung has pointed
out, Tappan believing that white collar crime is not legalistic, while Burgess
feels that it is not sociological.—Paul Tappan, "Crime and the Criminal,"
Federal Probation, XI, No. 3 (July–September, 1947) , 44. See also his "Who Is
the Criminal?" *American Sociological Review*, XII, No. 1 (February, 1947) ,
96–103. Also Ernest W. Burgess, in his Comments on Frank E. Hartung, "White-
Collar Offenses in the Wholesale Meat Industry in Detroit," *American Journal of
Sociology*, LVI, No. 1 (July, 1950) , 32–33.

general terms with the criterion of the crimes of the other class. The definition should not be the spirit of the law for white-collar crimes and the letter of the law for other crimes, or in other respects be more liberal for one class than for the other.[3]

Unless a broader interpretation of "crime" is used, it is impossible to deal analytically with diverse illegal activities which are punished in different ways according to one's occupation and social class.[4] This becomes more apparent when one considers that an apprehended burglar or robber is always punished by a jail sentence, a fine, or probation, whereas a doctor may be punished by having his license revoked, a lawyer by being disbarred, or a businessman by being enjoined by the government, being required to pay civil damages, having his license to do business suspended or, in some cases, as in impure foods, having his product seized and destroyed. All of these sanctions imply that such behavior is socially injurious, that punishment is involved, and that society is stigmatizing the offender. All illegal activity should be studied, regardless of the legal·categories, if we are to derive any meaningful generalizations about the nature of criminal or illegal behavior.[5]

---

[3] Sutherland, "White Collar Criminality," *loc. cit.,* pp. 5–6.

[4] Many people look upon crime as though it is something distinct and unique, rather undefined and regarded as abhorrent, with little recognition of its essential nature. Actually any crime, whatever its nature, is a type of human behavior which represents violations of certain conduct norms, value systems, which have been designated by society as legal conduct norms. Any violation of these legal conduct norms can be followed by the imposition of formal punishment of a variety of types. See Thorsten Sellin, *Culture Conflict and Crime* (New York: Social Science Research Council, 1938).

[5] This sociological conception of crime does not, however, include, as crime, behavior which is solely antisocial, injurious to society, unfair, greedy, but not necessarily illegal. For example, for a period after the termination of price control a widespread practice existed in the United States of reselling new cars as used cars. In most cases, as under price control, the price was far in excess of the list price and consequently sales of this type became known as the "used-car racket." Unethical as this practice might seem, it was not illegal and was not

There are a number of reasons for this difference in the sanctions applied for burglaries, for example, in comparison with the sanctions used for various white collar violations such as most of the black market. In the first place, many socially harmful activities committed by business were not made illegal until comparatively recent times. In fact, embezzlement and various forms of fraud, as compared with burglary and robbery, did not legally become crimes until the latter part of the eighteenth century.[6] As late as the period from 1887 to 1936, behavior such as the following was outlawed in this country: restraint of trade, misuse of trademarks, false advertising, impure foods and drugs, insolvency of banks by fraud or negligence of officials, sale of fraudulent securities, improper conduct of labor relations, and many other similar activities. Part of the reason for this tardiness was the fact that the general social, political, and economic philosophy of laissez faire and the belief in *caveat emptor* ("let the buyer beware") interfered with the development of needed legal prohibitions regardless of occupation or social class.

Second, it has frequently been difficult to get laws passed defining entirely as crimes certain socially injurious practices, such as price and rationing violations by businessmen, because of the public's unorganized resentment against such practices. Violations of law by businessmen are more often punished by

white collar crime. As another example, congressional investigators, at the end of 1947, revealed a great deal of speculation by traders in wheat, much of which was destined for European relief. This behavior was condemned by many, including the President, but such speculation was not illegal, except for employees of the Commodity Credit Corporation, and, therefore, not criminal. Thus, for it to be within the province of "white collar crime" there must be a law outlawing certain behavior.

[6] See Jerome Hall, *Theft, Law and Society* (Boston: Little, Brown & Company, 1935). The following sentence is from Livingston Hall, "The Substantive Law of Crimes, 1887–1936," *Harvard Law Review*, (February, 1937), 61–63.

civil and administrative sanctions than by fine or imprisonment. This difference in treatment arises, in part, from the fact that society does not sufficiently recognize the extent and consequences of business violations to warrant making nearly all the behavior criminal. Even in cases where the behavior is recognized as being serious enough to be punished by criminal action, the issue is frequently the enforceability of a criminal action rather than its appropriateness. There are several reasons for this apparent indifference on the part of the public. Business violations such as the black market are usually complex and their effect is diffused over a long period of time, whereas ordinary crime is overt and generally simple, the effects are easier for the public to visualize, and the perpetrators of the crime are easily discerned. Moreover, the extreme complexity of many violations of price and rationing regulations enabled some to conceal the essential criminality of their violations.[7] And finally, white collar crime like the black market usually does not receive the same publicity, particularly in the press, that ordinary crimes do and, therefore, does not arouse the same degree of organized resentment in the public. These difficulties inherent in dealing with illegal business activities as violations specifically of the criminal law have been well summarized by Mannheim.

First, the anti-social character of many human activities, as, for instance, of certain business transactions or methods of business organization, such as attempts to monopolize a branch of trade, may for a long while remain hidden from the eyes of the legislator and the public. Secondly, different social classes within the community may hold opposite views about the merits or otherwise of this or that form of human activity, whether it may be betting and

---

[7] See Sutherland, *White Collar Crime*, pp. 50–51.

gambling, or some aspects of the stock exchange business, or strikes, sleeping out, and dozens of others. Since, in a democracy, the efficient administration of criminal justice has to depend on the widest possible backing of the community at large, any such divergence of opinion will make the lawgiver reluctant to resort to penal methods. A third point: Even where universal agreement does exist as to the anti-social character of certain forces of behaviour, they may be regarded as unsuitable objects of the criminal law, either because penalizing them would mean interfering too much with the private lives of individuals, or because it would be technically too difficult.[8]

Third, legislation directed against the antisocial behavior of businessmen has been characterized by a tendency to pass more lenient laws and to enforce such laws in a differential manner according to the social status of the offender.[9] By not including a criminal sanction in certain laws, legislators have not only tended to avoid antagonizing businessmen, but have frequently allowed the fact that they are often of the same social group to influence the employment of the criminal sanctions where alternative punishments are available. There are, in addition, obvious legal difficulties in bringing a criminal action against a corporation, since all that may possibly be achieved, after a long-drawn-out suit with many technical difficulties, is a moderate fine for the corporation or a short jail sentence for an officer of the company. There is no indication, however, that the technical difficulties presented by black market cases were any greater than those for legal actions such as antitrust suits, tax cases, and others.

---

[8] Hermann Mannheim, *Criminal Justice and Social Reconstruction* (New York: Oxford University Press, 1946), pp. 5–6.

[9] See Richard C. Fuller, "Morals and the Criminal Law." *Journal of Criminal Law and Criminology*, XXXII (March–April, 1942), 624–630. Also see George Rusche and Otto Kirchheimer, *Punishment and Social Structure* (New York: Columbia University Press, 1939).

The black market is a good example of white collar crime,[10] for nearly all violations of OPA regulations actually constituted criminal acts from a sociological point of view.[11] Not only did Congress label such acts as socially injurious; these acts were punishable by the state. Violations commonly known as the black market were stated by Congress to be socially injurious, constituting a serious threat to our national security. If prices were allowed to become completely uncontrolled there might well be inadequate production of war commodities and facilities, profiteering from abnormal wartime market conditions, dissipation of defense appropriations by excessive prices, undue impairment of the standard of living of persons on fixed incomes, and a possible postwar collapse of economic values.

The general sanctions policy of the government in regard to black market cases clearly stated, with certain minor exceptions: "No case which discloses a violation shall be closed without the application of a formal sanction, e.g., criminal, license suspension, contempt, treble damage (suit or settlement), injunction or administrative suspension."[12] Thus there

---

[10] Such aspects of the black market as counterfeiting and theft of ration currency represented more closely the conventional type of criminality.

[11] Tappan disagrees with this conclusion and has stated with reference to black market violations: "The problem of definition becomes even more complicated when a given type of transgression is prohibited by civil as well as criminal statute and may be tried by a civil or equity court or even by an administrative agency with civil remedies ensuing. Consider, for example, an OPA violation which might be either a civil wrong adjudicated by an administrative agency or, if intentionally committed, could be prosecuted as a misdemeanor in a criminal court. Several questions may be raised about this situation to point up the difficulty of definition: (1) If there is mere accusation of a violation, has a crime been committed? (2) If a person be found guilty of unintentional violation by a board or by a civil court, has a crime been committed? Is the adjudicated defendant a criminal? (3) What if there is mere accusation, but of an intentional violation? (4) If a board, agency, or civil court make a finding that the accused had committed an intentional violation, would its finding constitute a conviction of a crime? Would its decision make the offender a criminal? (5) If found guilty of intentional violation by a criminal court, is the defendant a criminal?"—Tappan, "Crime and the Criminal," *loc. cit.*, pp. 42–43.

[12] *OPA Manual, Enforcement Operating Procedures,* Office of Price Ad-

was considerable variety in the sanctions available for controlling the black market, and there is no evidence that violations to which the criminal sanction was applied could, on the
whole, be clearly distinguished either in seriousness or in willfulness from those dealt with by civil and administrative sanctions. The facts seem to support the position that the government, for a variety of reasons to be discussed later, could
employ the criminal sanction in only a relatively small number
of selected cases and relied instead on alternative sanctions.

There was no uniformity in the sanctions applied in black
market cases. In thousands of cases involving almost identical
violations, administrative measures were sometimes used, and
at other times civil, and occasionally criminal, prosecution.
Cases involving evasive violations where there was definite
willfulness, such as falsification of records and inventories in
rationing cases, were sometimes handled with an injunction
suit or a suspension order proceeding, and at other times with
criminal prosecution. A detailed analysis of 122 black market
cases in the Detroit wholesale meat industry, which were dealt
with by criminal, civil, or administrative action, failed to show
any criteria by which one could distinguish the relative seriousness of offenses by the type of sanction. An examination of the
factual material about the offense showed that both civil and
administrative actions were used in cases involving definite
criminal behavior.[13] In an intensive survey persons were given
abstracts of black market cases where criminal or civil actions
had been imposed. The public tended to disapprove equally of

---

ministration (Multilithed) , Sec. 9–1501.02A. The exceptions were cases where
the violation was clearly trivial and inconsequential, no formal sanction was available under the law, the investigation had not been substantially completed, or an
enforcement exception was granted by the Deputy Administrator for Enforcement.

[13] Hartung, "White Collar Offenses in the Wholesale Meat Industry in
Detroit," loc. cit., p. 32.

both types of cases.[14] Another survey found that many businessmen felt that "fines" included not only monetary payments
imposed through criminal prosecutions, but also any other sums
collected by the OPA as settlements or as a result of civil judgments. In a 1945 survey of several hundred food wholesalers it
was found that 88 per cent of them could not distinguish between actual criminal fines and civil treble damage actions,
using the same term to apply to both.[15]

In considering nearly all black market violations as
"crimes" the question of criminal intent has often been raised.
The evasive nature of most black market and other white collar
violations indicates an awareness of the illegal nature of the
activities and repudiates the contention that most violations
were unwitting. While there is no question that most persons
who commit such white collar crimes do not wish to have their
actions designated as willfully "criminal," they generally regard
themselves as "offenders" against the law, and the issue consequently becomes merely a matter of labels rather than of
differences in the nature of the violation. Actually this element
does not need to be established in many criminal court prosecutions even at the present time, and statutes are increasingly
being enacted which do not incorporate this element of intent.
In many states persons may now be convicted of a criminal
charge for many crimes, such as adultery, bigamy, statutory
rape, selling mortgaged property illegally, and passing bad
checks without criminal intent being established.[16]

The question of proven willfulness, then, was not essential
in order to judge violations of price and rationing regulations
as crimes, although it might be well to point out the extent to

---

14 Hartung, "A Study in Law and Social Differentiation," p. 330.
15 "Opinion Survey of Food Wholesalers," cited above.
16 Livingston Hall, *op. cit.* Also Sutherland, *White Collar Crime,* p. 49.

which violations were probably intentional. Estimates by a group of food wholesalers in 1945, for example, showed that a third of them believed that most violations were deliberate. More specifically, 10 per cent felt that everyone violated deliberately, 14 per cent estimated over three fourths, and another 11 per cent felt that more than half of all violations were deliberate. Perhaps an even more empiric index of the willfulness of black market violations was the extent of evasive violations such as falsification of records in connection with side payments. When a violation was evasive there could be no doubt that it was intentional and that the person was familiar with the provisions of the regulation and the nature of the investigations, at least familiar enough to try to conceal his evasion. Of the group of food wholesalers interviewed in 1945 more than one out of five thought evasive violations were frequent.[17] Moreover, 57 per cent of the wholesalers interviewed in this survey stated that enforcement efforts were effective in securing compliance, indicating an awareness that many of their actions were intentional violations of the law. Even when violations of government regulations were intentional, many businessmen, while they may have regarded themselves as violators, often did not believe they had committed crimes, and therefore could not possibly be treated as criminals. Although this attitude was not unanimous among businessmen, it was general enough to make it obvious that among many business groups the mores were not involved in the black market. Such laws were largely *mala prohibita,* that is they were laws enacted without necessarily having full support of the persons concerned. The force of public opinion had not been sufficiently

---

[17] "Opinion Survey of Food Wholesalers."

developed to make them *mala in se* or laws which are not merely statutory enactments but actually regulate behavior which is bad in itself.

Actually there was more to it than this, for many black market violations were various types of fraud inasmuch as they constituted devices for obtaining money fraudulently by misrepresentation. Certainly fraud existed in the many cases, both at the consumer and retail levels, where goods were delivered to an unsuspecting person at prices above ceiling, or, in the course of business, the quality or quantity was not the same as invoiced. Although most cases were not legally fraudulent, in that the buyer usually knew he was paying an illegal price and was not actually being defrauded, there were many cases where if lack of good faith in the contract action could have been shown there might have been the right of recovery under existing state and federal laws even if the OPA statute had not been in existence. Many black market cases at the wholesale and manufacturing level also resembled extortion insofar as the retail purchaser was, or believed himself to be, unable to prevent the illegal transaction.[18] Moreover, as will be indicated in the following chapter, most violations of the price and rationing regulations were also violations of other laws where a criminal sanction was also provided.

During the five years of price control, 259,966 sanctions were instituted, of which only 13,999 cases involved criminal prosecution. (See Table 1.) The remainder consisted of 67,919 consumer's treble damages and 40,763 administrator's settlements or suits, or a total of 42 per cent; 52,297 suspension orders, or 20 per cent; 78,081 injunction suits, or 30 per cent;

---

18 Hartung, "A Study in Law and Social Differentiation," p. 98.

and 6,907 miscellaneous sanctions. In order to point out more clearly the punitive nature of each of these sanctions, as well as the nature of the problems involved in their use, each type will be discussed separately.

The Criminal Sanction

Criminal proceedings actually constituted lesst han 6 per cent of all OPA cases where sanction actions were started. Experience showed that it was impossible to use the criminal sanction in all cases where it could be used, as the following important factors had to be considered: (1) Criminal cases required much preparation, and both the Justice Department, which prosecuted such cases for the OPA, and the federal courts could not handle large numbers of cases. If the tens of thousands of potential criminal cases had been sent to the courts, the flood would have bogged down the Justice Department, to which criminal cases were referred for prosecution, the courts, and the OPA. As it was, even with careful selection of cases, the three thousand average OPA criminal cases annually constituted about a tenth of all criminal cases before the federal courts during the war years, a figure far greater than that of any other government agency. The federal government does not have the mass criminal procedures available to Canada and Great Britain, which are similar to a trial before a United States commissioner. In this country every federal case must be taken before one of the 190 federal judges in the ninety-three federal judicial districts. (2) Important also was the fact that the federal courts were generally several months behind in their civil and criminal cases, and this time lag was particularly serious in any attempt to control urgent wartime violations. (3) All criminal cases had to meet with the approval of the United States attorneys in each judicial district who had to institute prosecution.[19] Actually this approval was often either not granted or given reluctantly, thus necessitating the use of other sanctions. Moreover, the United States attorneys were often unfamiliar with OPA regulations and had little sympathy for the agency or its purposes, although they dealt with other business violations such as tax laws.

As a result of this careful selection, of the cases turned over to the Department of Justice for prosecution, convictions were secured in over 93 per cent. Of the 12,415 completed criminal cases from 1942 to 1947, only 815, or 6.5 per cent, were lost by the government. After conviction, however, extremely mild sentences were generally imposed on this selected group of offenders, which included some businessmen as well as criminals guilty of theft and counterfeiting of ration currency. For example, during the five-year period, of 11,600 persons convicted and sentenced, only 2,970, or 25.6 per cent, received imprisonment with or without a fine (Table 2). The remainder, or 74.4 per cent, were not severely penalized, 5,312 being fined and 3,318 placed on probation or given a suspended sentence. During 1944, of 3,486 persons convicted of violating price and rationing regulations, only 27 per cent received imprisonment or imprisonment and fine. Of the total convicted, 46 per cent received only a fine, and 28 per cent were placed on probation. The records of the Federal Bureau of Prisons show that between 1942 and 1949 only 558 persons were received for price violations and 48 for rent, all of whom would probably fall in the "white collar" class. (See Table

---

[19] "Whenever the Administrator has reason to believe that any person is liable to punishment under this [criminal] sub-section, he may certify the facts to the Attorney General, who may, in his discretion, cause appropriate proceedings to be brought."—*Emergency Price Control Act of 1942 and Stabilization Act of 1942 as Amended by Stabilization Extension Act of 1944*, Section 205 (b) , Office of Price Administration, July 1, 1944, p. 16.

20.) Of 132 Detroit wholesale black market meat violators, only 41 defendants were criminally convicted, only 15 of them receiving imprisonment alone or with a fine.[20] On one occasion the OPA general counsel, in testifying before the House Committee on Banking and Currency, stated that one of the practical difficulties in dealing with the meat black market was that there had not been anything like the extent of convictions "one would think desirable." He pointed out that a surprisingly large proportion of the cases of criminal conviction resulted in a fine which was often less than the proven amount of the illegal profits.[21]

Of 1,836 persons sent to federal prisons during the four year period 1944–1947 for all black market activities, 55.4 per cent received a sentence of six months or less. (See Table 21.) Only 328 persons, primarily businessmen, were sentenced to federal prisons for price violations during this period, and 211 of them, or 64.2 per cent, received a sentence of six months or less. Many received sentences of only a month or so. If we include those persons with short-term sentences of less than one year who were sent to nonfederal institutions (Table 20), the percentage serving minor sentences would be 71.0 for all violations, and 76.5 for price violations. During the year 1944 the heaviest jail sentences, with or without fines, imposed on slaughterers, packers, and wholesalers participating in the meat black market were as follows: one received a sentence of one year and a day, one received six months, two got three to six months, and two received sentences of three months or less. In most cases of more severe sentences there were additional

---

[20] Hartung, "White-Collar Offenses in the Wholesale Meat Industry in Detroit," *loc. cit.,* p. 213.

[21] *Hearings before the House Committee on Banking and Currency,* on Senate Resolution 502, Seventy-ninth Congress, First Session, p. 85.

Table 20

Federal Prisoners Received from the Courts for Violation of OPA Regulations, by Type of Violation and Class of Institution, 1942–1949

VIOLATION	TOTAL	1942	1943	1944	1945	1946	1947	1948	1949
ALL FEDERAL COMMITMENTS									
Total..........	3,189	2	199	805	1,250	540	235	125	33
Rationing:									
Gasoline......	{2,448}	..	107	514	819	{396	103	83	..
Other........		2	69	152	203				
Price control....	558	..	23	139	168	111	80	28	9
Rent control....	48	..	..	..	7	10	12	2	17
Other..........	135	..	..	..	53	23	40	12	7
TO FEDERAL INSTITUTIONS									
Total..........	2,081	2	121	470	819	379	168	93	29
Rationing:									
Gasoline......	{1,578}	..	78	322	543	{287	78	63	..
Other........		2	27	68	110				
Price control....	375	..	16	80	120	77	51	22	9
Rent control....	36	..	..	..	2	6	11	2	15
Other..........	92	..	..	..	44	9	28	6	5
TO NONFEDERAL INSTITUTIONS									
Total..........	1,108	..	78	335	431	161	67	32	4
Rationing:									
Gasoline......	{870}	..	29	192	276	{109	25	20	..
Other........		..	42	84	93				
Price control....	183	..	7	59	48	34	29	6	..
Rent control....	12	..	..	..	5	4	1	..	2
Other..........	43	..	..	..	9	14	12	6	2

SOURCE: Data furnished by United States Bureau of Prisons, Department of Justice, fiscal years ending June 30.

Table 21

OPA Violators Received from the Courts into Federal Institutions, by Type of Violation and Length of Sentence, 1944–1947

SENTENCE	TOTAL		PRICE CONTROL		RATIONING		OTHER OPA	
	NUM-BER	PER-CENTAGE	NUM-BER	PER-CENTAGE	NUM-BER	PER-CENTAGE	NUM-BER	PER-CENTAGE
Total	1,836	100.0	328	100.0	1,408	100.0	100	100.0
Less than 1 month. . .	33	1.8	26	7.9	7	0.5		
1 month. . .	138	7.6	44	13.4	89	6.3	5	5.0
2 months. . .	104	5.7	30	9.1	66	4.7	8	8.0
3 months. . .	176	9.6	28	8.5	134	9.5	14	14.0
4 months. . .	126	6.9	22	6.7	93	6.6	11	11.0
5 months. . .	14	0.7			12	0.9	2	2.0
6 months. . .	425	23.1	61	18.6	346	24.6	18	18.0
7–11 months	155	8.4	17	5.2	128	9.1	10	10.0
1–2 years. . .	477	26.0	70	21.3	386	27.4	21	21.0
2–3 years. . .	118	6.4	23	7.0	86	6.1	9	9.0
3–4 years. . .	44	2.4	5	1.6	39	2.8		
4–5 years. . .	3	0.1			3	0.2		
5 years or more. . . .	23	1.3	2	0.6	19	1.3	2	2.0

SOURCE: Data furnished by the Federal Bureau of Prisons, United States Department of Justice, for fiscal years ending June 30. This table covers the period from 1944–1947, while Table 20 is from 1942–1949.

factors involving moral judgments other than black market activity, such as selling contaminated meat.[22]

While one reason for these light sentences, which were almost trivial compared with the sentences given offenders who

---

[22] For example, a midwestern meat dealer was sentenced to two years and fined $500. He sold meat without obtaining ration points, purchased ungraded beef, and failed to prepare a base period statement of ceiling prices. Added to these violations, however, was the fact that the meat was butchered under unsanitary conditions. Some of the meat was partially spoiled and in one case came from an animal which had died of a disease. As a consequence of these violations his case received a lot of unfavorable publicity.

violate ordinary criminal laws pertaining to property offenses, was the lenient attitude of the court toward these offenses, another reason was the fact that most of the business offenders seldom had a criminal record. As the judges on occasion re-marked from the bench, they "would not make criminals of 'reputable' business men." Although this method of dealing lightly with the majority of violators who had no previous record may be in line with advanced criminological theory, it does raise certain basic questions about the role of the crim-inal law in a democracy. Actually the injury to society was far greater in many of these black market crimes, which often involved as much as several hundred thousand dollars or even several million, and the example of disobedience of law was far more flagrant than in the case of most ordinary robberies, burglaries, or larcenies. Moreover, as Hartung has pointed out, black market violations involved a feature which was not found in most criminal offenses but was of particular significance to the general public. By their very nature many violations in-volved "not merely one offense [by one individual or concern in the conduct of its business affairs] but began a progressive chain of offenses which did not stop until the ultimate con-sumer paid the financial amount involved in the offenses of the given chain."[23]

Another question raised by the imposition of these light sentences was the effect it generally had upon compliance. Actually the penalty of imprisonment, even for a short period

---

[23] Hartung, "White-Collar Offenses in the Wholesale Meat Industry in Detroit," *loc. cit.*, p. 30. It is interesting to note that by the end of June, 1945, 5,516 conscientious objectors had been sentenced to prison for terms of from one month to five years (with an average sentence of two and a half years), while four were only fined and 218 were placed on probation. See Lowell Edwin Maechtle, "A Socio-Psychological Study of the Adjustment Problems of Con-scientious Objectors in Civilian Public Service Camps during World War II," Ph.D. Dissertation, University of Wisconsin, 1952, p. 38.

of time, was the punishment most feared by businessmen, according to their own statements; yet it was seldom invoked as a deterrent for others. A survey of wholesale food dealers' opinions, for example, revealed that they considered imprisonment a far more effective penalty than any other government action, including fines.[24] In fact, some 65 per cent of them made such a statement. They made remarks such as the following about jail sentences: "Jail is the only way; nobody wants to go to jail." "Everybody gets panicky at the thought of a jail sentence." "A jail sentence is dishonorable; it jeopardizes the reputation." "It [jail] spoils the offender's reputation and frightens the other fellow." "The thing that puts a man to shame—closing his store and sending him to jail." These expressions are in marked contrast to the attitudes of the same men toward the imposition of fines and other monetary penalties: "They don't hurt anybody." "They're never missed." "People are making enough money nowadays to pay a fine easily." "The violators violate again, so they must not care about paying a fine." "It just comes out of the profits, like a tax." "They make so much in the black market they can afford to pay steep fines."

District enforcement attorneys of the OPA also felt the lack of this element of deterrence for, according to one survey, they reported that where sentences were generally adequate, observance of regulations was best, and that a converse situation existed where sentences were inadequate.[25] As an example, one concern was found guilty of handling over 300,000 pounds of meat in five months, with over-ceiling side payments of from 7 to 11 cents a pound. The convicted defendants were fined only $250 on each of six counts, and given a suspended sen-

---

[24] "Opinion Survey of Food Wholesalers."
[25] Unpublished survey by the OPA Enforcement Department.

tence of thirty days, to run concurrently on each of the six counts. As a result of this case the OPA district enforcement attorney reported that subsequent efforts of investigators to enforce the regulations were laughed at by businessmen. On the other hand, in one midwestern city two automobile dealers were fined $5,000 apiece, and in addition one was sent to a federal penitentiary for fifteen months, for selling used cars above ceiling. After this sentence numerous automobile dealers commented that they were not going to take any chances of facing a sentence such as that imposed on these violators, and better compliance resulted.

There were several other factors in the limited use of the criminal sanction and the lenient sentences imposed on black market business offenders. Many OPA enforcement attorneys were reluctant to ask for the criminal sanction because this might mean the loss of potential clients when the war was over. Price and rationing controls were temporary measures, and the attorneys were often afraid that criminal penalties would not only mean the possible loss of business from their clients but also from the entire social group from which the offenders came. Likewise, many of the federal and state judges, while not ordinarily faced with the loss of future clients, were much influenced by the opinion of businessmen within whose social strata they ordinarily move.

From the beginning of the agency until the end there was trepidation about using the strong enforcement measure of criminal prosecution against white collar black market offenders, a situation which at times seriously endangered the entire future of the government program. The failure to secure general support for the use of the criminal sanction from many persons in high governmental places had serious consequences, for no legislative enactments or administrative rules which prescribe certain behavior requirements of persons under the jurisdiction of a regulation have any value unless these rules and regulations are enforced. Perhaps, as Fuller has suggested,[26] strong enforcement of such laws and education as to their purpose will bring about greater consensus in society that crimes committed in commercial transactions are more serious than ordinary burglaries and robberies.

Injunctions

Because of these many difficulties it is no wonder that the government used alternative sanctions for cases which were equally criminal in the legal sense. The sanction most widely used to control price violations was the statutory injunction, a civil proceeding whereby the court ordered that certain illegal behavior be stopped, or forced compliance with certain provisions of the regulations. In the event a person failed to obey the injunction he could be held in contempt of court and if found guilty could be either fined, imprisoned, or both. Since an injunction was rather easily obtained, it was a particularly useful means of stopping violations where delay might lead to the continuance of such violation. Several courts, however, objected to the use of injunctions to hide more willful violations which might be punished more rightfully by other measures. In fact, in cases of substantive violations, it was later found necessary to couple the injunction with a treble damage suit, which will be discussed shortly, in order to recover damages for past violations. An injunction without a treble damage action to recover the amount of an overcharge might be compared to serving a hypothetical injunction on a bank robber as he comes out of a bank with his loot, preventing him

---

[26] Fuller, *op. cit.*

from further robbery but allowing him to retain the stolen money. In spite of the fact that all an injunction did was to require the defendant to comply with the law, business concerns frequently resisted the OPA's application for an injunction. Perhaps an injunction carried with it more stigma than is customarily attached to such an order.[27] Another significant factor in this opposition was the fear of possible contempt proceedings, for if a firm continued to violate the regulation it could be cited for contempt of court.

The Office of Price Administration filed 78,081 complaints for an injunction in connection with the enforcement of price regulations. Temporary injunctions were secured in 2,970 cases, and permanent injunctions in 48,899 cases. In only 1,606 cases, or 2 per cent, were injunctions denied by the courts. This was probably the greatest mass use of this sanction in a similar period in the federal government's history. In a typical year the Securities and Exchange Commission, the Federal Trade Commission, and the Food and Drug Administration together filed less than 150 injunction suits. In fact, on the average the OPA filed 50 per cent of all complaints for injunction in the federal courts during the war.[28]

The injunctive remedy was particularly useful in forcing the maintenance of records which were indispensable for the enforcement of the price regulations, particularly where hidden side payments or quality deterioration might be involved. However, the complexity of the OPA regulations and the burden placed upon some business concerns in order to comply

---

[27] See Sutherland, "Is 'White Collar Crime' Crime?" loc. cit., pp. 132–140, for the view that an injunction involves stigma and is punishment.

[28] Annual Report of the Director of the Administrative Office of the United States Courts. Report of the Judicial Conference of Senior Circuit Judges held at Washington, D. C., September 25–28, 1945 (Washington: Government Printing Office, 1945).

with them, often involving record keeping on several thousand items, soon brought up the question of the courts' discretion in granting or withholding an injunction where violations were shown to exist.[29] This situation was eventually clarified in the Hecht case[30] in which The Hecht Company, one of the largest department stores in Washington, D.C., was charged with failure to keep proper records on several thousand items of merchandise. The company agreed that this was true, but asserted that it maintained a large staff to comply with the regulations, that when informed of the violations it took immediate steps to correct them, and that it established controls to prevent their recurrence. The Supreme Court, taking the case on certiorari, handed down a decision essentially in favor of The Hecht Company, but added some qualifications which, in the long run, materially benefited OPA's effective use of the injunction. In his opinion, Justice Douglas stated that the court might have issued an order "retaining the case on the docket with the right of the Administrator, on notice, to renew his application for injunctive relief if violations recurred." The Supreme Court warned that the courts should generally grant injunctions and that the power of the court "must be exercised in light of the large objectives of the Act. For the standards of the public interest, not the requirements of private litigation, measure the propriety and need for injunctive relief in these cases."

Several factors were considered by the courts in granting injunctions. The existence of a prior record of violation was regarded as an important feature favorable to the government

[29] Portions of the material on legal issues were derived from Roach, *op. cit.* See also Jerome Count, "Enforcement Aspects of Price and Rent Control," *Administrative Law Service,* May, 1945.

[30] The Hecht Company v. Bowles, 321 U.S. 321. U.S. Supreme Court, February 28, 1944.

in a complaint for an injunction. Still another factor of importance in granting an injunction was evidence that the defendant knew the provisions of the regulations. Some judges, for example, were interested in learning if the business concern had any prior conferences with OPA personnel, whether it had been previously warned to cease violating, or whether at any time the concern had agreed to stop violating. Where there were such evasive violations as improper records which prevented the government from obtaining knowledge of the proper prices charged, the true quantity sold, the overcharges, or any other subterfuge, an injunction was generally granted. On the other hand, an injunction might be denied if the defendant had made every attempt within reason to comply, such as making frequent applications to the OPA for interpretations of proper pricing, demonstrations of the ambiguities in the regulations, requests to have the OPA determine the proper price, or a generally favorable attitude toward price control. Business concerns sometimes attempted to create the impression of good faith by introducing evidence that the manager, salesman, or other employees had been ordered to comply with the government regulations. Such instructions were disregarded where the OPA had taken enforcement action against the company in other jurisdictions, where violations had been called to the defendant's attention by the price panels or the district office, or where no disciplinary action had been taken by the business concern in the case of violations. The defense could not be offered that the regulation was difficult or that it worked a hardship, since this would constitute an attack upon the validity of the regulation, a matter which was exclusively within the jurisdiction of the Emergency Court of Appeals.[31]

---

[31] Provisions were included in the act for the protection of private rights through a protest of the regulation which had to be acted upon by the OPA

Where it appeared that there was only a single violation the court often denied an injunction, but where it looked as though there had been many an injunction was usually granted. The government frequently sought a blanket injunction on all regulations[32] when a business concern had violated one regulation. In genèral, the courts denied such injunctions, but in one case in 1944 a company was enjoined from any further violation of price regulations issued by the OPA. In this case the judge held that the defendant had been previously ordered to desist from violating other regulations, and that the previous record of the concern's compliance showed that it was guilty of several different types of violations. In one case the circuit court stated that "one who commits one series of acts will be likely to commit another of like character," and found, moreover, that there was a "close relationship and similarity between the acts committed and the acts sought to be restrained."[33]

Sometimes, although not generally, the courts refused to grant injunctions which were broader than the violations discovered. Thus in a case where a concern failed to keep a base period statement of shoe sales the judge refused in addition to enjoin the defendant from selling shoes at over-ceiling prices or from otherwise violating the shoe regulation. In another

---

Administrator within thirty days. In the event that the protest was not satisfactory a person could appeal to the Emergency Court of Appeals which was created by the act and consisted of three judges appointed by the Chief Justice of the Supreme Court from federal, district and circuit courts. This court had exclusive jurisdiction, subject to final review of the Supreme Court, of the validity of OPA price and rent regulations.

[32] Injunctive action to prohibit price violations did not form the basis for an injunction prohibiting rationing violations. Most of the latter involved largely suspension orders, although there were some injunctions.

[33] Bowles v. May Hardwood Company, 140 F (2d) 914, CCA 6th, February 25, 1944. In a sense this was an extension of the rule in the famous case of the National Labor Relations Board v. Express Publishing Company, 312 U.S. 425, 435: "It is a salutory principle that when one has been found to have committed acts in violation of a law he may be restrained from committing other related unlawful acts."

case a concern had been charged with selling hosiery at prices in excess of the regulations, and the court limited the injunction to certain types of hosiery sold by the concern rather than all hosiery. In another case the court granted an injunction limited to chicken, lobster, and gin as against the OPA request for a blanket injunction covering all food items. This decision was upheld in the Court of Appeals.

One of the major drawbacks of this sanction, however, was the fact that few injunctions were followed up to determine the firm's compliance with the court order. In the five years, 1942–1946, for example, only 564 contempt proceedings were brought, which is fantastically low considering the total of 78,081 injunctions outstanding. As one enforcement official commented, "Rather than continue to spread the country with a mass of injunctions of the type which should be discouraged, there is now a sufficient framework of injunction decrees to support substantial contempt cases. A reasonable number of successful contempt cases will revive the significance of the existing injunction decrees."[34]

Treble Damage Actions

Originally the price control provided two kinds of treble damage suits, a civil action brought in court involving the recovery of three times the amount of damages suffered either by a consumer or, in other types of cases, by the people of the United States. All of these suits had to be brought within one year from the date of the violation. One type of treble damage suit was the so-called consumer suit, actually a purchaser other than in the course of trade or business. A consumer of this

---

[34] Weekly Enforcement Letter No. 1 to Regional Administrators and Regional Enforcement Executives from George Moncharsh, Deputy Administrator for Enforcement, Office of Price Administration, September 10, 1945, p. 4.

type could sue a retailer for any violation and recover, in addition to attorney's fees, damages as determined by the court at an amount not more than three times the amount of the overcharge or an amount not less than $25 or more than $50, whichever was greater. This suit was never as extensively used as had been contemplated in the original act, and when it was renewed in 1944 the Price Administrator was also given the right to sue in the name of the consumer for recovery of damages. All of these suits could be settled by mutual agreement between the OPA and the defendant. The other type of treble damage action could be brought by the administrator for violations arising in the course of trade or business, that is, by manufacturing or wholesale concerns, and provided for damages amounting to three times the amount of the overcharge. The payments in these cases went not to the OPA but to the United States Treasury.

If the overcharges by a manufacturing or wholesale business were particularly great there was no question that the treble action, if proven, could be a severe penalty. Actually it was usually a far heavier monetary penalty than the imposition of a fine, although it involved less stigma. Typical fines imposed by the court in OPA cases were rarely over a few hundred dollars, or at the most a few thousand, whereas many administrator's treble damage settlements or suits were considerably greater. One of the most severe fines ever levied by a court in a case involving OPA regulations was about $100,000, but there were several treble damage settlements involving sums in excess of $500,000. One company settled a treble damage claim for overcharges on sales of woolen cloth for $2,065,842. As pointed out, however, the element of greater stigma involved in criminal prosecution and subsequent fine might have been more effective than the monetary loss, particularly if the firm's reputation were important. In addition, there were cases where the United States district attorneys were reluctant to prosecute even to achieve a small fine; hence the use of a stiff treble damage action was more effective.

The penal nature of the treble damage action is indicated by the fact that no money paid to the United States Treasury as the result of a treble damage settlement or suit brought by the OPA could be deducted as a business expense under the internal revenue statutes. In the case of all treble damage suits, however, Congress differentiated between violations which were not willful and negligent and those which were. If the defendant could establish the former contention, only the single amount of the overcharge could be awarded.[35] The defendants were not very successful, however, in establishing this so-called "Chandler defense," since the courts refused to consider it if the OPA could show evidence of side payments, falsification of records, tie-in sales, or other violations which demonstrated willfulness. The courts took a similar interpretation in some cases where there was an absence of proper records, failure to instruct employees, and other similar violations.

One interesting problem which arose in connection with consumers' treble damage suits was whether the consumer had

[35] The President issued a statement on the problem which this feature presented to enforcement: "The provisions of the Extension Act which give me the most concern are those relating to enforcement. No act is any better than its enforcement. No act, least of all a price control act, can be effectively enforced without the support of the people affected by it. But people tend to become careless in the observance of even a good law if it is not enforced against the fringe of chiselers who will violate a law whenever they think they can get away with it. I know that the Congress in relaxing the penalties against nonwillful violations are anxious to protect only those acting in good faith and not those who do not wish to know what the law requires of them. But I fear that the changes made will weaken and obstruct the effective enforcement of the law. I hope that experience may not justify my fear. But if it should turn out that the enforcing officers encounter serious difficulties in bringing chiselers and black-market operators to book, I shall ask the Congress to remove the difficulties." (Statement on June 30, 1944.)

knowledge of the overcharge and whether there was a refund or attempted refund of the overcharge to the consumer. If a consumer was found to have made numerous purchases knowing them to be at over-ceiling prices, with the sole purpose of recovering the amount of the damages, the courts generally decided against him. A somewhat similar situation was the Administrator's suit for treble damages where a seller in the meantime made a refund for the commodity. In one New York case after a violation was discovered the purchaser returned certain cigarette lighters to the seller and received a credit refund. The seller claimed that the administrator had no right to bring a suit involving these lighters, but the court stated that "a thief who steals his employer's funds, and who returns them to the till, upon discovery of his theft, cannot thus wipe out his crime. Neither can this defendant and one of his black market purchasers, through a rescission of their unlawful contract, put at naught the rights of the Administrator."[36]

Although many cases were brought under these provisions—in all 28,125 administrator's treble damage settlements and 12,638 suits and 33,612 consumers' treble damage settlements and 26,094 suits—rarely did a case actually recover anything like the amount of the overcharges taking place in this country. Bowles estimated food overcharges alone as at least a billion dollars a year. Yet the total amount collected during the war through treble damage actions and fines was slightly over 73 million dollars. Considering the number of consumers in the United States and the number of purchases made in a single day, the figure of approximately 20,000 consumers' treble damage suits annually was obviously considerably less than one might have expected in view of the extent of violations.

---

[36] Bowles v. Leventhal, 61 F. Supp. 144, U.S. District Court, Southern District of New York, March, 1945.

License Suspension Suits (Price)

License suspension suits, involving the legal suspension of a concern's right to sell products for varying periods of time, were considered suitable for serious price cases and were used only after at least two violations had occurred over a period of time. Such a proceeding was based on the reasoning that the issuance of a regulation automatically "licensed" all persons covered by it.[37] Where the concern was doing a business of over $100,000 and engaged in interstate commerce, such cases could be taken into federal courts. Cases involving smaller concerns were tried before state courts. A formal license warning notice was issued after the first violation, and only if this were followed by another violation could this sanction be instituted. License suspension proceedings differed from other sanctions in that there was a presumption on the part of the court that a prior violation had occurred for which the defendant had already been warned. Thus the court had a record of the concern's violations.[38] This type of sanction was used in certain cases where criminal proceedings were warranted, for it was considered by some even more appropriate because of its greater effectiveness.[39]

Not only was there a previous violation in the license suspension suit; the legal instructions for its use implied that it was a punitive action. This punitive consideration ordinarily affected the length of the suspension. The government's policy

---

[37] Originally the idea had been actually to issue licenses, but this became too cumbersome a procedure.

[38] As one judge phrased it: "I have read quite carefully the complaint setting forth that when the first visit was made about four months before, they made a spot check, they did not attempt to cover all the items and they found in those instances which they did investigate, a large number, an apparently planned, deliberate attempt to charge a little more than the ceiling price."

[39] OPA Manual, Sec. 9–1803.02A.

was not to seek a suspension of business unless it would presumably be for more than one month, for if the suspension were for only a few days it might, rather than be a penalty, furnish a "vacation" to the business concern. Furthermore, the policy was not to seek a suspension if it should fall within the defendant's slack business period. The government attorneys usually asked for an order suspending the business concern from selling any commodity governed by the regulation under which the violation occurred, not from selling all commodities. The *OPA Manual* listed several factors which should be taken into consideration in "determining whether the punitive effect of a license suspension is disproportionate to the subject's offenses . . . (a) the effect of suspension upon the subject's business and economic status; (b) the flagrancy, nature and extent of the violations found, including the relation between the first and subsequent violations; (c) the degree of economic compulsion to violate; (d) the existence of willfulness or indifference to price regulations."[40]

Most courts held that the original violation, which had resulted in a license warning notice, and the subsequent violation involved in the license suspension suit need not have been of the same regulation or order, of the same type such as selling or posting, or even of the same line of the defendant's business. The belief was that an over-ceiling sale was not only a violation of the maximum-price regulation, but also a violation of a "license" to sell the commodities. Many business concerns raised the issue of whether the courts should review the violation involved in the license warning notice as part of the license suspension suit, which would have meant that if a business concern could establish that the original warning notice should actually not have been sent, the suit might be

---

[40] *Ibid.*, Sec. 9–1803.02B.

dismissed. The law was quite clear, however, that the government alone was responsible for determining whether the concern had violated its license.

It was the policy of the government to use injunctions in connection with most license suspension proceedings, the purpose being to implement the suspension order. Two types of injunctions might be sought in connection with license suspension orders: one, an injunction prohibiting the sale of the commodities for which the defendant's license was suspended; the other, an injunction restraining violations subsequent to the reinstatement of the defendant's license. Contempt of court could be based, of course, upon a violation of the judgment suspending the license. The suspension order was primarily directed at the "license," and the first type of injunction restrained the business concern from selling during the period of the suspension. If the concern violated by selling during the period of suspension, contempt proceedings might be instituted. The second type of injunction, that of restraining the defendant from future violations of the regulations, was used because of the relatively short period of time of most suspension orders. If the defendant violated after the period of the suspension the OPA had to institute suspension order proceedings again, but if the concern was under a permanent injunction all that need be done was to bring a contempt action. There was some difficulty, however, in securing a future injunction in connection with a license suspension order.

Courts sometimes issued further specifications when they issued a suspension order. In some cases the business concern was ordered to post a conspicuous sign, in letters of a certain height, in front of the premises during the period of the suspension order, stating that the license to sell commodities had been suspended by the court for certain price violations. This was somewhat similar to the notices required in ration suspension order proceedings, which was an administrative action.

In the light of the early enthusiasm about the possible effectiveness of the license suspension sanction, it is interesting to note that actually it was the least used of all sanctions available to the OPA for enforcement purposes. Although the OPA issued 32,118 license warning notices up through March 31, 1945, only 1,013 suits for suspension of license were instituted, and of this total only 394, or slightly over a third, were prosecuted to judgment. Attorneys of the OPA were reluctant to use this sanction for various reasons. First of all, primary emphasis throughout the war continued to be on the use of the injunction. An injunction without limit as to time, regardless of whether the violation called for a suspension order, was considered by many attorneys as more effective than a complete suspension order for a short period. Second, there were actually two steps necessary in order to suspend a license, the license warning notice and then the license suspension proceeding. Third, the courts were reluctant to suspend licenses for periods long enough to produce compliance, and even if they were willing to do so the suspension of a merchant's license might seriously affect a particular community's economic life. Fourth, the fact that the state courts were given jurisdiction in cases of smaller dealers meant bringing cases before courts which were not only unfamiliar with the Emergency Price Control Act, but frequently sympathetic toward the defendant or even openly prejudiced against the OPA.

Rationing Suspension Orders

The most widely used sanction in rationing cases was the ration suspension order, a procedure whereby, after an administrative hearing before an impartial hearing commissioner, a person's right to deal in a given rationed commodity might be suspended for a period anywhere from a few days to the duration of the war. Such decisions could be appealed to the Washington OPA office and on a few occasions were appealed to the courts. In all, 52,297 ration suspension orders were issued. Such an order differed from a license suspension suit in that the latter was a judicial proceeding following a previous warning, whereas the former was entirely administrative and required no previous warning notice.

All rationing suspension order proceedings involved improper diversion of strategic supplies. Many of the cases involved supply shortages which had been covered by purchases of stolen or counterfeit ration currency from professional criminals; others represented false inventories of supplies on hand. A study of such cases under the Second War Powers Act, which were entirely administrative in character rather than a court procedure, would show that many of them, largely gasoline, meat, and sugar, involved extensive and evasive violations. Most of the cases were willful and could have been prosecuted under the criminal provisions of the OPA statute; yet the procedure of suspending an individual's business was a much more effective, and rapid, means of action.

In the use of this type of sanction it was not necessary for the OPA to prove willfulness, but such proof might affect the length of the suspension order. Of particular interest in considering this sanction was the Supreme Court decision in the Steuart Oil Case which upheld the validity of the suspension order proceeding.[41] In this case the company maintained that the suspension order was a penalty and that the OPA did not have authority to use penal action. The OPA contended that

[41] Steuart and Brother, Inc. v. Bowles, Price Administrator, 322 U.S. 398, 1944.

it was not a penalty, but rather a withdrawal of an allocation. The Supreme Court said that the suspension order was remedial but conceded that it was an injury to the person suspended. From the point of view of the arguments presented in this discussion, however, it would seem that the suspension of a business for periods ranging up to the duration of the war was a penalty regardless of the legal interpretation. To put a man out of business would appear to be as much a penalty as a fine.

In order to stay within this legal interpretation, the formal OPA instructions for the use of the suspension order proceeding stated that it was not a penalty, but rather a proceeding "to withdraw the right to deal in, receive, or use rationed commodities from persons who have diverted such commodities from essential civilian or military uses or have otherwise shown themselves untrustworthy to play an unrestricted role in a rationing program."[42] Having stated this and also having added that the suspension order should not be used as a substitute for criminal proceedings in cases of willful and flagrant violations but might be used as an adjunct to such proceedings, the instructions included this reservation: the suspension order "should be used only where it is necessary in the public interest to promote the national welfare, since its consequences may be severe."[43]

The following case illustrates representative suspensions ordered by hearing commissioners and indicates their serious nature.

Respondent, a gasoline dealer, was charged with purchasing gasoline rationing coupons and transferring gasoline to consumers without receiving coupons in exchange therefor. During the months of October, November, and December, 1942, respondent purchased

---

[42] *OPA Manual.* Sec. 9–1905.03.
[43] *Ibid.,* Sec. 9–1905.02.

gasoline ration coupons in violation of Ration Order 5C, paying for them at the rate of four to five cents a gallon. The seller, who was under arrest at the time of the hearing, testified that he sold to the respondent coupons covering 2,000 gallons of gasoline and that such sales of coupons were made on four or five different occasions. . . . respondent while denying the number of coupons so purchased by him did admit that he purchased some of them, explaining that he did so for the purpose of making up a shortage, and that he charged customers an additional amount over the regular price of gasoline to cover the cost of these coupons to him. The respondent further admitted that he sold gasoline and accepted in exchange therefor, coupons which were not valid at the time that they were accepted. The violations of the Gasoline Rationing Regulation of which the respondent is guilty are very serious. Solely for the purpose of gain he has sold gasoline to persons without coupons and he has used coupons purchased in violation of the Regulations for the purpose of replenishing gasoline thus sold; and has accepted coupons which were not valid at the time they were delivered to him. With the serious shortage of gasoline for essential driving, for war production and for actual military needs, the action of the respondent deserves severe condemnation and punishment.[44]

Although this discussion has dealt with the punitive aspects of the various measures available to the OPA in its attempts to control the black market it does not imply that sanctions are the most efficient way to control large segments of business[45] or any other social group. All effective social control must rely on the voluntary compliance with the regulations of society by the vast majority of the citizens. When men wish to violate the law they will do so in most cases, just as men who do

---

[44] From an OPA suspension order hearing on a Long Island, New York, case.

[45] See Max Radin, *Manners and Morals of Business* (Indianapolis: The Bobbs-Merrill Company, 1939), pp. 251-52.

not wish to violate the law could not be forced to do so. Formal punishment, whether criminal, civil, or administrative sanctions, often leads merely to cleverness in the means of evasion. Sanctions should be reserved only for the small minority of business violators.

CHAPTER TEN

Were Black Market

Violations Unique?

So much was said and written during the war about the price and rationing regulations and the nature and extent of the black market that many persons came to look upon such violations of government regulations by businessmen as unique in this country. Reports of congressional investigations and various government agencies charged with regulating business, as well as statements by many authorities in the field of business ethics and criminology, indicate that this type of activity certainly is neither new nor uncommon.[1] There is evidence that businessmen, although certainly not all of them, have violated, or are violating, peacetime laws. There is also evidence that there were violations of other wartime laws. An even more important consideration is the fact that most black market activities were not only violations of the wartime price and rationing laws, but also violations of other federal and local laws dealing with conspiracy against the government, protection of our currency, tax collections, pure food and drug regulations, marketing regulations, and weights and measures. Little publicity was given to these other aspects of law enforcement; hence many people believed that the black market was

---

[1] See, for example, Sutherland, *White Collar Crime.*

the first time that business concerns were violating laws to any considerable degree.

Peacetime Business Violations

Investigations have revealed criminal behavior in peacetime in banking, public utilities, the oil industry, the Stock Exchange, munitions, real estate, insurance, railways, reorganization committees in receiverships and bankruptcies, and politics.[2] These violations include embezzlement and misapplication of funds, misrepresentation in financial statements, tax frauds, short weights and measures, misgrading of commodities, misapplication of funds in receiverships and bankruptcies, manipulation on the Stock Exchange, wash sales by which the value of a security is fraudulently determined, transfer of deteriorated securities from the possession of a banker to a trust fund he administers, and bribery of public officials. Sutherland, in commenting on the extent and size of typical violations, has said:

The manufacturers of practically every class of articles used by human beings have been involved in legal difficulties with these commissions with more or less frequency during the last thirty years, including the manufacturers of the surgical instruments with which an infant may be assisted into the world, the bottle and nipple from which he may secure his food, the milk in his bottle, the blanket in which he is wrapped, the scales on which he is weighed, the flag which the father displays in celebration of the event, and so on throughout life until he is finally laid away in a casket which was manufactured and sold under conditions which violated the law.

---

[2] See numerous governmental investigations and reports of the past twenty years. Also see Sutherland, *White Collar Crime* and his *Principles of Criminology* (Philadelphia: J. B. Lippincott Company, 4th ed., 1947). Considerable consensus regarding the extensiveness of white collar crime exists among the writers of nearly all the leading textbooks in criminology.

The financial loss to society from white-collar crimes is probably greater than the financial loss from burglaries, robberies, and larcenies committed by persons of the lower socio-economic class. The average loss per burglary is less than one hundred dollars, a burglary which yields as much as fifty thousand dollars is exceedingly rare, and a million-dollar burglary is practically unknown. On the other hand, there may be several million-dollar embezzlements reported in one year. Embezzlements, however, are peccadilloes compared with the large-scale crimes committed by corporations, investment trusts, and public utility holding companies; reports of fifty-million-dollar losses from such criminal behavior are by no means uncommon.[3]

In a recent study, 70 large corporations, which with two exceptions are included among the 200 largest nonfinancial institutions in the United States, were reported to have had 980 decisions rendered against them for violations of government regulations.[4] This figure, including subsidiaries, was an average of 14 for each corporation. Sixty corporations had decisions against them for restraint of trade, 53 for infringement of patents, 44 for unfair labor practices, 28 for misrepresentation in advertising, 26 for rebates, and 43 for miscellaneous offenses. Sixty per cent of these adverse decisions were rendered in the ten-year period 1935 through 1944 when there was increased government enforcement of business regulations. After a careful examination Sutherland concludes that although 158 cases were dealt with by the criminal courts, in actuality crimes were committed in 779 out of the 980 cases, 583 being decisions by criminal and civil courts. Even if the analysis were restricted

---

[3] E. H. Sutherland, "Crime and Business," *Annals of the American Academy of Political and Social Science*, CCVII (September, 1941), 113. Reprinted by permission.

[4] Sutherland, *White Collar Crime*. Because of incompleteness of data and other factors, Sutherland mentions that this figure represents an undercount of actual cases.

to the criminal courts it would show that almost two thirds of the corporations had been convicted and had an average of four convictions each.

Violations of Other Wartime Regulations

Violations of the price regulations and rationing orders were by no means the only blight on the American scene during the war. The War Production Board, another wartime agency which also encountered violations, dealt with the allocation of priorities of scarce materials to business concerns, these allocations being made for the purpose of facilitating war production. In one case, for example, scarce nylon was allocated to a fairly large concern for making parachutes, but instead large amounts were diverted to the making of women's stockings. The violations of the War Production Board's orders were numerous and evasive. During 1944, the WPB made 26,434 investigations and discovered violations in three out of five cases. The violations were largely dealt with by admonitions and compliance conferences. Up to January 1, 1945, a total of 1,235 probation, consent, and suspension orders were issued on withdrawing allocations, and 258 cases were referred to the Department of Justice for civil or criminal prosecution.[5]

In addition to violations of specific regulations issued by war agencies there were frauds in connection with war contracts. The investigation of war profits by the Truman Committee[6]— later the Mead committee[7]—indicated that these violations,

---

[5] Material from unpublished reports of the War Production Board.

[6] *Investigation of the National Defense Program,* Senate Report 10, Additional Report of the Special Committee Investigating the National Defense Program pursuant to Senate Resolution 71, Pts. 1–14, Seventy-eighth Congress, First Session, 1943, and Pts. 15–20, Seventy-eighth Congress, Second Session, 1944.

[7] *Investigation of the National Defense Program,* Senate Report 110, Additional Report of the Special Committee Investigating the National Defense

while certainly not involving all concerns, were extensive. They included padded expense and personal accounts, bribery of public officials, and the manufacture of substandard products in order to secure greater profits. One postwar report compiled by Comptroller General Lindsay Warren charged overpayments or fraud in more than 5 per cent of all war contracts. Out of 4,789 contracts studied, the government was overcharged $4,350,000. On the basis of these figures it was estimated that the government was overcharged, or cheated out of, more than $60,000,000 on the 318,000 war contracts. One particular series of acts involving flagrant overcharges to the government is reported to have occurred in connection with navy purchases of Middle East oil. The Senate committee investigating these purchases stated that certain leading American oil companies, although operating as foreign subsidiaries which paid royalties to the countries concerned, made misrepresentations to the United States government, and overcharged the government on sales to the navy between 30 million and 38 million dollars during the period January 1, 1942—June 30, 1947: "The Committee is of the opinion that if the statement contained in the official Navy justification for the purchase of oil at $1.05 a barrel is true, that the oil companies represented to the Navy that they had doubled their royalty payment from 21 to 42 cents a barrel, then the Government clearly was defrauded because the royalty payments were not doubled."[8]

Black Market Dealings as Violations of Other Laws

As noted above, most black market activities were also violations of many other federal and sometimes state laws deal-

---

Program pursuant to Senate Resolution 71, Pts. 1–4, Seventy-ninth Congress, First Session, 1945, and Pts. 5–8, Seventy-ninth Congress, Second Session, 1946.

[8] *Senate Report No. 440*, Additional Report of the Special Committee·

ing with conspiracy against the government, protection of our currency, tax collections, pure food and drugs, marketing regulations, and weights and measures, as well as various other state and municipal laws and ordinances. In fact, prosecutions were occasionally made not under the price and rationing control regulations but under federal laws which also operated in peacetime. Some of these cases involved prosecution as conspiracy to violate a federal law,[9] submission of false reports to the government,[10] or counterfeiting a government document.[11] For ex-

---

Investigating the National Defense Program pursuant to Senate Resolution 71, Eightieth Congress, Second Session, April 28, 1948, Pt. 5, p. 32.

[9] "If two or more persons conspire either to commit any offense against the U.S. or to defraud the U.S. in any manner or for any purpose and one or more of such parties do any act to effect the object to the conspiracy, each of the parties to such conspiracy shall be fined not more than $10,000.00 or imprisoned not more than two years or both."—Title 18, Chap. 4, Sec. 88 (Sec. 37 *U.S. Criminal Code*).

[10] "Whoever shall make or cause to be made or present or cause to be presented for payment or approval to or by any person or officer in the civil, military or naval service of the United States or any department thereof or any corporation in which the United States of America is a stockholder any claim against or upon the Government of the United States or any department or officer thereof or any corporation in which the United States of America is a stockholder knowing such claim to be false, fictitious or fraudulent; or whoever shall knowingly and willfully falsify or conceal or cover up by any trick, scheme or device any material fact or make or cause to be made any false or fraudulent statements or representations or make or use or cause to be made or used any false bill, receipt, voucher, roll, account, claim, certificate, affidavit or deposition knowing the same to contain any fraudulent or fictitious statement or entry in any matter within the jurisdiction of any department or agency of the United States or of any corporation in which the United States of America is a stockholder shall be fined not more than $10,000.00 or imprisoned not more than ten years or both."—Title 18, Chap. 4, Sec. 80 (Sec. 35A *U.S. Criminal Code*).

[11] "Whoever shall falsely make, alter, forge or counterfeit or cause or procure to be falsely made, altered, forged or counterfeited or wittingly aid or assist in the false making, altering, forging or counterfeiting any bond, bid, proposal, contract, guarantee, security, official bond, public record, affidavit or other writing for the purpose of defrauding the United States; or shall utter or publish as true or cause to be uttered or published as true or having in his possession with intent to utter or publish as true any such false, forged, altered or counterfeited bond, bid, proposal, contract, guarantee, security, official bond, public record, affidavit or other writing for the purpose of defrauding the United States knowing the same to be false, forged, altered or counterfeited or

ample, conspiracy to possess gasoline ration coupons acquired unlawfully and to transfer such coupons unlawfully was considered a felony.[12] The forging of gasoline ration coupons in time of war when restricted civilian use was essential to sustain supplies for armed services was "sabotage" of the war effort and constituted a "fraud against the United States" within the section prohibiting forgeries for the purpose of defrauding the United States as an act of frustrating proper administration of this section and impairing the functions of government.[13]

BLACK MARKET DEALINGS AND INCOME TAX RETURNS. Each year there are reports of extensive violations and evasions of taxes not only by business concerns but by other segments of the population. The amount in taxes owed the federal government alone on January 1, 1948, has been estimated to have been from 5 billion to 8 billion dollars,[14] a figure which would include both avoidance and violation of the tax laws.

During the war the Bureau of Internal Revenue looked into the income tax aspects of black market violations. It also issued regulations to the effect that over-ceiling payments could not be deducted as legitimate business expenses but had to be taken out of profits.[15] This provision stated that such over-

---

shall transmit to or present at or cause or procure to be transmitted to or presented at the office of any officer of the United States any false, forged, altered or counterfeited bond, bid, proposal, contract, guarantee, security, official bond, public record, affidavit or other writing knowing the same to be false, forged, altered or counterfeited for the purpose of defrauding the United States shall be fined not more than $1,000.00 or imprisonment not more than ten years or both. —Title 18, Chap. 4, Sec. 72 (Sec. 28 *U.S. Criminal Code*).

[12] U.S. v. Strickland, 62 F. Supp. 468.

[13] U.S. v. Mullin, 51 F. Supp. 785; U.S. v. Rashin, 52 F. Supp. 343.

[14] "Hunt for Income Tax Evaders," *United States News*, December 5, 1947, pp. 23–24.

[15] Section 29.22 (a) —5. Also section 23 (a) —1, (1945–7–I. T. 3724). Making violations a nondeductible expense was an effective penalty in connection with the enforcement of the rulings of the War Labor Board. It is interesting to note that the Bureau of Internal Revenue in 1945 was able to secure from congressional committees a budget sufficient for five thousand additional investi-

ceiling payments could not be allowed, for income tax purposes, as a part of the cost of goods sold or as a business expense deduction. Since the Emergency Price Control Act made it unlawful to pay an over-ceiling price, at least in the course of trade or business, and also provided criminal penalties for willful violations, the Bureau of Internal Revenue would not recognize as a business expense any part of a price which exceeded the maximum price. In this connection the courts had previously held that a taxpayer may not obtain tax advantages from expenditures which are made in contravention of a well-defined public policy and this construction was expanded to include the price and rationing laws which prescribe particular types of conduct. In concluding its order the bureau definitely indicated that money paid to a seller in excess of the ceiling prices could not be deducted as a business expense and that to deduct it was a tax violation.

The foregoing cases support the conclusion that an amount paid to a seller of goods in excess of the legal price for such goods may not properly be recognized for tax purposes. The excess payments are not legitimately to be classified as a part of the cost of goods sold, and public policy decrees that no tax advantage may be derived from such expenditures. To allow the characterization of an amount in excess of the ceiling prices as a part of the cost of goods sold is to allow a mere form set up by the acts of the violators to distort the true nature of the payments so made and to encourage the consequent disregard of the anti-inflationary policies established by the Emergency Price Control Act. Accordingly, it is held that amounts paid in excess of ceiling prices established by the Office of Price Administration, in so-called black market transactions, may not be allowed either as a part of the cost of goods sold, or as a

---

gators for the purpose of investigating illegal war profits. The OPA never did have a staff of this size and encountered serious difficulties in securing even a few hundred additional persons.

business expense deduction, in computing income subject to Federal income taxation.[16]

The following case is illustrative of the attitude of the Bureau of Internal Revenue and the courts about illegal profits derived from evasive black market violations. During 1945 a New York meat retailer and his partner, who were unable to purchase meat at ceiling prices, purchased $4,200 worth of stock in a corporation called United Meat Company, Inc. Through this corporation they were able to purchase meat at ceiling prices, but they were also "assessed" additional amounts, making a total of almost $7,500 paid contributions to United in 1945. When attempts were made to report this amount, for income tax purposes, as cost of goods sold, the tax commissioner disallowed this expense, classifying the amount as a capital contribution by stockholders; hence an addition to the cost of their investment. The judge in this case made the following statement in disallowing this expense for tax purposes: "These payments were in addition to the top price permitted by the OPA. . . . If they are to be added as a part of the cost of the meat, then the total cost was in excess of a lawful price and it would be difficult to distinguish the transaction from 'black market' purchase. If that were true, then [it] . . . represented a scheme devised to avoid the letter of the law while . . . violating its spirit."[17]

The Bureau of Internal Revenue also prosecuted cases where deductions were made as a business expense, contrary to the tax regulations, of money paid in settlement of violations such as fines, as voluntary payments to the U.S. Treasury, or as the result of treble damage actions. The Bureau of Inter-

---

[16] From a letter from Commissioner of Internal Revenue, January 7, 1948.
[17] Alexander Eulenberg, "Influence of Public Policy on Deduction," *Taxes*, December, 1950, p. 1197.

nal Revenue made arrangements for the OPA Enforcement Department to furnish the names and addresses of all violators of the price regulations against whom a penalty of over five hundred dollars had been levied. The files of these violators were then checked by the Bureau of Internal Revenue for possible violations of income tax laws, and action was taken in many cases.[18]

While a large number of cases were dealt with in this general fashion, there is no doubt that this procedure could have been used much more extensively. One of the difficulties was that false books were kept recording sales and receipts.[19] Two wholesalers made these comments:[20]

Well, ma'am, you know today if every little grocery store and every concern would have to keep straight honest books, they figure the government would take a whole lot of the money, so a lot of them keep books, but not complete ones.

I would say that about half of them follow [the regulations], the rest of them ask for the difference in cash. The government loses a lot of money that way, the cash transactions are not in the books, and the government can't collect taxes, because there are no records. . . . The government is losing vast amounts of money on that alone.

Even after the war the volume of such violations was so great that tax authorities were disturbed as to how they could

---

[18] Information furnished by Commissioner of Internal Revenue, January 7, 1948. Since Section 55 (f) of the Internal Revenue Code prohibits the disclosure of information contained in federal income tax returns, except as provided by law, the OPA was unable to secure information from the bureau concerning black market transactions or concerns having greatly increased incomes. The regulations governing the inspection of returns (T.D. 4929, section 463c.33) made it possible for the OPA to inspect designated returns for the purpose of obtaining information to be used as evidence in its proceedings.

[19] Sometimes two sets of books were kept, one for the OPA and one for the Bureau of Internal Revenue.

[20] "Opinion Survey of Food Wholesalers," cited above.

possibly prosecute all these violations and still maintain post-war fraud work.[21] At the close of 1947, about a year after the end of the OPA, black marketeers were still being sought in large numbers for tax violations. "These include black-market deals on automobiles, liquor, textiles, sugar, poultry, meat and many other products. One man was found to have bought 3,900,000 pounds of rationed sugar for a fictitious candy manufacturing company. He resold the sugar at a huge black-market profit. Agents recently assessed him $310,000 for taxes, interest and penalty on those profits."[22]

ILLEGAL DIVERSION OF SUGAR. When sugar was illegally diverted in commercial channels during the war it constituted a violation of the laws governing the making of alcoholic beverages in the United States. The Alcohol Tax Unit[23] is charged with the enforcement of laws dealing with alcoholic beverages in the United States and thus is concerned with the disposition of large quantities of sugar. The law requires that any person who disposes of sugar or other substances used in manufacturing distilled spirits must submit returns showing essential details with regard to every such disposition. This includes not only refiners and wholesalers but also importers, jobbers, retailers, transporters, and users of these substances. Under this authority the government may require returns on all disposition of sugar or other raw material regardless of quantity, but usually indicates a minimum disposition which must be reported. Anyone convicted of willfully violating any provision of this law is subject to a fine of not more than $500 or imprisonment for not more than one year, or both.[24]

---

21 *Journal of Tax Research*, November, 1946.

22 "Hunt for Income Tax Evaders," *loc. cit.*, p. 24.

23 Bureau of Internal Revenue, U.S. Treasury Department.

24 Section 2811, Internal Revenue Code and also see Regulation 17, "Disposition of Substances Used in the Manufacture of Distilled Spirits," Bureau

Since the OPA was interested in sugar as a rationed commodity which was not to be diverted from legitimate channels, many cases of illegal sugar usage were violations of both the sugar rationing regulations and the Internal Revenue Code, and both agencies frequently worked together on these cases. When the sugar rationing regulations went into effect a joint investigative program was set up between these two agencies, and was given practically full-time attention by the raw materials investigators of the Alcohol Tax Unit. Representatives of the latter agency assisted in formulating the sugar rationing regulations and maintained close contact with the sugar enforcement officials of the OPA, this cooperation extending down through the field offices of the two agencies. The officials of the Bureau of Internal Revenue realized shortly after rationing began that the administrative and criminal sanctions embodied in the rationing regulations made enforcement of these enactments the best possible means of preventing the diversion of sugar into illicit distilling channels. This realization, together with the protests of business concerns against the great number of government reports required of them, led to the cancellation of practically all formal demands under the Alcohol Tax regulations for returns on the disposition of cane and beet sugar and to the substitution of OPA reports.

While checking sugar sales for its own purposes the Alcohol Tax Unit could also find out if such sales were made in violation of the sugar rationing regulations. The Alcohol Tax Unit, moreover, furnished information about sales without sugar certificates, "wash" sales, price violations, and the existence of, and the illegal sale from, undisclosed inventories. Not only was it helpful in enforcing price regulations on liquor and in

of Internal Revenue, United States Treasury Department (Washington: Government Printing Office, 1945).

training OPA investigators; it was of valuable assistance on many criminal conspiracy cases. In most instances actual prosecution was handled under OPA regulations, and in other cases by the Alcohol Tax Unit; in still other cases they prosecuted jointly under both laws.

Officers of the Alcohol Tax Unit obtained the first indictment, as well as the first conviction, for violation of the sugar rationing regulations. During the rationing period investigators of the Alcohol Tax Unit, in most cases independently but sometimes jointly with officers of the OPA, conducted 10,409 investigations of alleged sugar rationing violations, and in addition reported to the OPA 1,784 such violations disclosed in connection with liquor violation investigations. From the effective date of the sugar rationing regulations in 1942 to the close of the fiscal year on June 30, 1943, there were only 35 sugar rationing investigations made by the Alcohol Tax Unit; during the fiscal year 1944 there were only 98 such investigations; and during the fiscal year 1945, 123. But during the fiscal year 1946, after the program was reorganized so that the Alcohol Tax Unit took over a larger share of the sugar program, there were 5,056 investigations; and during the fiscal year 1947, 5,097 investigations. As a result of this joint program, in addition to the results obtained by OPA officers working independently, 505 persons were convicted of rationing violations and sentenced to serve 44,919 days in prison and to pay fines aggregating $486,572, with many of the largest cases still pending court action as of about the middle of 1948. In addition, 1,348 dealers were suspended from selling sugar because of lesser offenses.[25]

DETERIORATION IN QUALITY OF FOODS. Each year the federal Food and Drug Administration (Federal Security Agency), as

---

[25] Information secured from letter from the Deputy Commissioner of the Bureau of Internal Revenue, June 22, 1948.

well as similar agencies in many states and cities, deals with thousands of cases involving sales of processed commodities in which there are violations of the pure food and drug laws. The reports of this agency carry evidence of widespread violations of laws whose purpose is to safeguard the health and welfare of the nation. These cases involve sales of all types of foods contaminated by such things as filth and rodents, adulteration of products such as mixing mineral oil with various salad oils or mixing ground chick peas or cereal with coffee, short weights and deceptive containers, and dangerous, unsanitary, or misleading commodities of various types.

As has been pointed out elsewhere, quality deterioration of foods and misbranding of commodities became rather common types of evasive violations during the black market. Persons who engaged in such activities could in many instances have been prosecuted under the provisions of the price and rationing regulations as well as under the pure food and drug laws. When supplies became scarce many concerns were tempted to use substitutes which were often harmful to the consumer. Although this was sometimes done in order to manufacture substitute articles, in the main the purpose was to increase profits by illegitimate means. Cases of such violations, if detected by the OPA in the course of a price violation, were referred to the Food and Drug Administration, which also kept the OPA informed of violations. Under the sugar rationing regulations, for example, a canner of fruit was allowed 90 per cent of his base period sugar consumption, but there was no limit on the amount of his pack and, consequently, no limit on how he might use his sugar. By using a lighter syrup he could come out ahead and might even dispose of some of his extra sugar on the black market, but at the same time deteriorating the quality of the product. In a wartime report the Food and Drug Administration wrote:

Current shortages and price ceilings have greatly increased the temptation towards adulteration and misbranding. An endless variety of substitutes, imitations, diluents, preservatives, and extenders have appeared on the market, some with labeling either false or so insidiously devised that all but the most observant consumers are grossly deceived. Such cheats become more serious where the supply of commodities is limited and the consumer is obliged to curtail his food purchases. Violations in this field may affect not only the pocketbook but may actually impair the health of consumers through reducing nutritional values below minimum requirements.[26]

In spite of the wartime difficulties facing the limited staff of a few hundred investigators of the Food and Drug Administration, this agency furnished valuable assistance to the OPA in preventing consequent inflation by quality deterioration. The penalties it imposed during 1942 and 1943 on some 3,000 violators each year included jail sentences.[27] Persons who illegally deteriorated the quality of a product on the assumption that these were only violations of the OPA must indeed have been blind to the pure food and drug laws which prevail in peace and war, for violations of these federal laws carry a punishment of up to five years' imprisonment and a fine of $5,000, plus seizure of the commodity. The following wartime cases not only illustrate the type of activities of this agency but also the interrelated nature of its problems and those of the OPA:

---

[26] *Annual Reports, Food and Drug Administration, Federal Security Agency,* 1941–1942, 1942–1943, combined (Washington: Government Printing Office, 1943), p. 30.
[27] *Ibid.*

Other seizures on charges of economic violations in 1942 and 1943 included imitation fruit-type beverages sold in a manner to create the impression that they are pure fruit juices; canned sardines labeled as packed in pure olive oil when they were packed in corn oil infused with an olive oil flavor or in unadulterated corn oil; oysters in small containers, incorporating excessive water; "enriched" bread that contained no enriching ingredients; horsemeat from which the dealer had stripped the identifying labels; Japanese crab meat relabeled after importation, "packed in Siberia, Soviet Russia"; domestic cheese stamped with the words "Imported Swiss" or "Switzerland"; storage eggs misbranded as fresh eggs; short-weight retail packages of "nut meats" containing a material proportion of pumpkin seeds; cider vinegar debased with water, ascetic acid, and distilled vinegar; chicken loaf with skin and lung tissue substituted for chicken meat; white poppy seed colored to simulate a more costly variety; waffle and pancake sirup with glucose and corn sirup was subsituted for cane sirup. The sardine canner was fined $5,000, the horsemeat dealer $200, and the cheese packers lost their misleading Swiss stamps in addition to being fined $3,000.

Traffic in spurious olive oil and in salad oils falsely labeled as mixtures with olive oil received new impetus when foreign sources of olive oil were cut off by war conditions. Seizures in 1942 reached the highest point since the 1936 campaign to break up the racket in olive oil adulterated with tea-seed oil. Federal prosecutions were brought against numerous violators and the State and municipal officials were extremely successful in apprehending the surreptitious distributors of fake olive oil.

Price ceilings on scarce commodities have tempted unscrupulous concerns to offset by giving short weight or measure. While this type of violation is easy to detect, the field is so tremendous that the constant vigilance of both local and Federal food enforcement agencies is required. One of the principal short-weight items for which many shippers were cited during the Spring of 1943 was potatoes packed in bags. To circumvent the price ceiling by marketing short-weight potatoes meant that the receiver was forced to pay an increased price per pound. The largest number of short-weight seizures involved butter. Also seized in substantial quantities was packaged sauerkraut in glass containers containing a very excessive quantity of brine. Other short-weight or short-volume foods seized included smoked salmon, spiced herring, crab meat, preserves, marmalade, apple butter, canned chicken, peanuts, mixed nuts, olive oil, wheat germ, pimentos, spices, and pickles.[28]

Practically every state has a food and drug laboratory directed by a chemist affiliated with the state health or agriculture departments. In connection with their work, they tested the quality of various food products to ascertain whether such products were in agreement with the OPA specifications contained in the price and rationing regulations involved. Such inspections were especially helpful in meat cases, as in the sale of adulterated sausage or hamburger, where there might be an inclusion of say, 50 per cent fat rather than 28 per cent as permitted by the OPA. An OPA official in 1945 paid special tribute to these state officials.

The State Chemists have done a splendid job of checking the quality of ground meat products offered for sale within their states. Wartime shortages have seriously increased their problems. There has been a tendency on the part of many sellers to extend their supplies by resorting to such practices as increasing the fat content to excessive amounts in such products as sausage and hamburger. We hope that special attention such as that now being given these products by the Denver Regional Office and the Colorado State Chemists will put an end to the practice of marketing excessive fat in ground meat.[29]

---

[28] *Ibid.*, pp. 31–35.

[29] John J. Madigan, Assistant Deputy Administrator in charge of the OPA meat program, quoted in *Washington Letter*, Office of Price Administration, No. 32, May 31, 1945, pp. 4–5.

Such evasive violations of the price and rationing regulations as upgrading of meat, poultry, eggs, and other commodities passing in interstate commerce were not the sole concern of the OPA. The Production and Marketing Administration of the Department of Agriculture regulates the grading of certain commodities passing in interstate commerce, and this agency furnished invaluable assistance to the OPA in suppressing many black market activities. As commodities became scarce during the war many firms tended to upgrade them, and the mutual exchange of information between these two governmental agencies aided in the control of violations. The effectiveness of this arrangement, however, was partially lessened by the fact that some of the production in these commodities shifted from business concerns in interstate commerce to local concerns where there was no control by the Department of Agriculture. Federal licenses, for example, were issued by the Department of Agriculture to slaughter houses whose products were shipped in intrastate commerce, and some meat was later diverted from federally inspected houses to places where there were less controls.

COUNTERFEITING OF RATION CURRENCY. The counterfeiting of any United States government document is punishable under the Federal Criminal Code, and while the OPA dealt directly with cases involving ration currency these violations were technically not only violations of the Price Control Act and the Second War Powers Act, but of other federal laws as well. When professional counterfeiters during the war shifted largely from the counterfeiting of United States currency to that of ration currency issued by the OPA, the agency sought the assistance of the United States Secret Service, which is charged with protecting currency. As previously explained, the Secret Service furnished invaluable assistance to the OPA in training special agents, particularly in techniques for detecting counterfeits. During the rationing period the Secret Service conducted schools for the OPA in all regions and on a number of occasions furnished information regarding the *modus operandi* and personal history of professional counterfeiters. Moreover, the two agencies exchanged information wherever desirable. The Secret Service also assisted in detecting forged applications for rationed commodities.

STATE AND MUNICIPAL BLACK MARKET LAWS. Almost from the beginning the OPA realized that the size of its enforcement staff was not adequate for the job of controlling the rapidly expanding black market, and it made efforts to enlist the assistance of state and municipal governments. As early as 1942 the Enforcement Department had drafted a model black market law which stated, in effect, that any violation of an OPA regulation or ration order would also be a violation of a given state law or municipal ordinance. Chester Bowles, in a speech before the Conference of Mayors in January, 1944, pointed out the need for this type of legislation.

Now how about the actual enforcement of OPA price ceilings throughout the country? Our own enforcement staff is almost pitifully small. . . . In many cities and towns throughout the country we have been getting the finest kind of enforcement backing from local and state governments. In 18 cities today, there are local ordinances which establish the right of local courts to levy fines up to $100 and jail sentences up to ninety days for all those who sell their products above OPA ceiling prices or who transfer rationed goods without collecting ration stamps. I cannot urge you too strongly to introduce similar legislation at once in your own city. . . . A city ordinance which will allow your own local enforcement organization to render firsthand protection to the people of your city would, I am sure, be welcomed by your local citizens as a great step forward on your part in protecting them against the wartime chiselers' and gougers' profit. You will, of course, get some opposition from the local pressure groups who would prefer to see prices go higher. Probably they will say—"Why not leave the job of enforcing price ceilings to the Federal Government?"—"Why is it any business of ours?"

While the governors of the several states were asked to help, actually only a few states adopted such a statute, among them being New York, Wisconsin, Rhode Island, and Arizona. One probable reason for the reluctance of most states to adopt such a law was the realization that the enforcement of price and rationing regulations would involve many problems. In fact, in those states where the ordinance was adopted relatively little use was made of the statute, and the majority of such violations, when detected, were turned over to the OPA. This, of course, added somewhat to the enforcement manpower available to the federal government.

The OPA model enforcement ordinance was also enacted by some seventy-five municipalities, most of which were relatively small, although a few, like Cleveland,[30] Milwaukee, Detroit, and New York City, were large metropolitan centers. In general, like the states, the cities made comparatively little actual use of the ordinance after its enactment. Throughout the United States during the war, however, several thousand cases of prosecution under state statutes and local ordinances were reported to the OPA each year.[31] New York City, contrary to other cities, made extensive use of this ordinance, and in a single year (1944) there were 18,875 prosecutions of retailers by the New York Department of Markets. These cases were 98

---

[30] The Cleveland ordinance was later declared to be unconstitutional by the Supreme Court of Ohio.

[31] Because of reporting difficulties these figures represented only a portion of the total cases.

per cent successful, and $291,977 in fines, as well as jail sentences aggregating 899 days, resulted. The sheriff's office, in the three-months period ending January 15, 1945, prosecuted over 4,000 wholesale dealers, getting 2,688 convictions, with fines of $42,000 and jail sentences totaling 1,425 days.

THEFT OF RATIONED COMMODITIES AND SHORT-WEIGHTING. In addition to the black market cases falling under these state and local black market statutes which were enacted primarily for this purpose, there were, of course, certain cases which would have been prosecuted in all states under existing laws. For example, there were increased thefts of scarce commodities, particularly rationed commodities such as tires, and states and cities aided the OPA in keeping rationed commodities in normal legitimate channels by prosecuting these cases in the same way as other theft cases. In fact, the federal government on occasion turned over violators in possession of stolen rationed commodities to state agencies for prosecution. Unfortunately, the fact that little actual money was stolen in the rifling of ration boards made it difficult for the states to prosecute such cases severely. State and municipal police assisted in the detection of counterfeiters, although for the most part such cases had to be handled through federal laws. One advantage of state and municipal prosecution was the fact that the federal courts normally had a large backlog of cases and the states and municipalities could deal more quickly and effectively with persons who stole rationed commodities. Furthermore, this action removed the OPA from being actively involved in the case, a factor which sometimes interfered with conviction in areas where there was much prejudice against the OPA.

During the war the two thousand weights and measurements inspectors in the various states were useful in trying to prevent price and rationing violations in the form of short weights. These investigators were trained to inspect both retail and wholesale establishments for scales fixed to short-weight a commodity and, consequently, violating price and rationing regulations. A retailer with a faulty scale, for example, not only made illegal profits but could also build up an extra supply of sugar to sell favored customers.

CHAPTER ELEVEN

Explanations of
Black Market Violations

Our knowledge of crime today admittedly represents a biased sample of ordinary crimes, for there has been little analysis of white collar crimes. Most of the hundreds of thousands of offenses, like the black market, are not included in most criminal statistics, the persons who commit them are not found in numbers in our prisons where they might be studied, and most theories of criminal behavior have largely neglected this group of offenders. All too frequently analyses are made of individual criminals and delinquents without respect for extensive law disobedience at all levels of our society. In explaining the black market, therefore, we must proceed through relatively untraveled ground, mixing some speculation with fact and recognizing that we need more intensive study, including case histories and personal document material, before we can state specifically the "causal" factors involved.

In studying the "causal" factors in any type of antisocial behavior, whether it be ordinary or white collar crime such as black market offenses, it is important to keep in mind that from an abstract point of view all human behavior may be thought of as consisting of two kinds of personality traits, sociogenic and psychogenic, both of which are acquired from social experience through association with other persons. Sociogenic traits or attitudes are derived from the definitions of situations furnished by the culture or subcultures to which a person belongs, for example, a person's attitude toward law and property. Psychogenic traits, or general reaction patterns, are often referred to as basic personality traits, such as feelings of emotional security or insecurity. Both deviant and nondeviant behavior must be explained in terms of these components of personality.

Despite this, either many current studies of ordinary criminals have largely disregarded cultural influences and personality traits or such studies have failed to take into consideration that the same basic factors should also be present among white collar criminals such as black market offenders. On the basis of studies chiefly of offenders from the lower socioeconomic groups, theories have been advanced explaining criminal behavior as the result of childhood emotional insecurity or giving the more extreme Freudian interpretation of unrepressed primitive desires, sexual symbolism, guilt feelings, and abnormally close emotional attachments to mother or father. Similarly, attempts have been made to indicate the importance of poverty, bad housing, broken families, feeble-mindedness, and such media of mass impression as "comic books" in the lives of ordinary criminals and delinquents without reference to white collar offenders. Even more serious, however, are the occasional attempts to give criminal behavior a constitutional basis without establishing how such behavior could be inherited or what behavior among white collar offenders is inheritable. A valid theory of crime should apply to the ordinary criminal and the white collar criminal alike, to the burglar and the black market offender since both are violators of the law.

Limited Knowledge of Black Market Offenders

The only fairly comprehensive data available on the backgrounds of black market offenders are for those offenders sentenced to prison, which is, of course, likely to be an unrepresentative sample. If we assume, however, for purposes of argument that white collar offenders sentenced to prison are likely to be the more serious offenders, we do not have the same bias that often appears in connection with offenders sentenced to prison from the lower socioeconomic group who frequently include a disproportionate number of the uneducated and the poor as well as members of certain minority groups. Those sentenced for rationing offenses included a considerable number of criminals who had stolen or counterfeited ration currency, and those who committed price offenses were chiefly businessmen.

On the whole, the characteristics of the rationing offenders more closely approximated the characteristics of those who are sentenced for ordinary crimes. Rationing violators were younger than price violators, more frequently single, had less education, and were more likely to be Negroes. Price violators, who were nearly all from business, were not young men, as is the case with most men sentenced to prison. While a large proportion of men admitted to prison each year are under thirty, only one in ten persons sentenced to federal institutions for black market violations from 1944 to 1947 were of this age. A third were between thirty and forty, a fourth were between forty and fifty; 240, or about 13 per cent, were over fifty years old. (See Table 22.) Likewise, there was no concentration among the divorced and separated, as is the case with other typical prison admissions, since four out of five of the price offenders sentenced between 1945 and 1947 were married and only 6.5 per cent were single.

Table 22

OPA Violators Received from the Courts into Federal Institutions, by Type of Violation and Age, 1944–1947

AGE	TOTAL		PRICE CONTROL		RATIONING		OTHER OPA	
	NUM-BER	PER-CENTAGE	NUM-BER	PER-CENTAGE	NUM-BER	PER-CENTAGE	NUM-BER	PER-CENTAGE
Under 20...	24	1.3			23	1.6	1	1.0
20–29......	387	21.1	34	10.4	333	23.7	20	20.0
30–39......	711	38.7	96	29.3	580	41.2	35	35.0
40–49......	473	25.8	116	35.4	333	23.7	24	24.0
50–59......	205	11.2	74	22.5	118	8.4	13	13.0
60 and over.	35	1.9	8	2.4	20	1.4	7	7.0
Total	1,836*	100.0	328	100.0	1,408*	100.0	100	100.0

* This figure includes one case for which the age was unreported.
SOURCE: Data furnished by Federal Bureau of Prisons, United States Department of Justice, for fiscal years ending June 30.

Table 23

OPA Violators Received from the Courts into Federal Institutions, by Type of Violation and Marital Status, 1945–1947

MARITAL STATUS	TOTAL		PRICE CONTROL		RATIONING		OTHER OPA	
	NUM-BER	PER-CENTAGE	NUM-BER	PER-CENTAGE	NUM-BER	PER-CENTAGE	NUM-BER	PER-CENTAGE
Single.....	188	13.8	16	6.5	155	15.2	17	17.0
Married....	1,005	73.6	206	83.1	730	71.7	69	69.0
Common-law.	17	1.3	1	0.4	15	1.5	1	1.0
Widowed ...	14	1.0	2	0.8	12	1.2		
Divorced...	89	6.5	17	6.9	66	6.5	6	6.0
Separated..	51	3.8	6	2.3	38	3.7	7	7.0
N. R.*.....	2				2	0.2		
Total....	1,366	100.0	248	100.0	1,018	100.0	100	100.0

* Not reported.
SOURCE: Data furnished by Federal Bureau of Prisons, United States Department of Justice, for fiscal years ending June 30.

(See Table 23.) As might be expected, the education of price violators was quite high in comparison with that of the typical offender, one out of ten of those sentenced to one year or more between 1944 and 1947 having gone to college and one in three being a high school graduate. (See Table 24.) Ninety-six per

Table 24

OPA Violators Received from the Courts into Federal Institutions under Sentence of One Year or More, by Type of Violation and Last School Grade, 1944–1947

GRADE	TOTAL		PRICE CONTROL		RATIONING		OTHER OPA	
	NUM-BER	PER-CENTAGE	NUM-BER	PER-CENTAGE	NUM-BER	PER-CENTAGE	NUM-BER	PER-CENTAGE
College 4 years .	8	1.8	5	7.2	3	0.9		
College less than 4 years .	10	2.4	2	2.9	8	2.4		
High school....	43	10.1	13	18.9	28	8.3	2	10.0
High school less than 4 years .	88	20.7	16	23.2	67	19.9	5	25.0
Grade school...	276	65.0	33	47.8	230	68.5	13	65.0
Total.......	425	100.0	69	100.0	336	100.0	20	100.0

SOURCE: Data furnished by Federal Bureau of Prisons, United States Department of Justice, for fiscal years ending June 30.

cent of the price group of short- and long-term offenders were white, with only 12 being Negroes, while 162, or 11.5 per cent, of the rationing violators were Negroes, which is approximately their percentage of the general population. (See Table 25.)

Some persons have suggested that black market offenders were chiefly recruited from persons of recent immigrant background.[1] MacIver, in fact, has stated that the black market, as

---

[1] Many persons have even suggested to the author that those in the black market were nearly all Jewish, practically none being Gentile Anglo-Saxons. There is absolutely no basis for such a contention.

well as violations by businessmen in peacetime, can be explained largely in terms of inadequate incorporation of persons of recent immigrant origin into our American culture.

The statistics of crime reveal that groups that are for any reason unadjusted to or unincorporated within the larger community in which they live contain a larger proportion of offenders

Table 25

OPA Violators Received from the Courts into Federal Institutions, by Type of Violation and Race, 1944–1947

RACE	TOTAL		PRICE CONTROL		RATIONING		OTHER OPA	
	NUM- BER	PER- CENTAGE	NUM- BER	PER- CENTAGE	NUM- BER	PER- CENTAGE	NUM- BER	PER- CENTAGE
White......	1,639*	89.3	315	96.0	1,240	88.1	84	84.0
Negro......	190	10.3	12	3.7	162	11.5	16	16.0
Other......	5	0.3	1	0.3	4	0.3		
N. R.**....	2	0.1			2	0.1		
Total....	1,836	100.0	328	100.0	1,408	100.0	100	100.0

* These numbers include five Mexicans. ** Not reported.
SOURCE: Data furnished by Federal Bureau of Prisons, United States Department of Justice, for fiscal years ending June 30.

or at least of convicted offenders against the code. This rule applies to immigrant groups that cherish traditions alien to those of the environing culture. . . . For a similar reason groups that are assigned a status of lesser opportunity or social inferiority are likely to develop, especially in times of rapid social transition, a spirit of resentment against the exclusiveness of the dominant majority. This spirit becomes a rebellion against the whole social order as well as against the authority that sustains it. When this happens they lose their respect for law and are ready to violate it on any opportunity. Thus in the United States those who organize devices for frustrating the law, who sell illegal products or provide illegal services, *who in time of war conduct "black markets," and so forth, are frequently found to be members of such groups.*[2]

Actually there is no evidence to substantiate such a statement, and MacIver presents none. An examination of a random list of OPA violators shows no concentration by race, nationality, or religion in excess of the normal distribution in a particular trade. In certain trades such as apparel where a particular group of offenders may come largely from a certain cultural group, it will also be found that they constitute a large proportion of the persons normally engaged in that trade. Statistics on OPA enforcement activity indicated that the black market situation was widespread throughout the entire country regardless of the composition of the area. Statistics on 1,836 violators sentenced to federal prisons indicate that, in proportion to population, the East North Central and Western states had fewer. About one third of all price and rationing violators came from the northeastern part of the United States, one third from the South, one fifth from the North Central states, and approximately one twelfth from the West. (See Table 26.) The extensive peacetime violations of business laws and the political corruption engaged in by persons of all nationalities and religions should be sufficient refutation of such myths.

Selling, a psychiatrist, has even suggested that the black market can be explained in terms of certain personality traits: "Wartime crimes, particularly such offenses as the black market, have, so far as we have been able to see, been committed by persons who were *basically antisocial* and only needed the extra

---

[2] R. M. MacIver, *The Web of Government* (New York: The Macmillan Company, 1947), pp. 77–78. (Italics mine.) Copyright, 1947 by R. M. MacIver and used by the permission of The Macmillan Company.

stimulus of greater opportunity with a smaller chance of getting caught to turn toward antisocial activities."[3] This would seem to imply that not only ordinary criminals but the businessmen

Table 26

OPA Violators Received from the Courts into Federal Institutions, by Type of Violation and Area, 1944–1947

AREA	TOTAL		PRICE CONTROL		RATIONING		OTHER OPA	
	NUM-BER	PER-CENTAGE	NUM-BER	PER-CENTAGE	NUM-BER	PER-CENTAGE	NUM-BER	PER-CENTAGE
Northeast..	605	34.8	141	45.6	441	33.2	23	23.0
South......	649	37.3	61	19.8	569	42.8	19	19.0
North Central..	348	20.0	68	22.0	227	17.0	53	53.0
West......	136	7.8	39	12.6	92	6.9	5	5.0
Hawaii....	1	0.1			1	0.1		
Total....	1,739*	100.0	309	100.0	1,330	100.0	100	100.0

* This figure does not include 97 cases for which the judicial district was not furnished.

SOURCE: Data furnished by Federal Bureau of Prisons, United States Department of Justice, for fiscal years ending June 30.

who engaged in the black market had pronounced differences in personality structures. The fact that so many persons, with what may be assumed pronounced differences in personality traits, engaged in black market violations should disprove any assertion that they were all unusual from a personality point of view.[4]

---

[3] Lowell S. Selling, "Specific War Crimes," *Journal of Criminal Law and Criminology,* XXXIV, No. 5 (January–February, 1944) , 310. (Italics mine.)

[4] A survey of 113 studies of the personality traits of ordinary offenders and nonoffenders found that there was no evidence of a distinction in the personality traits of the two groups.—Karl F. Schuessler and Donald R. Cressey, "Personality Characteristics of Criminals," *American Journal of Sociology*, Vol. LV (March, 1950) .

The Black Market Cannot Be Attributed to Gangster and Shady Elements in Business

Then there was the common assumption that the black market was due primarily to the entrance of shady or gangster elements into American business. This public misconception about the black market seems to have arisen from the publicity program directed at arousing the country in a melodramatic fashion to the dangers of violations of price and rationing controls.[5] Such views have not been entirely confined to these sources, for a postwar study dealing with the relation of World War II to social disorganization surmises, but with no supporting evidence, that "certain wartime crimes, particularly those involving black market operations, may have been carried on by the criminal or quasi-criminal groups who normally would be engaged in more conventional criminal activities. Such behavior may merely represent the transfer of activity away from the traditional offenses, particularly those against property, toward activities which offer immediate return in wartime."[6]

One enforcement official, however, has stated: "I had thought, when I got into enforcement activities, and I think most people would, when we speak of violators and enforcement, we think of a racketeer. That has not been our experience. After all, who has the goods to sell? It is the person who

---

[5] Statements were made that organized racketeers were engaging in black market activities, and there were numerous magazine and newspaper articles, as well as motion-picture shorts, describing such cases. For example, the following statement about the meat black market was released by the Office of War Information and appeared in the Washington *Post*, March 5, 1943: "Another source of supply, the OWI said, is the rustler who rides the range at night, shooting animals where he finds them, dressing them on the spot and driving away with the carcasses in a truck."

[6] Francis E. Merrill, *Social Problems on the Home Front* (New York: Harper & Brothers, 1948), p. 181.

customarily is in the line of supply."[7] A former OPA administrator, writing on the black market in 1946, had this to say
about the violators:

> Criminal racketeers of the gangster variety have relatively little
> place in the wholesale chiseling now going on. They do not control
> our slaughterhouses, lumber mills, textile centers, and automobile
> agencies, nor do they have any interest in our retail stores and rail-
> roads. Current racketeering is largely in the hands of men and
> women with whom we have always done business.[8]

Even the meat black market which was widely thought of
as primarily a gangster racket, with hijacking and sales through
"blind pigs" as in the prohibition era, was found to have been
largely a product of ordinary business channels, although the
number of nonfederally inspected meat slaughterers increased
considerably during the war. In 1946 there was a significant
exchange of communications between the general counsel of
the National Independent Meat Packers Association and the
government official in charge of enforcing meat regulations, in
which the government official stated: "My point was, if you
read my testimony, that the black market consists of numerous
violations, none of them committed by the Capone type con-
spirator or meat bootlegger, but rather by established members
of industry, including members of your association and the
American Meat Institute."[9] Hartung, after studying the meat
black market in Detroit, concluded:

> First and most important, the meat black market was not a
> clandestine criminal organization parasitic upon the industry. It

---

[7] *Hearings before the Senate Banking and Currency Committee,* on Senate
Resolution 2,028, Seventy-ninth Congress, Second Session, II, p. 1679.

[8] Henderson, "How Black Is Our Market?" *loc. cit.,* p. 46.

[9] *Hearings before the Senate Committee on Banking and Currency,* 1946
Extension of the Emergency Price Control and Stabilization Acts of 1942, as
Amended, Seventy-Ninth Congress, Second Session, Pt. II, 1247.

did not hijack meat at various stages in the normal flow and sell it through blind pigs known to fortunate customers. It was most definitely not an excrescence upon the industry composed of racketeers coming from various criminal fields, or perhaps surviving from the prohibition era. Had this been the case, effective detective work could have uncovered it, and OPA would indeed have been remiss in not doing so.

Of the thousands of meat black marketeers proceeded against criminally, civilly, and administratively, the writer knows of none who were gangsters. Of the several hundred defendants in the Detroit area, only two had a previous criminal record, but neither of these could in any way have been regarded as a gangster. Neither of the convictions was for activities related to meat, and both had been committed outside of Michigan some years previously. Actually, then, the violations in this industry were committed by persons more or less well established in the different levels, from slaughterers to wholesalers and retailers. And the violations ranged from hardly more than traditional sharp practices to the most studied and deliberate attempts at conspiracy.[10]

In examining those price and rationing cases where criminal prosecution was instituted, which constituted a sample of flagrant cases, we find that less than one violator in ten was reported to have had any criminal record.[11] Those with criminal records probably represented chiefly thieves and counterfeiters of ration currency. Only somewhere between one in two and one in three persons sentenced for more than one year were known to have had previous institutional commitments.[12] Since these figures included dealers who violated the rationing provisions, as well as those professional criminals who stole or counterfeited the currency and the relatively few persons who

---

[10] Hartung, "A Study in Law and Social Differentiation," pp. 159–160.

[11] Unpublished OPA Enforcement Department data.

[12] Information furnished by the Federal Bureau of Prisons. In 1945, 45.5 per cent; 1946, 38.8 per cent; and 1947, 46.5 per cent.

were prosecuted for price and rent violations, the proportion of the last-named group who had a criminal record was probably even smaller. In fact, as has been pointed out elsewhere, one reason for the small number of prosecutions for price violations was that few of those violators had previous records of criminal behavior, thus making the possibility of conviction, or imprisonment, difficult. Among those persons with criminal records who violated the price regulations were some liquor dealers with a record of violation during the prohibition period. One case of this type represented a violation of the price ceilings on whiskey, and the offender was sentenced to the federal prisons for twenty-four months and fined $10,000. He had been engaged in bootlegging from 1926 to 1932, both as a liquor runner and a moonshine dealer. He operated five liquor stores in a fairly large southern city, and his black market profits were estimated at $30,979.

A somewhat different explanation, but with the same implication, was that those businessmen who engaged in the black market were chiefly either shady operators before the war or new elements, but not gangsters, entering business during the war. While it is true that some new businesses, for example, entered the meat and apparel black market, they constituted a relatively small proportion of the total business in the country. With few exceptions, businessmen and writers in various journals of business stated flatly that regular business was primarily responsible for the black market: "The big trouble in foods is that black markets are usually operated by regular merchants through regular channels of trade."[13] Statements of government enforcement officials, and an analysis of

---

[13] "Ceiling-Price Gyps," *loc. cit.*, p. 72.

black market cases, furnish further proof of this contention. While not definitely proving that the persons were either respectable or had always lived in these areas, in one particular study, where a tabulation was made of the residence of meat black market offenders, it was found that more than 80 per cent

Table 27

Distribution of Meat Black Market Offenders According to Desirability of Residence

RESIDENTIALLY DE-SIRABLE QUINTILE	NUMBER OF PERSONAL DEFENDANTS	PERCENTAGE OF TOTAL
1	62	48.4
2	41	32.0
3	15	11.7
4	4	3.1
5	6	4.7

Source: Hartung, "A Study in Law and Social Differentiation," p. 221. Index of residence desirability constructed by Detroit Bureau of Governmental Research on the basis of twenty criteria.

lived in the most desirable areas of the city. (See Table 27.) Of the ten who lived in the least desirable area, three lived in good downtown hotels.

Black Market Not Restricted to Certain Commodities or Business Areas

Many persons believed that the black market was characteristic of certain commodities such as meat and gasoline, or fields of business, but a survey of violations has indicated that the black market was not the outgrowth of unique conditions of any particular industry, the peculiar injustice of certain regulations, the squeeze at a particular level of trade, or the conditions prevailing in certain parts of the country. There were black markets in all types of commodities. Our analysis has shown that extensive violations occurred in at least twenty-one major commodity groups and in many minor ones, and in all sections of business. Farmers, packers, manufacturers, wholesalers, retailers, large and small companies—all participated in the black market and each one took his particular share of illegal profits. It is possible that the producers' and wholesalers' violations were the more flagrant insofar as their violations were subsequently reflected in the retailers' dealings with the consumer. Still the relative seriousness of violations cannot be definitely established empirically.

Black Market Primarily Due to Certain Cultural and Ethical Definitions in Business

If the black market cannot, therefore, be attributed to certain elements in our society, or as so many individuals flaunting the law, to what can we attribute such wholesale disregard of the law at the very time one should expect patriotic compliance? Certainly the situation out of which this black market arose was complex. While the problem was primarily one of social and cultural factors, as the discussion will show, also involved were problems of economics and the relation of government to business. Before going into the matter in more detail, however, it is important to understand how these activities spread, for this was one of the underlying causes of the black market.

Most black market violations appear to have their origin in behavior learned in association from others, unethical and illegal practices being conveyed in the trade as part of a definition of the situation and rationalizations to support these violations of law being similarly transmitted by this differential association.[14] This type of learning must be regarded as a pull between unethical forces favorable to black market violations on the one hand and the forces leading to legal behavior. The same process of acquiring criminal behavior operates among businessmen as it does among ordinary criminals who learn how to steal and make counterfeit ration currency and how to dispose of it. Such a theory does not explain all violations, however, and, as will be indicated later, other factors had an effect on such differential association.

Both the extensiveness of the black market and the kinds of violations indicate primarily subcultural transmission. Basically the black market appears to have been related to many practices current among certain elements in business during peacetime. Some of the black market represented "normal" business procedures which were outlawed by the government, while others represented unethical and illegal behavior which the government attempted to deal with during peacetime on a limited scale and whose extensiveness was probably accentuated by the opportunities afforded by the war. Among the practices that might be termed "normal" during peacetime were tie-in sales of certain commodities, the giving of excessive discounts or kickbacks to favored customers, and a certain amount of quality deterioration in products, particularly through up-grading.

We have indicated in the preceding chapter that peacetime violations of trade laws and regulations by businessmen are extensive. Some types of illegal practices current in peacetime are revealed in the reports of the Federal Trade Commission,

---

[14] By differential association is meant a person's contact with various cultural definitions. While the term usually refers to deviant or illegal cultural definitions, it actually signifies a relation between law-abiding norms and norms of disobedience to law and ethics. Also see Sutherland, *White Collar Crime,*. Chap. XIV.

which was established in 1914 to deal with unfair methods of competition in industry. There are many cases of false and misleading advertising, misbranding of commodities as to quality, purity, origin, source, attributes, or nature of manufacture, and their sale under names and circumstances which deceived the public. Many other violations come under such activities as procuring the business or trade secrets of competitors by espionage or by bribing their employees; making false and disparaging statements respecting competitors' products and business; conspiring to maintain uniform selling prices, terms, and conditions of sale through the use of a patent licensing system or combinations or agreements to fix, maintain, or depress prices; giving products misleading names in order to give them a value to the consumer which they would not otherwise possess; and shipping products at market prices to customers or prospective customers or to the customers or prospective customers of competitors without an order and then inducing or attempting by various means to induce the consignees to accept and purchase such consignments.[15] Sutherland found in his study that among the common illegal practices in business were violations of the antitrust laws and the fair labor practices laws, false advertising, illegal rebates, violation of trademark laws, the giving of illegal bonuses and commissions to officers and favored stockholders, "wash sales" of stocks and manipulation of the market to sell company securities, and false income tax returns.[16]

In some instances during the war almost the entire industry engaged in violations of particular types, as for example, the lumber industry in the South and the poultry industry in

---

15 See the annual reports of the Federal Trade Commission.
16 Sutherland, *White Collar Crime.*

the Delmarva Peninsula, "where a very high proportion of the business was transacted in flagrant and intentional violation."[17]

Many types of black market violations were picked up from conversations of businessmen and descriptions of violations appearing in trade newspapers and the general press. In most cases there was a remarkable similarity in the nature of the violations, particularly in certain evasive practices in the meat black market and the side payments in used-car violations. The extensiveness of the relations with the professional criminals in the gasoline black market indicates that knowledge of how to obtain illegal ration currency was acquired, in part, from other gasoline dealers. In some black market activities the pattern of violation was diffused from the supplier to the purchasing concern. In others there was actual collusion between buyer and seller. In still other cases large concerns diffused the violations among their subsidiaries. Competitors copied illegal practices not necessarily to stay in business but rather to take advantage of the additional profits afforded. The following cases illustrate, at least in part, the explanation of the violations through differential association.

1. An established commission agent in meat sales, who, as far as is known, up to that time had never participated in the black market, received a long-distance telephone call from a meat dealer in another part of the country. According to the telephone conversation, the latter asked how conditions were and "I told him that conditions were miserable and I was having a difficult time and I wished to goodness he would give me some meat to sell. At that time I said, 'I understand that you have been shipping some meat into ————.' " At this the meat dealer laughed and said, "So, you did wake up! How would you like to handle some meat?" The proposi-

---

[17] Mansfield, *op. cit.*, p. 256.

tion was then outlined calling for shipments invoiced at ceiling prices. Cash side payments were to be secured in ———— and instructions were given that no checks were to be taken or any receipts given for the cash. A contact man was to pick up the cash.

2. In a flagrant violation, scrap metal, essential to the armed services, was upgraded by the inclusion of tin cans and then sold as No. 1 scrap. The owners of this concern, which operated in several states, specifically instructed their employees to include tin cans in the material invoiced. They, moreover, instructed the employees in the manner of handling such scrap so that the tin cans would be concealed in the bundle and would not be visible upon inspection.

3. During 1942 two eastern tire salesmen were instrumental in organizing a state-wide ring which purchased, received, and transferred new rubber tires and tubes without exchanging rationing certificates. In this case the two principal defendants arranged a meeting with retail tire dealers, who later became involved also, and explained the method that they were using to transfer tires without surrendering rationing or replenishment certificates and advised them that they could get any tires they needed. The plan was to have signed blank billheads on printed stationery to be used as "sign-offs," giving the impression that the principals were bona fide agents when acquiring tires in large metropolitan centers. The tires were then sold to the retailers at a cash profit and then resold by the latter mostly in bulk sales. No certificates were to be used in transferring these tires, and no accurate records were to be kept of the transactions, since it was suggested that the retailers bill these tires to "phony" individuals or to defunct garages which had been out of business for many years. The eventual tire ring involved a large number of dealers in scattered cities and towns who disposed of thousands of tires through this illegal device.[18]

---

[18] Cases from unpublished Enforcement Department case material.

Many violations indicated such great ingenuity that they undoubtedly represented the assistance given by lawyers and others who helped work out a method of getting around or violating the regulations. Reports from informed persons indicated that advisers were hired by business concerns, or legal advice was sought, in order to discover just how close one could come to breaking a regulation without being subject to prosecution.[19] Numerous amendments to the various regulations, which were often the subject of ridicule by the press and various business interests, became necessary when ways and means of getting around them were devised.

Evidence of both consensus and organized behavior among certain business interests further supports the view that the black market was primarily a product of differential association. Examples of such organized behavior on the part of some businessmen were their planned violations, attitudes toward enforcement personnel, lack of condemnation for violators, reluctance to inform on black market violators, and their general failure to offer real support to the government program. Many black market offenses involved a close-knit chain of relationships between various levels of activity, for example, manufacturers, wholesalers, and retailers in textiles and apparel. Some activities tied together parent company and subsidiary. Other violations were organized on an extensive geographical basis, as in a used-car conspiracy, for example, which involved thirty-one persons centering around southern Illinois, the entire state of Kentucky, and Detroit. This conspiracy involved pick-

---

[19] Some attorneys were hired away from the OPA for this purpose. In most cases the attorney did not actually participate in a trial involving the OPA, which would have been contrary to the federal statutes prohibiting a former government employee from appearing against the government for a period of two years. This did not, however, deter such individuals from working behind the scenes in some law firms.

ing up used cars and redistributing them at over-ceiling sales throughout the country. In another case a postwar black market in wholesale food was operated out of a small Wisconsin city with a hotel room in New York as the eastern office of operation. Practically all dealings of the company were in the black market, including the sale of corn syrups, dextrose, butter and eggs, poultry and meats, and about 800 carloads of cheese. Payments were made in bills of small denominations to an agent who kept the room continuously in a New York hotel where these illegal payments were made.

There was also consensus among certain sections of business that the OPA enforcement staff was stupid and inefficient. Interviews, for example, with wholesale food dealers found most of them in agreement on this point of stupidity and inefficiency. Whether investigators displayed these characteristics is irrelevant here, for it would be difficult for potential violators to be objective. Certainly there was little indication that these people wanted, or tried to get, more intelligent and better trained enforcement officials.

If you give them more supplies the enforcing end will take care of itself. They need more enforcement officers that are of the intelligent type. A lot that they have now are qualified to join the Gestapo. Too many assume you're dishonest before they start.— Eastern grocery dealer.

I might abolish it [the OPA] entirely—now I'm not saying I would but I might—it sure needs a good overhauling. I'd cut the payroll to one third. Put more efficient men in charge. I had 14 coops of chickens marked hens and springs and the OPA man comes along and he looked at them and he said, "Are you sure those hens are not springs?" He didn't know hens from springs. Now you know he shouldn't have been trying to tell us how to run the chicken business if he didn't know hens from springs! I think it's wrong to have a twenty-eight-old lawyer who has just graduated from college come in trying to tell you how to run your business.— Midwestern poultry dealer.[20]

Although there were some instances where businessmen offered to help police their trades, a study of the testimony of representatives of business organizations before congressional committees, as well as of interviews with businessmen, indicates that nearly all statements were directed at the weakening of enforcement or in favor of outright repeal of the entire program because of its "failure." Conversations with the man on the street, discussions in the trade press, even the attitudes of many newspapers were such as to convince many a businessman that his fellows, as well as a majority of the public, shared his disrespect for the OPA. There is little evidence to indicate that leading representatives of many business trades made speeches or used other means to appeal for real compliance in their trades. Most efforts were directed at attacks on the OPA or toward achieving greater liberality in the regulations. When food wholesalers were asked what they would do to help enforce regulations, the following replies were typical:

Lady, it can't be done, not if they put a whole army of people to work. You are not going to get me to propose anything. I wouldn't be connected with that OPA, because it just isn't doing any good. In the first world war we just let supply and demand take care of the situation and we got along all right.—Midwestern meat dealer.

I wouldn't have any [suggestions] to give you. Before I'd take a job with the OPA I'd retire. There are too many parasites in the government now. You are doing your best to put me down on that question but no matter how you word it I won't offer any sugges-

---

[20] Cases taken from interviews, "Opinion Survey of Food Wholesalers," cited above.

tions on how to enforce something I don't believe in.—Midwestern grocery dealer.

I'm not in favor of the OPA regulations so I wouldn't want to make any suggestions as to how to force people to comply. But understand this: as long as there are OPA regulations I'll abide by them. [*Question:* Couldn't you suppose that you were in favor of them? Couldn't you make some suggestions under these circumstances?] No. It'd be too much of a strain on my imagination!— Midwestern grocery dealer.[21]

Some businessmen also displayed considerable consensus about black market violators, for there is little indication that many of them regarded such people, or, in fact, any violators of wartime regulations, as persons who had lost much face or prestige. At the height of the meat or apparel black market, for example, large sections of these trades stuck together. Nothing better illustrates the degree of organization and consensus among businessmen than their reluctance to testify against each other. One southwestern fresh fruit and vegetable dealer described it this way: "When a merchant buys, we tell him of all the over-ceiling fellows that we know about—but we don't report them to the OPA."[22] A Pittsburgh case illustrates this reluctance to inform on another businessman engaging in black market operations. After a local distributor of frozen meat and poultry had received a bill for a carload of poultry which he was expecting, he was approached by a black marketeer who had somehow learned of the shipment and offered him $3,000, plus the price of the poultry itself, if he would make this carload over to him. Although the poultry dealer refused the offer, saying he "couldn't look at his own face in the mirror" if he

---

21 *Ibid.*

22 "Opinion Survey of Food Wholesalers." This behavior was certainly not true of all businessmen, as the OPA received numerous complaints of violations.

did such a thing, since his own son was "over there fighting for us," he did not report the offer, nor could he be persuaded by the OPA to reveal the name of the man who had approached him.[23]

Despite numerous rationalizations and protestations, the tradition of not testifying against others was effective. As one OPA official well familiar with this practice put it, "they will not directly tattle on their competitors." There were occasional cases of informing against particularly bad chiselers and newcomers, but in general, when they were faced with the problem of punishing certain persons in order to clear up a particularly bad black market situation, it was extremely difficult to persuade businessmen to testify. Even persons being milked by numerous violations of suppliers in the form of upgrading and tie-ins with worthless commodities would rarely testify. While undoubtedly some of this reluctance, particularly among retailers, involved the fear of being cut off from supplies, this explanation does not sufficiently account for the degree of this solidarity. Some businessmen felt that the trade would disapprove of behavior which might undermine a solid front against the government as well as interfere with supplies. In one criminal case in 1944 involving one of the leading wholesale liquor dealers of a large city, the government maintained that he was charging over-ceiling prices and engaging in extensive tie-in sales. Although this had been admitted by retailers to the investigators, not a single one in a long parade of retailers on the witness stand confirmed such violations.[24] This was true

---

[23] From OPA Information Department data.

[24] It appears that if business concerns had been sufficiently well organized or had been particularly inclined to exert collective pressure upon their suppliers they could have forced compliance with the regulations. This is indicated by the fact, which was frequently heard, that many large concerns, particularly chains, forced compliance by their suppliers on the ground that they would not

even where they were not having direct business dealings with the suspected offenders. Realization that the OPA was a legal agency and part of the government of the United States was a disconcerting thought which many an associate of a businessman helped him to overcome.[25] To speak with only those sharing similar attitudes served to reinforce a belief and did not bring it out into the light of logical scrutiny.

Most of the sellers subject to controls were businessmen unaccustomed to such outside interference in the operation of their businesses, and in many instances resentful of it on principle. Moreover, the vast majority of them were respected members of their community. They were not professional criminals—on the contrary, they were regarded and regarded themselves as staunch supporters of the constituted order. Since the regulations being enforced often set new and unusual restrictions on customary practices, violations of these restrictions did not in themselves seem heinous offenses, either to the violators or to the public generally. . . . Firms in trouble frequently found influential friends and character witnesses to intercede for them.[26]

Criticisms of Differential Association as a Complete Explanation of the Black Market

While it is likely that most cases of violations of price and rationing regulations, where there had been continuous and intimate association with unethical and illegal differential norms and at the same time some isolation from other norms, can be satisfactorily explained by a theory of differential asso-

pay over-ceiling prices for the commodities they obtained. The small merchant, however, unless organized, had difficulty in exerting such control.

[25] In fact, to counteract the misconception that the OPA was something different from other agencies of the government, nearly all OPA materials, such as stationery, legal notices, as well as many of the forms used in enforcement cases, employed the phrase "The United States Government."

[26] Mansfield, op. cit., p. 257.

ciation, there are several limitations in such a general theory as an explanation for *all* cases.[27] Such a theory does not adequately explain why some individuals who were familiar with the techniques and the rationalizations of black market violations, and were frequently associated with persons similarly familiar, did not engage in such practices. It is doubtful whether any businessman could participate in a given line of business for any length of time, either in peacetime or in wartime, without acquiring a rather complete knowledge of the illegal practices in his trade. This was particularly true of black market practices as a subject of much general conversation at this time. Certainly besides talking with competitors and customers a businessman had ample opportunity to read of techniques of black market violations in the average newspaper and trade journal. It is difficult to explain, therefore, why thousands of business concerns, even in those commodities where one may have expected greater violation, appeared to have complied rather fully with the wartime regulations. In some instances it appears that variables other than continuous and extensive contacts with norms favorable to crime, as opposed to unfavorable definitions as Sutherland has suggested, must be introduced to explain the violation. Differential association discounts not only personality factors but also questions of various pressures from suppliers and even sometimes from consumers leading to violation. The question of restriction on profits must also be considered. Inefficiency of government, "red tape," and other factors are also not taken into account in such an analysis.

The theory of differential association, moreover, does not allow sufficiently either for the independent invention of a

---

[27] Sutherland, for example, has suggested differential association as a universal explanation of all white collar crime. See his *White Collar Crime,* Chap. XIV.

complex black market technique or for the need for acquiring any technique for those black market violations which were extraordinarily simple. The validity of this particular statement should, of course, be ascertained by further detailed study of a number of black market case histories. Certainly many black market violations, involving similar techniques, appeared in isolated areas. In many violations only a single person seems to have been involved. There was, for example, ample evidence to indicate that rather complex evasive violations of rent regulations appeared in relatively isolated areas. Apparently they were independently devised, since ordinarily association between landlords is limited.

It seems likely that there were occasions when attitudes favorable to law violations were selectively incorporated or rejected on the basis of the individual's general personality pattern. By this it is suggested that *some,* but by no means all, persons tended to accept or reject black market opportunities according to their basic personality make-up. Some of these general personality patterns, which probably were important in accounting, in some instances, for participation, or lack of participation, in the black market, were egocentricity, emotional insecurity or feelings of personal inadequacy, negative attitudes toward other persons in general, the relative importance of status symbols of money as compared with nationalism, and the relative lack of importance of one's personal, family, or business reputation.[28] Many of these basic attitudes are

---

[28] Illustrating the role which psychogenic traits might play in black market violations is the following case. The middle-aged owner of a grain company, with no criminal record of previous arrests or convictions, stated that he had to buy black market corn in order to keep his customers, who were badly in need of grain. He claimed he made only 1 per cent profit on the corn after paying over-ceiling prices. He secured the grain by hiring another man to act as his contact man with the farmer. The buyer was paid a commission for all the corn he secured. The owner would write a check for the ceiling price and then write

derived from the culture, and thus cultural emphasis lends additional support to attitudes which may have also been a product of early differential experience.[29] Moreover, these attitudes, which are often in conflict, may have been the result of the different integration of the several social roles which each individual plays in society.[30] This fact has been pointed out by Sellin: "An important function of etiological research is, there-

another check for the over-ceiling amount, entering only the first check on his books.

His attitude at the time of the arrest was very antagonistic, and he claimed that if he hadn't "shot off his mouth" he would have gotten off with a lighter sentence, because "the government doesn't like it when you talk back." The reports of the neighbors stated that he was a "high-pressure" fellow. It is clear from the record that this man made every attempt to deceive the enforcement officers. The offender felt that he was not guilty of any wrongdoing, because the government had no right to shut him off from the regular market and he felt that all regulations were null and void, and for this reason he couldn't see any reason why he should obey them. On more than one instance he remarked, "This is all the bunk." The dealer stated that the government could not put him out of business and that he would continue to buy corn at whatever price he had to pay, ceiling price or no ceiling price. He thought that the government should be charged with "restraint of trade." In this case the defendant had almost developed a persecution complex and thought that everyone was at fault except himself. The offender had an exaggerated feeling of importance, was a "smart aleck," and regarded himself as a "big business man."—From a case record.

[29] Another difficulty in differential association as a universal explanation of the black market is that the theory tends to overemphasize the more recent developments, notably in connection with his business occupation, in the individual's personality rather than the importance of childhood behavior patterns in the formation of personality. These early behavior patterns may well be important enough to counterbalance or play a part in the acceptance or rejection of illegal attitudes involved in later association with the antisocial conduct of those participating in the black market.

[30] Another criticism of differential association as a complete explanation of black market violations is that, according to this theory, behavior is largely accounted for in terms of a single social role or part the person plays in society, which in the case of black market violations was that of a businessman. The same individual might have played a variety of other social roles, and behavior such as that involved in violating or not violating the law may well have involved an integration of several conflicting roles. In the case of offenders of the lower socioeconomic classes there is likely to be more similarity in the behavior of different roles in which the person is engaged. When considering offenders of the white collar class, such as most of those engaging in the black market, there is probably less similarity in the several roles.

fore, the formulation of generalizations which permit us to differentiate the violator from the conformist, in terms of personality structure or growth process."[31] Several others besides Sellin have suggested that this is one of the most crucial issues in criminological research.[32] Perhaps before finding a final answer to this question criminology will have to wait on further understanding of the nature of personality differences.

Sutherland has stated, however, that he believes the variation in crimes of a group of corporations which he studied was not the result of personality factors.[33] For example, corporations which have violated the antitrust laws have been doing so for over forty years. He cites, as further evidence, that a comparison of the number of philanthropists and public-spirited citizens on boards of directors at various times shows little difference in the extent of violation. The fact that the composition of boards of directors varies from one concern to another indi-

---

[31] Sellin, *op. cit.*, p. 40. "Ultimately, science must be able to state that if a person with certain personality elements in a certain configuration happens to be placed in a certain typical life situation, he will probably react in a certain manner, whether the law punishes this response as a crime or tolerates it as unimportant."—*Ibid.*, pp. 44–45.

[32] Walter C. Reckless, *The Etiology of Delinquent and Criminal Behavior,* Bulletin No. 50 (New York: Social Science Research Council, 1943), pp. 51–52, 62–63, 64–67, 70–73, and 81. "Whether this proposition [differential association] can be maintained is doubtful, although future research will have to be the judge. The necessity for discovering differential response, which is something more than frequency and consistency of contacts and which assumes that personality and experience act selectively on exposures to behavior patterns, has already been mentioned. Differential association and differential response are more likely to occur together than either one singly and separately."—*Ibid.*, p. 62. See particularly the discussion by Ernest W. Burgess in Clifford Shaw and Henry McKay, *Brothers in Crime* (Chicago: The University of Chicago Press, 1938). Sutherland, "The Relation between Personal Traits and Associational Patterns," in Reckless, *The Etiology of Delinquent and Criminal Behavior,* pp. 131–138. Marshall Clinard, "Criminological Theories of Violations of Wartime Regulations," *loc. cit.*, pp. 258–270. Also his "Rural Criminal Offenders," *American Journal of Sociology,* L (July, 1944), 38–45. A. R. Lindesmith and H. W. Dunham, "Some Principles of Criminal Typology," *Social Forces,* XIX (March, 1941), 307–314.

[33] Sutherland, *White Collar Crime,* p. 265.

cates that personalities have little bearing on violation. These conclusions, however, have been reached with only preliminary research and, while true in many cases, cannot be taken as evidence that personality has no bearing at all on violations. Even a casual study of many prominent violators of government regulations would reveal some definite antisocial personality traits. The fact that boards of directors appear similar does not mean that one individual may not have dominated the decisions which the board reached.

Economic Factors in the Black Market

Having examined the role of differential association in the black market, it is important to investigate the explanations and rationalizations or reasons put forth by businessmen for their disregard of the price and rationing regulations. We have already pointed out that most of these violations were not looked upon as crimes by businessmen, although they actually were and should be treated sociologically as criminal acts. Even if their acts were against the law, however, many rationalized that the law could be evaded or openly broken if it were unjust. They complained that under these wartime anti-inflation laws it was impossible to make profits. This complaint, namely, that government controls did not allow business to make profits and that in order to maintain their businesses they had to engage in black market practices, was one of the most widely held explanations for the black market. The following comments by businessmen are characteristic: "If a man can't make a living legitimately he is going to make it illegitimately." "The war has nothing to do with it—just provide business with a fair profit and business will be done legitimately." "I know that 99 per·cent start out honest but these new regulations make men dishonest. A man becomes a thief when he is hungry." "They've

Table 28

National Income and Profits before and after Taxes,
All Private Corporations, 1929 and 1939–1947

(Billions of dollars)

YEAR	TOTAL NATIONAL INCOME *	CORPORATE PROFITS BEFORE TAXES	CORPORATE PROFITS AFTER TAXES		
			TOTAL	DIVIDEND PAYMENTS	UNDISTRIBUTED PROFITS
1929	87.4	9.8	8.4	5.8	2.6
1939	72.5	6.5	5.0	3.8	1.2
1940	81.3	9.3	6.4	4.0	2.4
1941	103.8	17.2	9.4	4.5	4.9
1942	136.5	21.1	9.4	4.3	5.1
1943	168.3	24.5	10.4	4.5	5.9
1944	182.4	24.3	10.8	4.7	6.1
1945	181.7	20.4	8.7	4.7	4.0
1946	179.3	21.8	12.8	5.6	7.2
1947	202.5	29.8	18.1	6.9	11.2

* National income is the total net income earned in production by individuals or business. The concept of national income currently used differs from the concept of gross national product in that it excludes depreciation charges and other allowances for business and institutional consumption of durable capital goods.

SOURCE: Data from the Department of Commerce, published in *The Economic Report of the President,* January, 1949 (Washington: Government Printing Office, 1949).

got overhead to pay and all that, so if they can't get the stuff any other way they've got to do it illegally." "It would be easier to enforce regulations if ceiling prices were allowed to go higher on certain articles so that a man could make a half-way decent living." An examination of the facts fails to show much validity in this explanation, for profits were generally high during the war period at all levels of production and distribution.

WARTIME PROFITS. Generally, business made higher profits, business activity was at a higher level, and business failures were far lower under price and rationing controls than at any previous time, including 1929. While it is true that some business concerns suffered loss of profits, they were a small minority, and the over-all figures show large profits for business. The total national income rose from 72.5 billion dollars in 1939 to slightly over 180 billion in 1944 and 1945. Profits of private corporations, before taxes, increased from 6.5 billion dollars in 1939 to an average of 22.5 billion dollars in the 1944–1945 period, and even when allowance is made for increased wartime taxes we still find that corporate profits were almost twice as great in the 1944–1945 period. (See Table 28.) Corporate profits in trade after taxes as a percentage of sales did not decline during the war years. In 1939 they amounted to 1.5 per cent and were 2.3 during the 1944–1945 period. (See Table 29.) Industrial production during the war years was over twice as great as in 1939. (See Table 30.) Durable goods manufacturing was over three times as great in some years, the index for non-durable goods being between 158 and 176. While there were 13,664 business failures in 1940, there was an annual average of 1,016 during the 1944–1945 period. (See Chart 2.)

The above figures include all industries, but if we compare manufacturing, wholesale, and retail profits in 1939 with those during the war years we find the same general picture of greatly increased profits and fewer failures. Wholesale profits before taxes in 1944 were over three times greater than in 1939, and retail profits were over four times as great. (See Table 31.) If adjustments were to be made for increased taxes the wartime index would still be several times greater. Wholesale profits after taxes were 1.3 per cent of sales and in the war years 1.7 per cent, while retail profits increased from 1.7 to approxi-

mately 3.0 per cent between 1944 and 1945. (See Table 29.)
There were 1,361 failures in the wholesale trade in 1940, and

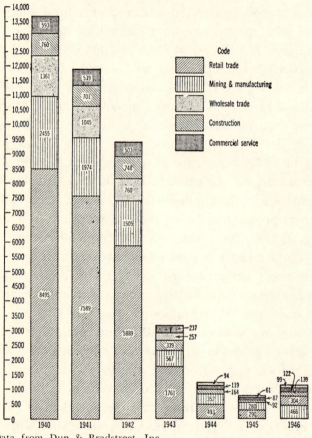

CHART 2

INDUSTRIAL AND COMMERCIAL FAILURES, BY INDUSTRIAL GROUPS
AND INDUSTRIES, 1940–1946

Data from Dun & Bradstreet, Inc.

an average of 78 in the 1944–1945 period. (See Chart 2.) Almost
8,500 retail establishments failed in 1940, while in 1944 the
number was 164 and in 1945 only 92. These figures hardly

Table 29

Corporate Sales and Profits, as Per Cent of Sales, 1939–1947

(Millions of dollars)

YEAR	TOTAL			WHOLESALE			RETAIL		
	CORPORATE SALES	CORPORATE PROFITS* AFTER TAXES	PROFITS AS PER CENT OF SALES	CORPORATE SALES	CORPORATE PROFITS AFTER TAXES	PROFITS AS PER CENT OF SALES	CORPORATE SALES	CORPORATE PROFITS AFTER TAXES	PROFITS AS PER CENT OF SALES
1939	42,262	641	1.5	21,314	276	1.3	20,948	365	1.7
1940	46,638	785	1.7	23,532	349	1.5	23,106	436	1.9
1941	57,081	1235	2.2	29,707	567	1.9	27,374	668	2.4
1942	55,184	1160	2.1	29,026	480	1.7	26,158	680	2.6
1943	57,616	1293	2.2	30,306	501	1.7	27,310	792	2.9
1944	61,023	1376	2.3	32,311	548	1.7	28,712	828	2.9
1945	65,005	1518	2.3	34,746	589	1.7	31,159	929	3.0
1946	85,920	2849	3.3	44,648	1053	2.4	41,272	1796	4.4
1947	98,322	2799	2.8	49,926	1011	2.0	48,396	1788	3.7

* After federal and state income and excess profits taxes.
SOURCE: Computed from *The Economic Almanac* for 1949.

317

indicate an extensive squeeze on retail dealers by the black market activities of wholesalers.

Net corporation profits before taxes were not only extremely high at manufacturing, wholesale, and retail levels but in almost all commodities, including a number of commodities

Table 30

Industrial Production Index, 1939–1947

(*1935–1939 = 100; seasonally adjusted*)

YEAR	TOTAL INDUSTRIAL PRODUCTION	MANUFACTURERS		
		TOTAL	DURABLE	NONDURABLE
1939	109	109	109	109
1940	125	126	139	115
1941	162	168	201	142
1942	199	212	279	158
1943	239	258	360	176
1944	235	252	353	171
1945	203	214	274	166
1946	170	177	192	165
1947	187	194	220	172

SOURCE: Data from *The Economic Report of the President.* January, 1949 (Washington: Government Printing Office, 1949).

where there were extensive black markets. Net profits before taxes in lumber and timber in 1944 were over eight times as great as in 1939, paper and allied products four times, retail apparel and accessories over ten times; even retail filling station profits were up 81 per cent over 1939. (See Table 32.) The magnitude of the increase in profits would still be great if calculated after taxes. Some indication of the favorable profit situation in rents, for example, was given in previous chapters. There were a few failures in a number of manufacturing com-

Table 31

Corporation Net Profits, before Taxes, by Major
Industrial Groups, 1939–1944
(*Index numbers: 1939 = 100; all money figures in millions
of dollars*)

YEAR	MANUFACTURING		WHOLESALE		RETAIL	
	PROFITS	INDEX NUMBER	PROFITS	INDEX NUMBER	PROFITS	INDEX NUMBER
1939	$ 3,580.1	100	$ 329.9	100	$ 405.5	100
1940	6,317.0	149	437.2	133	535.4	132
1941	10,439.3	292	904.4	274	997.0	246
1942	13,659.6	382	1,037.0	314	1,326.5	327
1943	16,593.7	463	1,190.5	361	1,647.8	406
1944	14,864.3	415	1,215.5	368	1,787.9	441
1945	10,256.8	286	1,216.3	368	1,889.5	467

SOURCE: Computed from *Statistical Abstract of the United States, 1942–
1948.*

modity lines where there were extensive black markets, although it might be contended that these failures were due to
the fact these concerns did not engage in black market activities. (See Table 33.) For example, only 2 textile manufacturers
and 17 manufacturers of apparel and other finished textile
products failed in 1945, as compared with 97 and 571 in 1939.

Some interesting comments on the economic factors accounting for these high profits are indicated in the following
statements by businessmen.[34]

One thing, ceilings have eliminated the great losses we used
to take in this business, overnight practically. We used to buy a car
[load] on Saturday and maybe on Monday the price would drop so

[34] "Opinion Survey of Food Wholesalers."

Table 32

Index Numbers of Corporation Net Profits,
by Industrial Groups, 1939–1944

(*Index numbers: 1939 = 100*)

INDUSTRIAL GROUP	1939	1940	1941	1942	1943	1944
Lumber and timber products...	100	336	914	1,074	969	886
Furniture and finished lumber products...	100	145	315	330	324	378
Paper and allied products...	100	180	349	353	392	410
Drug stores (retail)...	100	148	239	476	640	595
Apparel and accessories (retail)	100	183	429	706	951	1,017
Furniture and house furnishings (retail)....	100	158	404	621	704	628
Filling stations (retail)...	100	124	236	186	172	181

SOURCE: *Statistical Abstract of the United States, 1942–1948.* Before taxes.

bad we would lose thousands of dollars. It's the protection against the dropping of prices that has made it possible for us to make more money under price regulation than we ever did before.—Midwestern fresh fruit and vegetable dealer.

If it were not for the OPA we would have been out of business long ago. There's no comparison in the prices in this war to what they were in the last. OPA is absolutely necessary though it makes operating more expensive and there's a lot of red tape. But it has held the prices and kept us in business so we shouldn't howl too much.—Western grocery dealer.

Table 33
Failures in Six Manufacturing Groups, 1939–1946

TYPE OF INDUSTRY	1939		1940		1941		1942		1943		1944		1945		1946	
	NUM-BER	RATE PER 1,000	NUM-BER	RATE PER 1,000	NUM-BER	RATE PER 1,000	NUM-BER	RATE PER 1,000	NUM-BER	RATE PER 1,000	NUM-BER	RATE PER 1,000	NUM-BER	RATE PER 1,000	NUM-BER	RATE PER 1,000
Food and kindred products	636	12.2	400	7.4	423	7.6	274	5.0	79	1.5	30	0.6	14	0.3	28	0.5
Textile mill products	97	19.4	92	20.0	36	7.7	28	6.0	4	0.9	5	1.1	2	0.4	1	0.2
Apparel and other finished textile products	571	28.0	519	27.5	401	21.0	262	13.6	81	4.4	25	1.2	17	0.7	26	0.9
Lumber and timber basic products	93	4.1	79	3.5	36	1.5	35	1.4	17	0.6	31	1.0	22	0.7	24	0.6
Furniture and finished lumber products	142	13.8	225	21.8	175	15.6	136	11.8	53	4.2	26	1.9	27	1.8	35	2.1
Paper and allied products	32	12.8	37	14.8	15	6.0	19	7.3	10	4.0	3	1.2	5	1.9	2	0.7

SOURCE: Marketing and Research Division, Dun & Bradstreet, Inc., 1947.

Table 34
Net Earnings of Meat-Packing Industry, 1935–1947

PERIOD	NET WORTH (000,000)	TOTAL SALES (000,000)	NET EARNINGS (000,000)	PER CENT RETURN		EARNINGS PER 100 LB.	
				ON NET WORTH	PER DOLLAR SALES	LIVE WEIGHT	DRESSED WEIGHT
5 year average 1935–1939	$705	$3,045	$ 25	3.55	0.82	$0.11	$0.19
5 year average 1940–1944	766	5,118	64	8.35	1.25	0.19	0.35
1940	721	3,158	42	5.85	1.34	0.15	0.27
1941	746	4,066	65	8.66	1.59	0.22	0.40
1942	779	5,781	67	8.64	1.16	0.20	0.37
1943	783	6,181	72	9.17	1.16	0.20	0.36
1944	802	6,404	72	8.93	1.12	0.19	0.35
1945	917	5,744	52	5.62	0.90	0.18	0.29
1946	945	6,145	143	15.17	2.33	0.48	0.75
1947	975*	9,200*	138*	14.20*	1.50*	0.42*	0.67*

* Estimates by American Meat Institute.

SOURCE: Net Worth, Total Sales and Net Earnings reported by the Packers and Stockyards Division, United States Department of Agriculture. Earnings per 100 lb. live and dressed weight are approximations calculated by the American Meat Institute, covering commercial slaughter. Table reprinted from *American Meat Institute Bulletin*, May 28, 1948.

On the whole, profits in the meat industry were not nearly as great during the war as in other commodities. The meat business, however, has always been noted for its small margin and small profits per unit. Data compiled by the United States Department of Agriculture showed that profits during the war period were higher than before the war. The meat industry made profits equal to 0.82 cents for 1 dollar of sales in 1935–1939, while in 1944 the profits were 1.12 cents for 1 dollar of sales. (See Table 34.) Using 1935–1939 as a base, net earnings to net worth in 1943 and 1944 varied between two and three times as great. As further substantiation of this argument, on various occasions the meat regulations were challenged according to law, as constituting a hardship, but the various decisions before the United States Emergency Court of Appeals almost uniformly upheld the profitability of operations under the meat regulations.[35]

The contention, then, of generally losing money cannot be established. Indeed these figures on profits, large as they are, consist for the most part of legitimate profits, and doubtless do not include a considerable proportion of black market dealings which were not reported in income tax returns.[36] Industries with exceptionally heavy violations, as, for example, textiles, also showed heavy profits. In many commodities violations ex-

---

[35] Elkinton, *op. cit.*, pp. 184–206.

[36] In fact, several contemporary articles attributed the riotous postwar living to persons who had made large wartime profits, as in the following item in *Newsweek:* "Nobody knew where all the money came from: few cared. Undoubtedly the bulk had been amassed in four war years of black-marketing, but nobody could prove it. All that anybody seemed reasonably certain of was that $5 would get you lunch; a $1,000 bill, judiciously employed as a common under-the-table fee, might get you a $50-to-$100-a-week two-room apartment. Cab drivers were pocketing $300 and more a week of this spendthrift cash; a smart haberdasher could report the theft of a $1,500 necktie without eliciting more than a grunt from hundreds of nocturnal roisterers sweating out hangovers on the hot beach."—*Newsweek,* March 4, 1946, pp. 22–23. Also see *Time,* March 4, 1946, p. 23. Both of these accounts were about Miami, Florida.

tended into all lines of business and were often industry-wide rather than confined to a few individual concerns. Fortunately, we have a study which adds evidence to this conclusion. After interviewing several hundred Chicago producers and distributors of consumer goods, Katona concluded that sales and profits were not related to price violations.[37]

OTHER ECONOMIC FACTORS. Undoubtedly certain economic factors contributed to some violations, but they appear to have been emphasized far more than the evidence warrants. In a system of controls as extensive as these, not all concerns were able to make a profit even if the general profit picture was favorable. The application of controls in a largely uniform fashion, involving the regulation of various sizes and types of business, undoubtedly made staying in business and obeying the law two irreconcilable objectives in some instances. Particularly difficult were the pressures at various levels of business by the violations of suppliers. Some wholesalers, for example, in overcharging, or utilizing tie-in sales, contributed to the predicament for the retailer, who then had to sell at a loss or violate the law.

The alternatives to violating the law in such a situation were either to reduce profit margins and absorb some cases of overcharge—and many did just that as they do in peacetime under somewhat similar circumstances—or to expose the supplier to the OPA and testify against him, an action seldom taken. If there were repercussions, such as having supplies cut off, several concerns could have banded together not only to prevent this squeeze but to promise retaliation after the war. There was also the drastic possibility which some patriotic men did follow, and that was to give up dealing with this supplier or go out of business entirely.

---

[37] Katona, *op. cit.*, p. 165.

Statements have been made that large firms generally complied with the regulations, while small ones did not. It has been suggested that large firms were better able to absorb any squeeze, considered their reputations more carefully, were more aware of their social responsibilities, employed so many persons that violations could not possibly have been kept secret, were more frequently and thoroughly investigated, and had larger staffs to become familiar with and explain all regulations. Small firms, on the other hand, were thought to be more liable to a squeeze, to have little reputation to lose, not to keep adequate records and, therefore, to be able to make frequent cash transactions to hide violations and so were not as frequently investigated by the OPA. This explanation, while perhaps valid in some individual cases, does not appear to be substantiated by the facts, and sometimes these arguments were even reversed. No over-all conclusion can be drawn, for many large concerns did violate, whereas many small ones did not. Although the findings were inconclusive, a survey which investigated this particular problem among Chicago business concerns suggested that the size of the firm alone did not appear to be an important factor in violation.[38]

There is no evidence to indicate, then, that businessmen generally had to choose between making a living and entering the black market. Economic restrictions did interfere with the size of the profits and to this extent increased black market activity, but they did not cause it.[39] In general, the price ceil-

---

[38] *Ibid.*, pp. 128–129.

[39] In this connection one magazine carried a supposedly true story involving an interview with a textile merchant in the club car of a Miami—New York train. Finding that the businessman was wearing a one-thousand dollar necktie, the interviewer asked him how he got the money. After he described a sordid tale of black market dealings in textiles of a particularly flagrant nature, in violation of the regulations of the War Production Board and the OPA, the businessman was asked, "Couldn't you have made pretty good money if you

ings did not produce losses, but merely restricted even greater profits, which were available from illegal rather than legal dealings, offering great temptation particularly when others were dipping into the "gravy." Thus many businessmen regarded failures to make the most money possible from a sale as a "loss" which might be regarded as perfectly "normal" economics were it not for the fact it was a violation of the law.

The Role of Government in the Black Market

The government contributed in several ways to the extensiveness of the black market, but like the economic factors, these considerations cannot be thought of as a "cause" of the black market. First, the nature of the price and rationing laws was significant in explaining some violations. In some respects the statute represented a major change forced upon American society and the chief reason for expecting its support came from the fact that we were at war and compliance would help us win it. It was unfortunate that there were some who were not as much interested in contributing to the war effort as in making large profits. Although many laws had been passed in the interests of large groups of our citizens, the emergency Price Control Act was actually the first one to affect practically everyone in this country. The federal trade regulations, the Securities and Exchange Act, the Food and Drug Act, and even the National Labor Relations Act directly affected relatively small groups, although indirectly a great many people benefited, if only theoretically, without having to make any particular personal sacrifice. Furthermore, some of the restrictions put upon

---

hadn't gone in for the angles?" "Of course," he replied, caressing his tie, "but then I'd be wearing only a hundred dollar tie instead of a thousand dollar one."— Potomacus, "The Thousand-Dollar Necktie," *New Republic*, March 25, 1946, pp. 407–409. Ties costing this amount of money were a fad and served as a method of displaying wealth at a time when luxuries were not plentiful.

each of the groups in America were contrary to certain fundamental ideological thinking right up to the passage of the law.

The government itself made mistakes in the issuance and enforcement of these economic controls, although the most serious blunders occurred in the early period of price and rationing controls. Admittedly the problem of price and rationing control was an extremely complex one, as the black market in meat vividly demonstrated. Obviously it is virtually impossible during a war situation to work out an ideal control situation without regard to the urgencies of time, manpower shortages, facilities, and the opinion of both the public and the persons immediately affected by the control program. Without proper enforcement, however, it was difficult to impose earlier and more far-reaching controls over the entire economic system, including wage and price controls. It was also a mistake not to have done more to encourage an even distribution of supplies nationally to take limited supply pressures from certain areas. There were many rather stupid procedures and an unnecessary amount of reporting work or red tape. The absence of hard-hitting enforcement work in dealing with the early black market contributed to a general disrespect for the OPA during much of its existence. Yet nearly all business had previously been under some form of peacetime regulation and subject to government reports. The extent of violations in many commodity areas would seem to disprove the contention that bad regulations alone accounted for most violations, unless one wishes to take the position that all regulations were technically bad.

In addition, because of insufficient manpower, technical skill, and other factors, enforcement efforts throughout the war were generally inadequate to deal with the size of the problem and the black market. Businessmen saw competitors and others making additional profits from illegal activities without being punished, and others felt the impact of the "squeeze," with the government relatively impotent to deal with it. Many businessmen felt that any enforcement efforts of the government destroyed the effectiveness of informal compliance, and some went so far as to maintain that the individual businessman was at liberty to do as he wished and that it was up to the government's enforcement officers to apprehend him.

The enforcement actions which the government did take were undoubtedly too weak. Not only was the actual criminal sanction insufficiently employed, but civil and administrative actions did not recover anywhere near the amount of profit derived from the black market throughout the war.

The government failed to enlist adequately the voluntary support of business and sections of the public in dealing with the black market, even though many efforts were made in this direction. Many businessmen did not voluntarily accept the fact that practices which were legal before the war had become illegal by a temporary law. The public did not seriously condemn violators, with the exception of the ration currency violations. When the amount of the violation was trivial, the public was particularly tolerant, not realizing the aggregate effect of such practices. The sabotage of the government's efforts to control inflation by numerous vocal and irresponsible lobbyists and politicians, representing special interests rather than the consumer, helped to confuse rather than clarify the situation. A government official described this situation in the summer of 1943:

The public is, to a large extent, doubtful of the need for OPA regulations, ignorant of their provisions, and skeptical of their fairness. This is due to a number of factors. In large measure it can be attributed to unwarranted and unfair attacks by business interests, by congressmen and congressional committees, by newspapers, and by various pressure groups. Much of this stems from purely political motives.[40]

There appears, however, to be little substance to the charge that OPA personnel "fixed" many cases because of political considerations. Some black market cases were "fixed" through friends and through political influence, and bribes were taken by some attorneys and investigators, but for the most part the "fix" does not appear to have been involved in most enforcement actions. In terms of the total number of cases or the large number of personnel, cases involving bribery appear to have been but a small percentage[41] and could not have materially affected attitudes toward the government.

---

[40] Report on Enforcement to Chester A. Bowles, Senior Deputy Administrator, by Thomas I. Emerson, Associate General Counsel for the Office of Price Administration, August 9, 1943, p. 2.

[41] A small staff of investigators was assigned to the OPA Administrator whose work involved the detection of cases involving bribery and other corruption among OPA personnel and the very knowledge of this fact was partially effective in keeping such cases at a minimum. Another factor was the high caliber and integrity of most top-level wartime government appointments. Probably more important still was the fact that most employees thought of themselves as doing "war work."

CHAPTER TWELVE

The Black Market and Disorganization in Our Society

Probably the most important factor to be taken into consideration in an analysis of the black market is the general social and cultural conditions in which these wartime controls were operating. In fact, the black market might be looked upon as one symptom of social disorganization in our modern society. From the beginning of time the major problem of society has been the achievement of consensus, of agreement on social values.[1] Social disorganization represents a lack of consensus in values, the extent to which members of a society fail to have common understandings on fundamental issues.

The relativistic nature of social values in modern society, with its emphasis on individual choice, has put great strains, even in wartime, on social organization and democracy, both conditions resting essentially on general agreement about fundamental social objectives. Under these conditions the significance of laws becomes relative, some to be selectively obeyed accord-

---

[1] Louis Wirth, "Ideological Aspects of Social Disorganization," *American Sociological Review*, V, No. 4 (August, 1940), 473. Certainly a "common sociological orientation for the analyses of all social problems may thus be found in the conflict of values which characterizes every social problem."—Richard C. Fuller and Richard R. Myers, "Some Aspects of a Theory of Social Problems," *American Sociological Review*, VI, No. 1 (February, 1941), 25.

ing to whether one believes in them; others to be disobeyed if one does not. This absence of consensus on fundamental values in our society is illustrated in these pulls between group objectives and individual self-interest and disregard for personal integrity, and between national welfare and individual materialism. On the one side has been respect for law and on the other side disrespect for law if it stood in the way of individual material success, as in the case of the black market.

Processes of urbanization are largely responsible for this underlying lack of consensus in modern society and for the presence of the black market. America today shows the effects of a rapid transition from a rural to an urban way of life.[2] Human relationships have become more and more impersonal, and individualistic interests have tended to replace actions motivated by the general welfare. Social contacts are heterogeneous, with various competing value systems, and the goals of life are centered around pecuniary objectives. Consensus cannot be as easily achieved voluntarily by personal influences; hence it depends chiefly upon formal laws. Thus a situation has arisen in this country which has been favorable not only to extensive crime among lower socioeconomic groups but to the black market and other white collar crimes. The interests of many a businessman have changed from those of a local entrepreneur and tradesman to those of a participant in a larger impersonal society where the rules of the game are kept by an impersonal "government."

This lack of consensus and this conflict of values, apparent in interest groups and in the general public, can also be seen in the conflicts centering around the government's efforts to con-

---

[2] Louis Wirth, "Urbanism as a Way of Life," *American Journal of Sociology*, XLIV, No. 1 (July, 1938) 1–24.

trol the black market.[3] The black market represented a different value to each person, in terms of what he believed, and each person accordingly looked upon the numerous controls, as well as their violation, in a different way. Some people looked upon the government program of controls as immoral restrictions on private enterprise; some regarded them simply as laws to be obeyed; some considered them wartime measures necessitated by limited supplies; others believed that no sacrifice would be too great if it would ensure destruction of our enemies. These individual attitudes were reflected in actions taken individually and collectively either to promote compliance with the government's wartime program or to flaunt it. Whereas the public in general supported these controls, as shown repeatedly in surveys, many persons individually contributed to the expanding black market. While on the one hand business interests in general had a poor record of compliance, some businessmen had excellent records in this respect. This lack of consensus about the purpose of the government's enforcement program against the black market is illustrated in the following exchange between OPA Administrator Bowles and Senator Taft of Ohio after the latter had stated that the OPA operated on the assumption that businessmen were "crooks":

MR. BOWLES: That is an absolutely fantastic statement. I have been in business and Dr. Ney has been in business, and certainly we know what business is.

SENATOR TAFT: But you have been converted into a Government bureaucrat. I am not criticizing you personally, but the attitude of OPA today, as I get it from everybody who comes to me, is that the businessman is presumably a crook; that if he is trying

---

[3] For a discussion of the conflict of some other values in our society, see John A. Cuber and Robert A. Harper, *Problems of American Society: Values in Conflict* (New York: Henry Holt and Company, 1948).

to make a profit he is greedy—and that is another term you use there. The implication is that anybody who complains is a member of a pressure group; at least, that is the impression you have created on business.[4]

This general confusion in values, indicative of social disorganization implicit in the black market, can be seen more clearly in an examination of the major justifications commonly advanced by some businessmen as excuses for their violations and accepted by some segments of the general population. One of the most frequently advanced justifications was that these violations were not crimes and should not be considered as such or punished as such. We have already shown that the United States Congress, in making price and rationing controls into law, specifically stated that violations were socially injurious and subject to punishment, making the criminal sanction available for willful violations. One aspect of this value conflict was whether "crime" and "criminal" should be restricted to overt crimes and to those who, in their personal characteristics, fit the stereotype of the criminal who commits such crimes as robbery, burglary, or larceny. The consensus in our society has not yet reached the stage of considering business violations as crimes or their violations as criminal acts, even though they were, on the whole, willful and evasive transgressions of the law.

Even this value conflict was linked with the social differentiation in our society, for when confronted with actual descriptions of black market violations rather than abstractions, the public and business apparently differed greatly in their judgments of the seriousness of the offenses. As a result of a test of this nature, Hartung found that marked differences existed

---

[4] *Hearings before the Senate Committee on Banking and Currency,* Inflation Control Program of OPA, Seventy-ninth Congress, First Session, 1945, pp. 29–30.

between the public and members of the wholesale meat industry in the degree to which they would impose civil and criminal sanctions on types of black market violations.[5] He attributes this lack of consensus to social differentiation in our society, substantiating, he believes, Durkheim's thesis of the division of labor, namely that attitudes toward civil law are an index of social differentiation within a society.[6] Hartung found that the public made no distinction between black market cases dealt with by criminal action and those dealt with by civil. There was a significant difference between the attitudes of the public and businessmen in regard to civil cases; the public would treat civil black market cases much more severely than would businessmen. Businessmen and the public on the whole agreed that the criminal cases were justified; finally, members of the industry differed significantly among themselves in their attitude toward criminal cases.

Another common justification advanced by black market operators for their violations, and a further indication of some of the serious value conflicts in our modern society, was that the government had no right to interfere in the conduct of their business. According to this contention, our society has always encouraged individual enterprise, and these controls interfered needlessly and unjustifiably with the private individual's management of his own business. Generally there was much prosperity throughout the country during the war, salaries were high, and business should be entitled to as large a share of this income as it could get. Thus business, being controlled by a law which it considered unjust and regulations which it termed

---

[5] Hartung, "A Study in Law and Social Differentiation," Chaps. VI and VII, particularly pp. 292–293, and 330–334. Persons interviewed represented a random sample, and criteria of significant differences were applied to the data.

[6] George Simpson, *Émile Durkheim on the Division of Labor in Society* (New York: The Macmillan Company, 1933).

stupid and confusing, might be selective in its obedience to law and violate government regulations at will. Yet it would not be fair to businessmen to suggest that they were alone in their selective obedience to law, for such disobedience is characteristic of our culture. "The public attitude seems to be that one should use his own discretion as to obeying the laws, ... Thus there has developed a code of selective obedience of law. Some crimes are taboo in certain circles, but the crimes that are taboo in one circle may not be in another circle."[7]

Were this selective obedience to law to be followed to its logical conclusion by all groups in a society, obviously there would be a complete breakdown of law and order and the termination of the democratic process. This does not imply that everyone must believe in all laws, nor even that most laws must have universal support; rather it is suggested that if one believes in the democratic process and desires some degree of social organization a law should be obeyed by everyone as long as it is a law. Any philosophy that the law does not apply to certain groups or is unfair and therefore should not be obeyed suggests sentiments dangerous to the whole principle of majority rule in a capitalist democracy. Under such a system we assume that laws are passed to promote the general welfare, after free debate and by majority vote. Any group has the right to lobby against any law, assuming that such lobbying is fair,[8]

---

[7] Sutherland, *Principles of Criminology*, p. 180.

[8] "If we had been unwilling or unable to resist their [lobbyists] irresponsible efforts, price control would have collapsed many months ago. There are 1,500 registered lobbies in Washington, and a heavy proportion of them, I imagine, at one time or another, has aimed all its guns at the OPA, at least it seems that way. Certainly this is no news to the members of the Senate and the House of Representatives who have been forced to bear the brunt of their efforts. But my two and a half years of conflict with some of the country's outstanding lobbyists has not been discouraging. On the contrary, I have arrived at two rather happy conclusions from the standpoint of a healthy democracy. First. Rarely do these professional lobbyists fully represent their industry or

and everyone has a right to test the legality of a statute in the higher courts[9] or to seek amendment or outright repeal.

A situation wherein labor laws can be violated by unions because they consider the law to be unjust or to put unwarranted restrictions on their freedom, where farmers can defy laws affecting their behavior, and where businessmen flaunt laws affecting them, even though each is in agreement that the law should be obeyed by the other group, indicates that an organized society or an orderly democratic process can be continued only with extreme difficulty. When the United Mine Workers defied a court injunction in 1947 and were fined $3,500,000 (later reduced by the United States Supreme Court to $700,000) and again in 1948 were fined $1,400,000, farmers and businessmen generally thought this was justifiable, as the miners should have complied with the law. When farmers, during the last depression, defied the farm mortgage foreclosure laws, or at other times stopped milk trucks in transit and dumped their contents in order to keep up prices, other groups became seriously disturbed. When thousands of businessmen flaunted the price and rationing control laws, defied court injunctions, and, when apprehended, escaped stiff sentences, this behavior was considered right and proper by many of them but condemned by labor unions and many segments of the public. If each group or each class decides for itself

---

trade. Often they build OPA bonfires over the radio and in the press simply to establish their own reputation as accomplished firemen with the industries whom they represent. The thoughtful men in the industries which employ them are often well aware of this. Second. The most powerful group of all is still the collective opinion of all of our people."—Testimony of Chester A. Bowles, Administrator, Office of Price Administration, at the *Hearings before the Senate Committee on Banking and Currency*, Inflation Control Program of OPA, Seventy-ninth Congress, First Session, 1945, p. 16.

[9] In the case of price and rationing controls, the major legal issues were decided in favor of the OPA by the Emergency Court of Appeals and the Supreme Court rather early in the history of price control. On the average the OPA won about 95 per cent of all cases brought into federal courts each year.

whether the will of the majority applies to it, democratic society loses its ability to act effectively.

The implications of this attitude can be seen more clearly if one considers ordinary crimes. Many persons who engage in such crimes as robbery, burglary, or gambling not only consider the laws applying to them as unjust and too severe, but often have a number of rationalizations to support this opposition. Among these justifications are the brutality of the police, the corruption of political officials and the courts, as well as the general dishonesty of the public. Undoubtedly the black market has furnished ordinary criminals with sufficient justifications for their violations of law for many years to come. As a warden of one of our state prisons put it in 1946: "What am I supposed to do, retrain people to be honest in a dishonest world of black markets and frauds?"[10] Even juvenile delinquency cannot be effectively dealt with unless adult models also obey the laws and not expect youths to be the models of society.[11]

If this dilemma in the imposition of controls in a democracy cannot be resolved by democratic means in which the minority, such as business or labor, bows to the will of the majority, then what are the alternatives? Can the general public and honest businessmen be protected by the growth of business ethics and the development of a profession of business, plus the stronger arm of governmental action against the activities of small numbers of dishonest businessmen? No democratic society can continue to exist in the face of wholesale flaunting of the law by persons whose aim is to gain special privilege, whether it be labor, business, or organized racketeers. "Government has the primary responsibility of safeguarding the whole

---

[10] Made in the course of a talk to the author and his students.

[11] Marshall B. Clinard, "Secondary Community Influences and Juvenile Delinquency," *Annals of the American Academy of Political and Social Science,* CCLXI (January, 1949) , 42–55.

against the part, and in our world of organized interests this responsibility has grown ever more comprehensive and more complicated."[12]

Another indication of the widespread social disorganization implicit in the black market was the common rationalization that it was all right to violate the law if one could get away with it. This justification of illegal activities was held by many not only with reference to the black market but in relation to other laws as well. As one businessman put it: "Nobody pays any attention to laws whether he is a businessman, labor leader, or just a citizen. The problem is to keep from getting caught."[13] Certainly in their daily contacts businessmen could see that many black market activities were being countenanced, that there was a general failure to assist in the enforcement of the law, and that offenders who were apprehended did not lose status among their groups. There was even dissemination of ways to violate, and general disdain was shared by many for the agents of the government. Many of them contended that the government, by taking over the formal policing of business, actually destroyed the effectiveness of informal compliance by businessmen, so that it was then up to the enforcement officers to apprehend violators. Certainly those who rationalized in this fashion could not have realized the consequences of this philosophy, for the belief that the government must force entire compliance with the law or not at all is entirely out of accord with the assumed relation of law to the citizenry. Enforcement is supposed to be employed only against the exceptional violator.

One solution might have been to call it a hopeless task and repeal the law, with the possibility of military defeat and eco-

---

12 MacIver, *op. cit.*, pp. 349–350. Reprinted by permission.
13 Excerpt from an interview.

nomic chaos. Another might have been to turn over to business its own policing. This possibility was obviously inadvisable because of the complexity of our industrial economy and the fact that business simply had no way of regulating itself to the extent required under price and rationing controls. Furthermore, business does not yet have fully developed professional ethics. One recent writer has aptly described this situation:

> Business instinctively resists external controls which interfere with its freedom of action, first, on the ground that such restrictions prevent the operation of the business at full economic efficiency and, second, on grounds of principle. . . . In thus resisting the tyranny of the state, businessmen are on sound ground, but what they fail to concede is that the exercise of their rights as individuals lays upon them corresponding obligations to society which guarantees these rights. Too often there is denial that any such obligations exist, and the naïve belief persists that the public good will best be served where each individual promotes to the limit his own self-interest.[14]

Even where trade associations existed and where certain trade practices had been declared unethical by the group, these were often no more than policy statements of "ethics" and fair standards: "Agreements persist only to that point where it becomes profitable for some party to break them. A low-cost producer will not long stick to an agreed-upon price or allocation of business which protects a competitor at his expense. No practical, efficient method for policing and enforcing such agreements has been discovered."[15] One prominent trade association executive has referred to this problem in this way:

---

[14] Edward A. Duddy, "The Moral Implications of Business as a Profession," *Journal of Business*, XVIII, No. 2 (April, 1945), 70–71.

[15] Quoted in Temporary National Economic Committee Monograph No. 18, *Investigation of Concentration of Economic Power*, Trade Association Survey, Senate Committee Print, Seventy-sixth Congress, First Session, 1941, p. 52.

"Yes, we have a code of ethics. It's something like the Ten Commandments, a nice thing to refer to but something which we do very little about. When it comes to unfair competition any smart businessman can beat it. There are lots of ways."[16]

Not only did business have no way of controlling such a tremendous program; the whole fallacy of this position in regard to the OPA was amply demonstrated during World War I and the prestatutory period of price and rationing controls of World War II, when business groups had an opportunity to police themselves and failed. Furthermore, the history of price control showed that the prices of unregulated commodities rose faster, even allowing for the black market, than those of regulated commodities. After OPA controls expired, efforts of industry to prevent the tremendous increases in prices which took place were fruitless, and "gray" markets were extensive. A midwestern wholesale poultry dealer aptly summed up the situation: "It [OPA enforcement] has an effect, as a whole. If no effort was made for enforcement the whole thing would break down soon. The one who did try to live up to the law would get disgusted watching the unjust flourish in peace and quit trying to co-operate."[17]

These value conflicts took place not just in a democratic society but in a democratic society at war. Whereas one might well have anticipated a tremendous surge of national unity in view of the wartime pressures, neither nationalism, public opinion, nor government enforcement activity could cope successfully with the black market. In the United States, in contrast to a number of other nations, the wartime goal was that of national expediency or practical necessity.[18] Winning

---

[16] *Ibid.*, p. 57.

[17] "Opinion Survey of Food Wholesalers."

[18] Morale, which has been described as a "disposition to act together toward a goal," may be of three types: those directed toward goals, representing

the war was not recognized as a romantic or sacred goal, despite endless propaganda directed toward these symbols; rather, most Americans felt it was a job that had to be done, the quicker the better. The American people seemed to have achieved considerable solidarity in respect to this goal; yet there was an indication of poor morale in that there was "an unwillingness on the part of given people to understand what it required of them by the war necessity or, in the face of such an understanding, a refusal to act on the basis of it. Such unwillingness and refusal indicate a divided group, a rejection of the goal of the group enterprise, the absence of cooperative feeling."[19]

It appears that among all groups of our people during the last war collective sentiments were mobilized to achieve the goal of overcoming the enemy, and practically all people were in substantial agreement about the necessity for avoiding inflation, allocating essential supplies, and sharing limited consumer goods. Yet there existed contrary motivations of individualism when the program was applied to specific business concerns or consumers. To that extent the black market indicated that the morale of America was not what it might have been. In fact, it might be said that the black market was both an indication of reduced morale and a cause of reduced morale in various segments of the population, even among those not directly affected by the violation.

Interviews with a group of food wholesalers during the war revealed how strong were materialistic aspirations among some businessmen. There was a fairly prevalent belief that desires

---

practical expediency; romantic; or sacred.—Herbert Blumer, "Morale," in *American Society in Wartime,* edited by William F. Ogburn (Chicago: The University of Chicago Press, 1943) , pp. 211, 218–222.

[19] *Ibid.,* p. 227. If the United States had encountered more serious reverses on the pattern of the Battle of the Bulge, one might have seen a clearer test of the degree of morale in American society. Under such conditions black market violations might have declined.

for profits generally should not be curbed, even in a national emergency.[20] Less than one out of ten of these food wholesalers indicated patriotic motives had much to do with compliance; although similar views were expressed by gasoline dealers, they were not as pronounced. The most important reasons for complying were fear of enforcement action and respect for law. Other major reasons were fear of injuring their reputations and the reasonableness of the regulations in terms of adequate profits. Materialism is not limited to some businessmen, as was indicated by the attitude of many consumers toward items under price control. Some purchased items at above-ceiling prices, not because they needed them for essential purposes, but rather because of the status which possession of a scarce article gave them. Senator Tobey, who later became famed for his righteous indignation at the Kefauver hearings on organized crime, had some blunt things to say about the role of the "paltry and dirty dollar" in the black market.

It is perfectly understandable why the people would rise up and condemn Congress and the OPA. We have in this country a law passed by the Congress and signed by the President, and it is the law of the land, enacted to save this Nation, as far as possible, through human agencies, from the dangers of inflation. The OPA has made a lot of absurd rulings—I will put it that way, in a kindly spirit—a lot of incongruities and abnormalities in administration. But it has tried to do a good job. We have a state of mind, according to the comments of my friend on my right, impelling people to patronize the black markets. It takes two to make a black market. What is lacking in this matter is a moral fiber on the part of the American people to be outraged at those men and agencies

---

[20] "Opinion Survey of Food Wholesalers."

who make the paltry and dirty dollar crucify the law and bring stigma upon the administration.[21]

Such attitudes were obviously derived from powerful value systems in our culture. An explanation of this conflict between the sentiments of group welfare in wartime and individual sentiments must be sought in the emphasis on the latter in peacetime. The consequences of such individualistic and materialistic emphasis, coupled with value systems emphasizing disrespect for law, are to produce crime, whether among the lower socioeconomic groups or the white collar groups, in peace or in war. Such a view helps us to explain illegal behavior as diverse as organized criminal activities, the acceptance of bribes by college basketball players, the tax scandals involving government officials and politicians, and their bribery by racketeers and some businessmen. Hermann Mannheim, while not writing specifically about the black market, has stated a fundamental explanation of it:

The criminologist who tries to lay bare the principal driving forces making for crime in a given society cannot fail to place a rather heavy responsibility at the door of this "acquisitive society" itself. This verdict is by no means intended to relieve the individual concerned of any blame for his criminal actions, but it nevertheless implies that the share of the individual may become comparatively insignificant from the sociological point of view.[22]

While the public generally gave verbal support to price controls, although not as frequently to the OPA, there is little

---

[21] *Hearings before the Senate Committee on Banking and Currency,* on the 1946 Extension of the Emergency Price Control and Stabilization Acts of 1942, on Senate Resolution 2,028, as amended, Seventy-ninth Congress, Second Session, 1946, II, p. 1673.

[22] Hermann Mannheim, *Social Aspects of Crime in England between the Wars* (London: George Allen & Unwin, Ltd., 1940), p. 186.

evidence that persons ostracized business violators either during or after the war. While details on a black market violation during the war might be meager, a single theft or robbery case might occupy several columns in a newspaper. This emphasis was, of course, a reflection of the inconsistency of the attitudes of the public regarding the relative importance of these two types of situations. Yet, from a logical point of view, there was no question about the relative importance of the two crimes. If it can be assumed that the war effort was of paramount importance in a wartime situation and that the country was mobilized to achieve a single objective, then the greatest danger lay in the failure of over-all coordination of the war economy and not so much in crimes involving injuries not as serious to the nation as to a few individuals. One might even argue with Durkheim[23] that ordinary crimes, since they often reinforce the collective sentiments against lawbreaking, contribute something to the strengthening of the group, particularly in wartime. It is conceivable, however, had the wider use of the criminal penalty been possible in connection with black market violations, since there was less stigma to the other penalties, that the jail sentence might have brought forth more direct public condemnation.

The solution to the black market problem could not have been achieved alone by formal enforcement measures by government. There is no indication that widespread compliance with government regulations could be secured even if the most drastic enforcement measures had been adopted on a grand scale. The problem is much deeper than enforcement, for there is the broader problem of what can be done about the extensive crime and delinquency in America among all groups, including

---

[23] Émile Durkheim, *The Rules of Sociological Method,* edited by George M. Catlin (Chicago: The University of Chicago Press, 1938), pp. 65–73.

business. There are fundamental processes and contradictions in our society of which the black market is only one symptom. On the basis of such an approach, efforts should be directed at curbing such individualism in our society as is inimical to group objectives, bringing about more personal primary relationships between individuals and groups, shifting status objectives from money and materialism to other more social and national objectives, and developing public realization that consensus in the long run can be neither achieved nor maintained in a democracy exclusively by formal law. On all of these questions society is divided. It has reached no fundamental agreement as to the nature of the social values which should be followed now on the relation between special interests, government, and the general welfare. Until a greater degree of consensus can be achieved by citizen discussion of the nature of accepted social values, with a full realization of the social consequences of courses of action, we cannot hope to achieve any adequate compliance with law, whether involving ordinary crimes or the black market.

CHAPTER THIRTEEN

In the Future

All of us would have liked to hope that the black market activity just described is past history and will never again occur, but after the Korean war began in 1950 the reinstitution of price controls, with the possibility of later rationing, has made a serious black market a real threat once again. Since there are several variables, it is difficult to predict how the black market will develop, particularly as to details. Any estimate of the future must be based on whether there will be a series of small· wars, a continued "cold war," or all-out hostilities. This time the severity of economic controls and compliance with them are more related to the nature of a future war than during World War II.

In any event, a number of issues are present in our situation today that were not as pronounced during World War II. First, possibility that the war will be carried to the home front, together with the increasing mechanization of modern warfare, is likely to make civilian controls assume a much greater importance. The threat of atomic warfare means not only the destruction of civilian manpower, but also the large-scale destruction of production facilities, lines of transportation, and of stockpiled supplies, all of which are equally important from a military standpoint. Likewise, the armed forces are far more mechanized and their consequently greater war needs for such supplies as steel, rubber, and gasoline mean less goods available

for civilians. Moreover, strict rationing of many more commodities seems a foregone conclusion in the event of serious
hostilities. This limited civilian supply problem is likely to
create greater pressures for black market activities; however,
a greater sense of urgency on the home front, coupled with a
more active civil defense corps, might make for better compliance among all groups. On the other hand, provided we do
not encounter an all-out war, the tremendous expansion in our
production facilities since 1940 will make it possible for us to
turn out a much larger proportion of civilian goods to war
supplies than we did during World War II and thus prevent
serious black market pressures.

Second, there were marked differences in the economic
situation at the time controls were instituted in 1951 as compared to 1941. Instead of there being a general situation of considerable unemployment and moderate inflation, controls have
been put into effect when there is relatively full employment
and great inflationary pressures have developed. Certain restrictions in the Defense Production Act passed in 1950, which resulted from the usual drive of special interests in Congress, who
see not the national welfare but an opportunity to make additional profits out of war, have been a severe handicap. The
price of agricultural commodities had to be kept at parity
on the highest price between May 24 and June 24, 1950. Standardization of production and grade labeling was forbidden, the
government could not prevent a manufacturer from shifting to
a higher price line, and any forced channeling of production
into certain areas was implicitly forbidden. Restrictions were
later placed by Congress on rollbacks of prices as well as on
the imposition of livestock slaughtering quotas.

The situation initially has meant that while the price
levels of most concerns were quite favorable to them at the

time controls were imposed on prices and wages, the pressures for higher wages and higher prices may become acute if more of the economy turns to defense. On a long-term basis the government's problem of combating inflation and enforcing economic controls, therefore, looks much more serious, especially if it must support both a civilian and a war economy for a prolonged period of time. Regardless of how much the present crisis deepens, expenditures for armaments of at least fifty billion dollars a year, as compared with about six billion in 1941, for ourselves and our allies can be expected for some time to come, with resultant pressures of this additional available money on more limited consumer goods. At the present time we are spending at the rate of slightly over one sixth of our national income for defenses, as compared with about one fourteenth in a somewhat similar defense period ten years ago. Higher taxes and tighter credit controls will drain off some of this money. With considerable inflation already with us and more to be expected, however, those who advocate uniformly higher taxes and similar methods of draining off surplus purchasing power fail to appreciate the plight of our lower income groups, many salaried persons, and those living on annuities who may not have the surplus funds to pay extra taxes or black market prices.

In the third place, we have had experiences with both economic controls and a black market. While it appears that the government, as a result of this experience, could do a more efficient piece of work in establishing controls, the situation in which these controls must operate appears to have deteriorated over that prevailing during World War II. The difficulties of any attempt to reinstate price and rationing controls have been increased not only by the wanton disregard for law that occurred last time but by other factors such as the subsequent revelation of the huge profits made not only from the black market but from other war frauds. Even persons in high places were found to be involved. It is likely that the public, which last time gave considerable support to economic controls, now feels confused and hopeless about the present situation. After the war there was little public discussion of the wartime black market; if anything, both civilians and veterans were led to believe that strikes by labor during World War II were a far more important wartime threat than the black market.

In the postwar period persons who had made illegal profits during the war used the money to build houses, buy cars, expand their businesses, or purchase other material goods. Certain filling station operators who had engaged in the worst possible black market dealings with professional hoodlums once again advertised how well they looked out for the public interest through various services. Other black market operators, who had actively aided our enemies even more than they would have as members of the latter's armed forces, told of their unselfish devotion to America and the free enterprise system. Although he probably did not lose money during the war, the honest businessman who had obeyed the law for patriotic or other reasons was not able to acquire nearly the amount of money or material goods that those who participated in the black market gathered for themselves. He did, however, have a clear conscience. Unfortunately, our society does not reward, in terms of higher status, persons who are honest under such temptation.

As for business, the previous black market has provided not only a series of techniques for violation but also a number of excellent rationalizations. Those who wish to violate should now know how to do it, and may proceed on the premise that the possibility of detection is limited, the penalty slight, and the disapprobation of other businessmen almost nonexistent. The honest law-abiding businessman of the last war is, therefore, in a difficult dilemma. It is possible that the danger of inflation, previous experience with economic controls, and the threat of communism may engender much more support for compliance than in the previous war, when such efforts were more closely associated in the minds of businessmen with the New Deal.

It is impossible to determine what the effect of this black market has been on general compliance with laws regulating commerce, for we have no adequate indices of white collar crime. Widespread disrespect for a law breeds further disrespect for the power of the government to enforce any laws. Certainly such widespread disobedience as the black market during World War II has affected many segments of the populace, leading some to compare the black market with conditions during prohibition. While the effect on disobedience to law may be similar, there were significant differences between the black market and the bootlegging of prohibition days. The National Prohibition Act was a peacetime law directed at extremely personal behavior, behavior which nearly everyone, and not merely those engaged in the violations, regarded as not being essential for the country's welfare. Dealers in illicit alcohol, moreover, were seldom reputable businessmen but were frequently men of shady reputations or men with a background of organized crime. Many who engaged in bootlegging were new to the liquor business. Price and rationing controls, on the other hand, are necessary wartime measures and are backed by considerable popular and governmental support; moreover the black market largely involves legitimate businessmen who before the war had been engaged in manufacturing and selling the commodities they later sold in the black market.

The experiences of World War II should have meant a more realistic start in the enforcement of regulations before violations and disrespect for the government's economic controls were allowed to develop. Unfortunately, this has not been the case. As before, we tried several months of appeals for restraint on the part of business and a general program of voluntary controls. It was a total failure, and Congress finally passed the 1950 Defense Production Act which, with all its drawbacks, nevertheless provided enforcement powers for violations. Regulations were then issued, however, without a proper enforcement staff being available and with the initial period being characterized, as in the past emergency, merely by threats of strong action, followed by little if any punitive measures. Part of this can be explained by the fear that Congress might not renew the act and by inability to estimate the extent of public support. The latter has always been a serious problem, for there were differences last time and there are differences now between what powers the government needs to control inflation and what Congress thinks the public will accept. Sometimes both are wrong in estimating public reaction. As Bosch wrote about rationing in the last war:

> There may be a gap between public willingness "to go along" and the interpretation of Government officials of the degree of that willingness. It seems apparent, for example, that Government and Congressional leaders misjudged the extent to which the public was willing to embrace rationing during World War II in the interest of the general war effort. Public opinion polls and government surveys of public attitudes in the case of food rationing at least revealed high public acceptance of the program throughout the war period.[1]

---

[1] Bosch, *op. cit.,* p. 456.

Despite all these difficulties, the government seems to be in a stronger position to do the administrative job of controlling inflation and enforcing price and rationing controls than before, when the task was unique for this country. This time the government has had an opportunity to profit from experience. A considerable body of knowledge has been accumulated about American business practices and procedures. Consequently, wage and price controls, production, and taxation can be more efficiently coordinated to control inflation. Not only can regulations be much more quickly issued; they should be more fair and at the same time more enforceable. Moreover, some of the uniform business procedures worked out by the OPA may be normal trade practices today; if not, their reapplication should not be difficult.

A number of more specific issues not faced last time will have to be faced eventually if the black market is to be controlled. One of these is the need for the greater standardization of manufactured articles, as was done in Great Britain. Production according to standard designs but still carrying the trade name is absolutely necessary if quality deterioration is to be avoided. The forced channeling of supplies into areas in short supply and with increased population pressures must also be accomplished; otherwise distribution of goods tends to follow cheaper distribution costs, which may not always lead to the areas where the supply situation is most critical and where consequent pressures for a black market are great.

Of paramount importance is the size of the enforcement staff. It is impossible to know how serious a black market exists without an adequate staff. A staff of from 6,000 to 10,000 persons would appear to be the minimum for such a gigantic task, although from the experience in World War II it is doubtful if Congress would sanction such a number. Considering the fact that some war plants will employ far more men, that several million men will be in the armed services, and that such controls are essential to a wartime economy, this does not seem too large a staff for our nation to spare from its manpower supply or too large a figure from the standpoint of expenditures. Nevertheless, it may be difficult to recruit competent and experienced men for price and rationing work because of the ridicule and stigma which was heaped upon their predecessors during World War II.

Further efforts should also be made to increase and coordinate, as well as to give specialized training to, various other federal, state, and municipal authorities who might be of assistance in dealing with the black market. The more local interest that can be enlisted, provided national policy considerations are not interfered with, the greater the possibility of success in an enforcement program. Certainly we could not allow the extensive field autonomy that existed in the recent attempt to control the black market, when national enforcement considerations were often flaunted locally. The use of citizen volunteers in actual enforcement work raises other problems. Admittedly they were used primarily to augment enforcement manpower as well as to aid in mustering citizen support behind the efforts to deal with the problem. If professional manpower were to be increased and become more highly trained, the wide use of citizen volunteers could be largely avoided. Certainly to provide such persons, among whom there is rapid turnover, with adequate technical knowledge draws away valuable assistance from the regular enforcement program. The idea of citizen participation is sound, but to accomplish the intended purpose sufficiently would mean an even greater number than was the case in World War II. The imposition of penalties by citizen tribunals is, moreover, a delicate problem, and what may be accomplished in terms of increased assistance and evidence of public support for the program can be outweighed either by laxness on their part or by mistakes which antagonize businessmen.

Enforcement actions this time should initially be directed toward bringing about compliance along lines most essential to the over-all national program. Enforcement should be concentrated from the beginning at the producing, manufacturing, and wholesaling levels, so that price squeezes can be prevented from spreading through the economic pyramid. Likewise, wherever feasible, enforcement should be directed at those commodities vital to the national program instead of dissipating efforts in various unproductive directions. Some systematic method of sampling various classes of business for investigation should be devised; for this a list of previous black market offenders or groups of concerns who had violated other government regulations would be useful. Constant vigilance should be exercised over those who have entered a particular business field since the advent of controls, on the supposition that many entered to secure illegal profits. Nonfederally inspected slaughterers should be thoroughly regulated and new concerns largely prevented from entering the industry. Constant research should be carried on to ascertain the effectiveness of enforcement programs, and to learn the attitudes of businessmen toward this work. Research directed at commodity fields where compliance is good might reveal some significant factors in trade practices, regulations, incentives, and enforcement policy applicable to other fields.

Adequate control of the black market must be based on the realistic position that some businessmen extensively violated government regulations before the advent of such controls and that the government must deal vigorously and effectively with

them. Methods must be devised to convince the general population, as well as business, that white collar crimes are as much
crimes as are the more customary forms of crime, and that they
are even more economically and socially injurious. The greater
use of sanctions, together with rigorous sentences, might help
to label black market activities more effectively among the
public, businessmen, and professional criminals as actually abhorrent to our society. Penalties such as the criminal sanction,
treble damage suits, injunctions, and administrative actions
likewise could be made more severe, although the latter penalties do not carry quite the stigma that the criminal sanction
carries. It is possible that legislation might be introduced for
the handling of small jail and fine cases by United States commissioners.

Most businessmen believe in price controls—provided they
are in another line of business, although there is a growing
recognition that without controls in a wartime economy the
value of the dollar and the value of investments would decrease
rapidly. But there is no conceivable way in which government
can force all citizens or all businessmen to comply with any law.
Such a police force would result in a "police state." Price and
rationing controls must be based on the acceptance of the inherent right of a democracy to legislate for the general welfare.
The government can help make such laws acceptable by a
widespread publicity program, it can attempt to direct public
thinking in support of its program and its agents, and it can
constantly publicize the actions it has taken against violators.
In the long run, however, a price and rationing law must be
supported by the groups most immediately affected, regardless of commodity lines or business levels. The cooperation
of businessmen must be voluntary and must involve the
majority of them; businessmen themselves must strive to

achieve support for the program. A second failure would endanger national security and would raise the possibility of the government's being forced to take over a considerable part of both war production and the distribution of goods. If a similar gasoline black market, for example, arose again it is possible that the government might of necessity have to commandeer supplies and distribute them to civilians through government-operated supply depots.

Even though not too effective to date, trade associations must take a more active part in any compliance program, whether in connection with the black market or with other government enforcement programs. They must formulate certain principles of fair dealing with the government and with the public and seek, by threat of internal action, to secure compliance among the trade. They must actively assist the government to achieve its objectives by detecting, publicizing, and punishing flagrant violations committed by the members. This means that trade associations must work out ethical principles with teeth in them regardless of whether or not it involves breaking the curtain of secrecy which often prevails about violations of government regulations. Most of all, standards of professional honesty must be developed that will stigmatize the offender who has broken the rules of the game, both economically and socially—something that was not achieved either during or after the black market of World War II. A well-known criminologist has stressed the necessity for internal controls within business to prevent white collar crimes.

Control of sharp, evasive, and fraudulent practices in business will have to develop externally, that is, by boycotting and reporting of white-collar violators by their victims (other businessmen, buyers, and consumers) as well as internally, that is, within the world of business and its various organizations and associations.

. . . Businessmen, through their own organizations and associations, must also become vitally concerned with the ethics of doing business and the ways of rendering service to the public. In several quarters of well-established and highly organized business, strong internal controls over members by associations is developing, whereby businessmen through their own collective pressure can hold their colleagues in line. Ethical business practices are what is needed to combat white-collar crime, although it is realized that this is difficult to bring about in some highly competitive enterprises, in wild-cat operations, and in businesses which have not developed a strong association.[2]

It is unfortunate that in the five-year interval between the termination and reinstitution of price controls there was so little discussion of this major problem by business groups, the public, and government, for in the final analysis no really effective control over the black market can be achieved without the active cooperation of all. There were, for example, few discussions by businessmen as to what should have been done or what could be done in the future to avoid this blot on them as a group or to prevent serious wartime dislocations in the economic life of our nation. In the final analysis any solution of the black market must come through the efforts of businessmen, leaving to government only a fringe of violations which cannot be dealt with by any other means.

It was the lack of reward for the honest businessman, or condemnation for the dishonest, that makes one fearful of a serious black market in any similar all-out war. Many businessmen who refused to deal in the black market learned that honesty does not always pay, and men new in business since the war still remember the stories of extensive, lush, and illegal black

---

[2] Walter C. Reckless, *The Crime Problem* (New York: Appleton-Century-Crofts, Inc., 1950), pp. 500–501.

market profits during the war years. For these reasons we may expect not less, but more, violations; not half compliance, but considerably less than half. In a future emergency where large-scale destruction of essential commodities occurs this situation may be fatal. If the emergency were a war involving new methods of total destruction, without even the degree of centralized governmental control available in the recent war, chaos is likely. On the other hand, the horrors of an atomic war might drive the American people to choose between the sentiments involving the general welfare and the personal goals of individualism and materialism. The consequences of a failure to reach consensus on this issue might, in another national emergency, be much more costly than it was in World War II.

Appendix

Classification of Price, Rent, and Rationing Violations

(AS OF 1944)

Part A. Violations of price regulations

I. By the seller
   A. Direct price ceiling violations
      1. Straight sale over ceiling without evasion
      2. Sale without required OPA approval of individual price
      3. Incorrect establishment of base period or formula ceiling
   B. Evasive price violations, i.e., indirect over-ceiling sales involving use of methods to cover up or hamper detection of violation
      1. Quality deterioration without comparable reduction in price
         Upgrading; changes in specification without required OPA approval; changes in brands; reduction in quality, performance, or services; changes in style of processing; changes in style of packaging or canning; reduction in servicing of commodity; charging for fictitious goods or services

2. Quantity reduction without comparable reduction in price

> Reduction in size of canned or prepackaged commodities; short-weighting; weight rigging; charging for fictitious goods or services

3. Tie-in sales of one commodity with another
4. Payments in addition to regular transaction (cash on the side)
5. Underevaluation

> Underappraisal of trade-ins; underpayment for goods or services purchased from the buyer

6. Price differentials

> Changes in the classification of purchasers; refusing to ship in quantities required by purchaser; splitting orders, etc.

7. Terms of sale

> Refusal to accept cash; discontinuance or reduction of trade discounts, allowances, and privileges; credit allowance to seller as additional payment

8. Excessive charges for transportation

> Misapplication of basing points; improper computation of shipping charges; trucking charges; unnecessary routing; delivery charges

C. Records and reports violations

1. Simple failure to comply with records and reports requirements

> Failure to prepare, incomplete, or improper, late filing of: base-period records, current records, prices with OPA, periodic reports, records of particular transactions; failure to label or mark, to give itemized invoices, sales slips, or receipts, to post prices, to apply for license, to display license

2. Failure or intentional refusal to comply with records and reports requirements with purpose of covering up substantive violations

Failure to prepare, incomplete or improper, falsification, destruction, late filing, back-dating of: base-period records, current records, prices with OPA, periodic reports, records of particular transactions; failure to label or mark, to give itemized invoices, sales slips, or receipts, to post prices, to apply for license, to display license

II. By the buyer (in the course of trade or business where regulations prohibit)

A. Straight price over-ceiling payments

B. Over-ceiling payments by evasive means, i.e., indirect over-ceiling purchases involving use of methods to cover up or hamper detection of violation

Part B. Violations of rent regulations

I. Direct rental overcharges; over-ceiling rent

II. Evasive or indirect rental overcharges

1. Side payments
2. Prepayments, or payments in advance
3. Security deposits
4. Elimination of customary discounts
5. Separate rental of apartment and furniture with the total over the maximum rent
6. Tie-in agreements
7. Fictitious sales
8. Reduction in services or charges
9. Fictitious services and charges
10. Altering rates of payment
11. Altering units of rental
12. Overcharges because of claims of fictitious exemption from the regulations

13. Bonuses, commissions, rewards, and gratuities
III. Evictions contrary to OPA regulations
    1. Exclusions from possession by removal of furniture, equipment, or discontinuance of services; lock-out
    2. Failure to give notice to vacate
    3. Eviction for fictitious reason
    4. Improper notice of eviction
IV. Violations of record-keeping and reporting requirements such as registering
    1. Simple failure to comply with records and reports requirements
       Failure to prepare, incomplete or improper, late filing of: registration, base-period records, current records, records of particular transactions (change of tenancy) ; failure to give receipts
    2. Neglect or intentional refusal to comply with records and reports requirements with purpose of covering up substantive violations
       Failure to prepare, incomplete, or improper, falsification, destruction, late filing, back-dating of: registration, base-period records, current records, records of particular transactions (change of tenancy) ; failure to give receipts

Part C. Violations of ration orders

I. By the seller
  A. Improper transfers
    1. Transfer of rationed commodity without receipt of proper amount of ration currency (except theft)
       Sale, gift; diversion of stock; in violation of freeze order; personal use; transfer as another commodity by false billing

2. Transfer of rationed commodity in exchange for invalid ration currency

Transfer prior to or after valid date of currency; failure to have coupons endorsed; improper ration currency value; falsifying endorsement

3. Transfer of lesser amount or more deteriorated quality of rationed commodity than represented by ration currency received

4. Wrongful acquisition, possession, or use of a rationed commodity

Unexplained inventory shortage; transfer of rationed commodity during effective period of suspension order from dealing in rationed commodities

5. Improper acquisition or possession of ration currency

Covering inventory shortage with purchased ration currency; failure to turn in currency that has been surrendered for purchases; detaching ration currency on deposit with dealer prior to delivering commodity (pretailoring)

B. Improper selling practices

1. Discrimination among legitimate purchasers of rationed commodities

2. Failure to hold for freeze order or refusal to permit inspection of commodity, such as tires, etc.

3. Transferring ration commodities to a purchaser known to be in default

C. Ration banking violations

1. Establishment of account

Failure to open; improper bank; improper documentation

2. Overdrawing account

3. Writing checks on nonexistent accounts

4. Improper deposits
Invalid coupons; material other than ration currency

5. Improper method of deposit
Falsification of contents; improper deposit envelopes, etc.

D. Records and reports violations
1. Simple failure to comply with records and reports requirements
Failure to prepare, incomplete, or improper, late filing of: base-period records, current records, records of particular transactions; failure to give itemized sales slips or receipts, to keep an inventory, to apply for allotment or replenishment

2. Neglect or intentional refusal to comply with records and reports requirements with purpose of covering up substantive violations
Failure to prepare, incomplete, or improper, falsification, destruction, late filing, back-dating, alteration of: base-period records, current records, records of particular transactions; failure to give itemized sales slips or receipts, to keep an inventory, to apply for allotment or replenishment

II. By the buyer (either in the course of business or as a consumer)
A. Improper transfer, acquisition, use, or possession of ration currency (except theft)
1. Sale
2. Gift
B. Wrongful possession or transfer of rationed commodity
C. Acquisition of commodity without ration currency (except theft)

D. Acquisition of commodity with improper ration currency

    Misuse of ration currency by invalid date; failure to endorse; inadequate ration currency value

E. Improper use of commodity

    1. Using for purposes other than authorized

        Nonessential driving, rights obtained for previous owner, relative, etc.

    2. Falsification of application for rationed commodity

        Occupation, ride-sharing, inventory, mileage readings, necessity

III. Theft, counterfeiting, alteration, destruction of ration currency

A. Theft

    1. Theft of ration currency

        Theft; by OPA or ration bank employees; by persons charged with destruction of used currency

    2. Theft of rationed commodity

    3. Sale of stolen ration currency

    4. Purchase of stolen ration currency

    5. Possession of ration currency

B. Counterfeiting of ration currency

    1. Counterfeiting of ration currency

    2. Possession of counterfeit ration currency

C. Alteration, mutilation, defacement, or unauthorized destruction of ration currency

Bibliography

Books

Arnold, Thurman W. *The Folklore of Capitalism.* New Haven: Yale University Press, 1937.

Backman, Jules. *Experience with Wartime Subsidies.* Washington: Citizens National Committee, Inc., 1945.

——. *Rationing and Price Control in Great Britain.* Washington: The Brookings Institution, 1943.

Barnes, Harry E. *Society in Transition.* New York: Prentice-Hall, Inc., 1939.

——, and Negley K. Teeters. *New Horizons in Criminology.* New York: Prentice-Hall, Inc., 1944.

Blumer, Herbert. "Morale" in *American Society in Wartime,* edited by William F. Ogburn. Chicago: The University of Chicago Press, 1943.

Bosch, Leon A. "Meat Rationing: World War II," Ph.D. Dissertation, Northwestern University, 1948, School of Commerce, Department of Marketing.

Brown, Lawrence G. *Social Pathology.* New York: Appleton-Century-Crofts, Inc., 1942.

Burgess, Ernest W., and Harvey S. Locke. *The Family.* New York: American Book Company, 1945.

Cuber, John A., and Robert A. Harper. *Problems of American Soci-*

ety; Values in Conflict. New York: Henry Holt and Company, 1948.

Durkheim, Émile. *The Rules of Sociological Method,* edited by George E. Catlin. Chicago: The University of Chicago Press, 1938.

Elkinton, Charles M. "The Meat Industry: Economic Characteristics Revealed by Price Control." Unpublished Ph.D. Dissertation, University of Wisconsin, Madison, Wisconsin, 1947.

Exner, Franz. *Krieg und Kriminalitat in Osterreich.* New Haven: Yale University Press, 1927.

Fuller, Richard. "Social Problems," in Robert E. Park, *Outline of the Principles of Sociology.* New York: Barnes & Noble, 1939.

Gillin, John L. *Criminology and Penology.* New York: Appleton-Century-Crofts, Inc., 3d ed., 1945.

Hall, Jerome. *General Principles of Criminal Law.* Indianapolis: The Bobbs-Merrill Company, 1947.

————. *Theft, Law and Society.* Boston: Little, Brown & Company, 1935.

Harris, Seymour E. *Price and Related Controls in the United States.* New York: McGraw-Hill Book Company, Inc., 1945.

Hartung, Frank E. "A Study in Law and Social Differentiation: As Exemplified in Violations of the Emergency Price Control Act of 1942 and the Second War Powers Act, in the Detroit Meat Industry." Unpublished Ph.D. Dissertation, University of Michigan, Ann Arbor, Michigan, 1949.

Kallet, Arthur. *Counterfeit.* New York: The Vanguard Press, 1935.

————, and John F. Schlink. *100,000,000 Guinea Pigs.* New York: The Vanguard Press, 1933.

Katona, George. *Price Control and Business.* Cowles Commission for Research in Economics, Monograph No. 9. Bloomington: The Principia Press, Inc., 1945.

Knight, Frank H. *The Ethics of Competition and Other Essays.* New York: Harper & Brothers, 1935.

Lever, Harry, and Joseph Young. *Wartime Racketeers.* New York: G. P. Putnam's Sons, 1945.

Linton, Ralph. *The Study of Man*. New York: Appleton-Century-Crofts, Inc., 1936.

Lynd, Robert S. *Knowledge for What?* Princeton: Princeton University Press, 1946.

———, and Helen Merrill Lynd. *Middletown*. New York: Harcourt, Brace and Company, 1929.

——— and ———. *Middletown in Transition*. New York: Harcourt, Brace and Company, 1937.

MacIver, R. M. *The Web of Government*. New York: The Macmillan Company, 1947.

Mannheim, Hermann. *Criminal Justice and Social Reconstruction*. New York: Oxford University Press, 1946.

———. *Social Aspects of Crime in England between the Wars*. London: George Allen & Unwin, Ltd., 1940.

Merrill, Francis E. *Social Problems on the Home Front*. New York: Harper & Brothers, 1948.

Parsons, Talcott. "The Motivation of Economic Activities," in *Essays in Sociology*, edited by M. C. W. Hart. Toronto: University of Toronto Press, 1940.

Radin, Max. *Manners and Morals of Business*. Indianapolis: The Bobbs-Merrill Company, 1938.

Reckless, Walter C. *The Etiology of Delinquent and Criminal Behavior*, Bulletin No. 50. New York: Social Science Research Council, 1943.

———. *The Crime Problem*. New York: Appleton-Century-Crofts, Inc., 1950.

Rusche, George, and Otto Kirchheimer. *Punishment and Social Structure*. New York: Columbia University Press, 1939.

Sellin, Thorsten. *Culture Conflict and Crime*. New York: Social Science Research Council, 1938.

Shaw, Clifford, and Henry McKay. *Brothers in Crime*. Chicago: The University of Chicago Press, 1938.

Simpson, George. *Émile Durkheim on the Division of Labor in Society*. New York: The Macmillan Company, 1933.

Sutherland, Edwin H. "Crime," in *American Society in Wartime,* edited by William F. Ogburn. Chicago: The University of Chicago Press, 1943.

———. *Principles of Criminology.* Philadelphia: J. B. Lippincott Company, 4th ed., 1947.

———. *The Professional Thief.* Chicago: The University of Chicago Press, 1937.

———. *White Collar Crime.* New York: The Dryden Press, 1949.

Taft, Donald R. *Criminology.* New York: The Macmillan Company, 1942.

Watkins, Myron W. *Public Regulation of Competitive Practices in Business Enterprise.* New York: National Industrial Conference Board, Inc., 3d ed., 1940.

Articles

"American Economic Mobilization," *Harvard Law Review,* Vol. LV (1942).

Anonymous. "Confessions of a Black Market Butcher," *Saturday Evening Post,* August 24, 1946.

"Black Market, The," *Collier's,* June 6, 1942.

"Boom, The," *Fortune,* June, 1946.

Bowles, Chester. "The Deadly Menace of Black Gasoline," New York *Times Magazine,* July 30, 1944.

———. "Theft by Counterfeit," *Newsweek,* March 27, 1944.

Carsel, Wilfred. "Rent Enforcement in the Office of Price Administration," undated, *circa* spring, 1945.

"Ceiling-Price-Gyps," *Business Week,* June 26, 1943.

Cherne, Leo M. "America's Black Market," *Saturday Evening Post,* July 25, 1942.

Clinard, Marshall B. "Criminal Behavior Is Human Behavior," *Federal Probation,* XIII, No. 1 (March, 1949), 21–27.

———. "Criminological Theories of Violations of Wartime Regulations," *American Sociological Review,* XI, No. 3 (June, 1946), 258–270.

———. "Rural Criminal Offenders," *American Journal of Sociology,* L (July, 1944), 38–45.

———. "Secondary Community Influences and Juvenile Delinquency," *Annals of the American Academy of Political and Social Science,* CCLXI (January, 1949), 42–55.

———. "Sociologists and American Criminology," *Journal of Criminal Law and Criminology,* XLI, No. 5 (January–February, 1951), 549–577.

Count, Jerome. "Enforcement Aspects of Price and Rent Control," Pike and Fischer's *Administrative Law Service,* May, 1945, Articles and Reports Section, 585–621.

Cressey, Donald R. "Criminological Research and the Definition of Crimes," *American Journal of Sociology,* VLI, No. 6 (May, 1951), 546–551.

"Daffy Gray Market, That," *Fortune,* May, 1948.

Duddy, Edward A. "The Moral Implications of Business as a Profession," *Journal of Business,* XVIII, No. 2 (April, 1945), 64–65.

Emerson, Thomas I. "Ration Robbers," *American Magazine,* September, 1943.

Eulenberg, Alexander. "Influence of Public Policy on Deductions," *Taxes,* XXVIII, No. 12 (December, 1950), 1189–1202.

"Expanding Livestock Production Makes Controls Unnecessary." (Chicago: American Meat Institute, October 25, 1950).

Frank, Lawrence K. "Society as the Patient," *American Journal of Sociology,* XLII, No. 3 (November, 1936), 335–344.

Fuller, Richard C. "Morals and the Criminal Law," *Journal of Criminal Law and Criminology,* XXXII (March–April, 1942), 624–630.

———, and Richard R. Myers. "Some Aspects of a Theory of Social Problems," *American Sociological Review,* VI, No. 1 (February, 1941), 24–32.

Ginsburg, David. "The Emergency Price Control Act of 1942: Basic Authority and Sanctions," *Law and Contemporary Problems,* School of Law, Duke University, IX, No. 1 (Winter, 1942), 22–60.

Hall, Jerome. "Crime as Social Reality," *Annals of the American Academy of Political and Social Science,* CCXVII (September, 1941), 1–14.

Hall, Livingston. "The Substantive Law of Crimes, 1887–1936," *Harvard Law Review,* L, No. 4 (February, 1937), 616–633.

Hartung, Frank E. "White-Collar Offenses in the Wholesale Meat Industry in Detroit," *American Journal of Sociology,* LVI, No. 1 (July, 1950), 25–35.

Henderson, Leon. "How Black Is Our Market?" *Atlantic Monthly,* July, 1946.

"Hunt for Income Tax Evaders," *United States News,* December 5, 1947.

Hutchins, Robert M. "Ideals in Education," *American Journal of Sociology,* XLIII, No. 1 (July, 1937), 1–15.

Lindesmith, Alfred R., and H. Warren Dunham. "Some Principles of Criminal Typology," *Social Forces,* XIX (March, 1941), 307–314.

"Meat Makes News," *Time,* April 30, 1945.

Potomacus, "The Thousand-Dollar Necktie," *New Republic,* March 25, 1946.

"Rackets in Lumber Industry: Black-Market Raid on Supply," *United States News,* September 13, 1946.

"Raid Meat Cache," *Business Week,* May 5, 1945.

"Rations and Racketeers," *New Statesman and Nation,* March 29, 1941.

"Rents and the Real Estate Lobby," *Fortune,* June, 1947.

Richardson, J. Henry. "Consumer Rationing in Great Britain," *Canadian Journal of Economics and Political Science,* VIII (February, 1942), 69–82.

Rutledge, J. Howard. "The Little OPA's," *Saturday Evening Post,* May 15, 1943.

Schuessler, Karl F., and Donald R. Cressey, "Personality Characteristics of Criminals," *American Journal of Sociology,* LV (March, 1950), 476–484.

Selling, Lowell S. "Specific War Crimes," *Journal of Criminal Law and Criminology,* XXXIV, No. 5 (January–February, 1944), 303–310.

Sparlin, Estal E. "The Possible Significance of OPA Price Panels," *Social Forces,* XXIV, No. 2 (December, 1945), 220–223.

Stewart, Maxwell S. "The Maze of the Black Market," *Survey Graphic,* XXXII, No. 10 (October, 1943), 377–380.

Sutherland, Edwin H. "Crime and Business," *Annals of the American Academy of Political and Social Science,* CCXVII (September, 1941), 112–118.

———. "Is 'White Collar Crime' Crime?" *American Sociological Review,* X, No. 2 (April, 1945), 132–140.

———. "White Collar Criminality," *American Sociological Review,* V, No. 1 (February, 1940), 1–12.

Taeusch, C. F. "Business Ethics," *Encyclopedia of the Social Sciences.* New York: The Macmillan Company, 1930, III, 111–113.

Tappan, Paul W. "Crime and the Criminal," *Federal Probation,* XI, No. 3 (July–September, 1947), 41–44.

———. "Who Is the Criminal?" *American Sociological Review,* XII, No. 1 (February, 1947), 96–103.

"Too Much Fat," *Business Week,* June 10, 1944.

Toombs, Alfred. "Ration Racketeers," *American Magazine,* August, 1942.

Wirth, Louis. "Ideological Aspects of Social Disorganization," *American Sociological Review,* V, No. 4 (August, 1940), 472–482.

———. "Urbanism as a Way of Life," *American Journal of Sociology,* XLIV, No. 1 (July, 1938), 1–24.

Wright, Chester W. "American Economic Preparations for War, 1914–1917 and 1939–1941," *Canadian Journal of Economics and Political Science,* VIII (February–November, 1942), 157–175.

Reports

Annual Reports of the Commissioner of Internal Revenue. Washington: Government Printing Office.

Annual Reports of the Director of the Administrative Office of the United States Courts. Washington: Government Printing Office.

Annual Reports of the Federal Trade Commission. Washington: Government Printing Office.

Annual Reports of the Food and Drug Administration. Washington: Government Printing Office.

Annual Reports of the Secretary of the Treasury on the State of the Finances. Washington: Government Printing Office.

Annual Reports of the Securities and Exchange Commission. Washington: Government Printing Office.

Office of Price Administration. *Basic Manual for Enforcement Investigators.* Multilithed, 1944.

———. *Opinions and Decisions.* Washington: Government Printing Office, 1944–1947, 6 vols.

———. *A Manual of Price Control.* Lecture Series Delivered at the Training Program for Price of the Office of Price Administration. Washington: Government Printing Office, 1943.

———. *Quarterly Reports* (1–22). Washington: Government Printing Office, March 31, 1942, through May 31, 1947.

Office of Temporary Controls, Office of Price Administration. *Historical Reports on War Administration: Office of Price Administration.* Washington: Government Printing Office. These publications are listed below:

Miscellaneous Publication No. 1.   *Chronology of the Office of Price Administration.*

Miscellaneous Publication No. 2.   *Minutes of the Price Administration Committee.*

Miscellaneous Publication No. 3.   *OPA Bibliography, 1940–1947.*

General Publication No.   1.   *The Beginnings of OPA.*

General Publication No.   2.   *A History of Ration Banking.*

General Publication No.   3.   *Wartime Apparel Price Control.*

General Publication No.   4.   *Field Administration of Wartime Rationing.*

General Publication No. 5. *OPA and the Public Utility Commissions.*

General Publication No. 6. *Studies in Industrial Price Control.*

General Publication No. 7. *Problems in Price Control: Pricing Standards.*

General Publication No. 8. *Problems in Price Control: Pricing Techniques.*

General Publication No. 9. *Problems in Price Control: Changing Production Patterns.*

General Publication No. 10. *Problems in Price Control: Stabilization Subsidies.*

General Publication No. 11. *Problems in Price Control: Legal Phases.*

General Publication No. 12. *Problems in Price Control: National Office Organization and Management.*

General Publication No. 13. *Studies in Food Rationing.*

General Publication No. 14. *Volunteers in OPA.*

General Publication No. 15. *A Short History of OPA.*

Roach, John C. *Manual for Enforcement Attorneys of the Office of Price Administration.* Multilithed, 1946.

Temporary National Economic Committee Monograph No. 18. "Investigation of Concentration of Economic Power," *Trade Association Survey,* Senate Committee Print, Seventy-sixth Congress, First Session, 1941.

Thatcher, Harold W. *Planning for Industrial Mobilization, 1920–1940,* Office of the Quartermaster General, General Administrative Services Division, Historical Section, Q.M.C. Historical Studies, No. 4, August, 1943.

Uniform Crime Reports, Federal Bureau of Investigation, United States Department of Justice. Washington: Government Printing Office.

United States at War, The, No. 1 of the Historical Reports on War

Administration, United States Bureau of the Budget. Washington: Government Printing Office, 1947.

Congressional Hearings

United States Senate

Hearings before the Subcommittee of the Committee on Appropriations, Seventy-ninth Congress, Second Session, 1946.

Hearings before the Subcommittee of the Committee on Appropriations, Second Deficiency Appropriation Bill for 1945, Seventy-ninth Congress, First Session, 1945.

Hearings before the Subcommittee of the Committee on Appropriations, Urgent Deficiency Appropriation Bill for 1946, Seventy-ninth Congress, Second Session, 1946.

Hearings before the Committee on Banking and Currency, Emergency Price Control Act, Seventy-seventh Congress, First Session, 1941.

Hearings before the Committee on Banking and Currency, Extension of the Emergency Price Control Act of 1942, Seventy-eighth Congress, Second Session, 1944.

Hearings before the Committee on Banking and Currency, Inflation Control Program of OPA, Seventy-ninth Congress, First Session, 1945.

Hearings before the Committee on Banking and Currency, 1946 Extension of the Emergency Price Control and Stabilization Acts of 1942, Seventy-ninth Congress, Second Session, 1946.

Hearings before the Committee on Banking and Currency, on Senate Resolution 231, Temporary Suspension of Meat and Perishable Meat Products, Seventy-eighth Congress, Second Session, 1944.

Investigation of the National Defense Program, Senate Report 110, Additional Report of the Special Committee Investigating the National Defense Program, Seventy-ninth Congress, First Session, 1945.

Investigation of the National Defense Program, Senate Report 10, Additional Report of the Special Committee Investigating the National Defense Program, Seventy-eighth Congress, First Session,

1943, also Parts 15–20, Seventy-eighth Congress, Second Session, 1944.

Investigation of the National Defense Program, Senate Report 440, Additional Report of the Special Committee, Eightieth Congress, Second Session, 1948.

House of Representatives

Hearings before the Subcommittee of the Committee on Appropriations, Second Deficiency Appropriation Bill for 1944, Seventy-eighth Congress, Second Session, 1944.

Hearings before the Committee on Banking and Currency. Seventy-seventh Congress, First Session, 1941.

Hearings before the Committee on Banking and Currency, Extension of the Emergency Price Control Act, Seventy-eighth Congress, Second Session, 1944.

Hearings before the Committee on Banking and Currency, on House Resolution 5,270, Seventy-ninth Congress, Second Session.

Hearings before the Committee on Banking and Currency, on Senate Resolution 502, Seventy-ninth Congress, First Session, 1945.

Hearings before the Committee on the Judiciary, on House Resolutions 85, 86, 91, and House Joint Resolutions 245, 98, Seventy-ninth Congress, First Session, 1945.

Hearings before the Special Committee to Investigate Food Shortages for the House of Representatives, Food Shortages, Seventy-ninth Congress, First Session, 1945.

Hearings before the Special Committee to Investigate Gasoline and Fuel-Oil Shortages, Seventy-eighth Congress, First Session, 1943.

Second Intermediate Report of the Select Committee to Investigate Executive Agencies, House Report 862, Seventy-eighth Congress, First Session, 1943.

Index

Index